Columbo

spin offs

A production of the Console-ing Passions book series
Edited by Lynn Spigel and Racquel J. Gates

Columbo

Make Me a Perfect Murder

AMELIE HASTIE

DUKE UNIVERSITY PRESS *Durham and London* 2024

Printed in the United States of America on acid-free paper ∞

Project Editor: Liz Smith

Designed by A. Mattson Gallagher

Typeset in Warnock Pro and News Gothic by Westchester Publishing Services

Library of Congress Cataloging-in-Publication Data

Names: Hastie, Amelie, author.

Title: Columbo : make me a perfect murder / Amelie Hastie.

Other titles: Console-ing passions book series. Spin-offs.

Description: Durham : Duke University Press, 2024. | Series: Spin-offs |

Includes bibliographical references and index.

Identifiers: LCCN 2023026652 (print)

LCCN 2023026653 (ebook)

ISBN 9781478020677 (hardcover)

ISBN 9781478025450 (paperback)

ISBN 9781478027591 (ebook)

Subjects: LCSH: Falk, Peter, 1927–2011. | Columbo (Television program) | Television

broadcasting—History and criticism. | Detective and mystery television programs—History

and criticism. | Columbo, Lieutenant (Fictitious character) | BISAC: PERFORMING ARTS /

Television / Genres / General | PERFORMING ARTS / Television / History & Criticism

Classification: LCC PN1992.77.C583 H378 2024 (print) | LCC PN1992.77.C583 (ebook) |

DDC 791.45/72—dc23/eng/20230810

LC record available at https://lccn.loc.gov/2023026652

LC ebook record available at https://lccn.loc.gov/2023026653

Cover art: *Columbo*, "Make Me a Perfect Murder," 7:3; Feb. 25, 1978. Image: Photofest.

this one's for me

Contents

acknowledgments   ix

prologue: humble origins and dogged returns   xv

Introduction: Murder by the Book   1

1   Mapping the Detective: Falk's Early Drives   24

2   Best-Selling Mystery Team: *Columbo* and Televisual
Collaboration   38

3   "I'm Fascinated by Money": Rank, File, and Gumshoe Detection   72

4   Special Guest Stars: Hollywood Icons and Repeat Offenders   95

5   Between Columbo and Cassavetes: A Familial Pack   119

6   An "Obsessive Preoccupation with Gadgetry": *Columbo*'s Investigation
of Media Technologies   144

7   Columbo's Reign: Of Life and Death and Detection   172

Epilogue: Loving and Leaving *Columbo*   197

notes   201

bibliography   219

index   225

Acknowledgments

In one of our conversations about *Columbo* over the years, cocreator of the series William Link asked me to please not title this book *Just One More Thing*. I promised him I wasn't even considering it, though I will inevitably turn to Peter Falk's catchphrase throughout the volume, and I can't avoid it in these acknowledgments, as every time I've imagined thanking those who have supported, inspired, and informed me throughout the long process of research and writing, there is always one more name to add to a very long list.

But let me begin, first and foremost, with Mr. Link, who spoke to me on several occasions by telephone and in person to offer background, share stories, answer my questions, and just plain motivate me. He and his ever glamorous wife, Margery Nelson, welcomed me into their home more than once; humbled by their kindness and worried I might be a pest, I perhaps did not take as much advantage of their graciousness as I might have, but the hours I spent talking with Mr. Link were some of the most delightful moments I spent while writing this book—which is saying something, given the ongoing pleasure of writing about a series that I have long loved. I regret that he did not live to see the final project, and I hope that I have been able to do his and Richard Levinson's great minds and great compassion justice here.

My love of the series began when I was a child, watching it with my parents (Claudette and Frank) and my two brothers (Matt and Bowman), all of whom have enthusiastically supported my work over time. Along with my mom, both my stepdad John Beahrs and my niece Katie have also been some of the most ardent and industrial familial supporters of my research over time. I am grateful to have a family who (mostly) takes my work seriously, especially my mom, who cheered me on over the years as I attended to my favorite detective.

My research and writing have taken place across two academic institutions—among beloved colleagues and friends at the University of California–Santa Cruz (UCSC) and then at Amherst College, where my students and further institutional support have together allowed this work to flourish. I have benefited from grants from the UCSC Institute for Humanities, the UCSC Arts Research Institute, the Amherst College Faculty Research Award Program, the Amherst College English Department, and the Gregory Call Academic Intern program. Four Amherst students in particular went above and beyond as my academic interns, and I would like to thank them for not only their research assistance but also their collaboration at key junctures of my work. To the inimitable Alison Fornell, who amassed materials on technologies and television over the summer of 2012, who developed an acute understanding of my work, and who raised the bar for what a student and a research assistant could potentially be; to Maeve McNamara who mastered an extraordinary research method that no one else has ever been able to fully reproduce and who cheerfully (and productively!) accompanied me to Los Angeles for a review of scripts at the Writers Guild Foundation in 2018; to Kiera Alventosa who worked carefully with me on the final chapter of the book, applying her interdisciplinary approach to research, and whose entire family supported her own work on *Columbo*; and to Sam Hood, who was the first person to read the entire manuscript over his winter break in 2019–20, who continued to read with me as I revised, and who offered insights and suggestions beyond his years. With additional thanks to academic interns Grace Kanija, Max Suechting, and, most especially, Sabrina Lin, as well as an extra shout-out to Kiera, Maeve, and Sabrina, who made up the glorious "Team Columbo" in 2018–19! And, finally, a special thanks to Carolina Cordon for her timely assistance with images.

I would like to thank various friends and colleagues across my primary institutions and well beyond: Aline Akelis (my *Columbo* viewing partner in Brooklyn), Miranda Banks, Rebecca Barden, Caetlin Benson-Allott, Barb Bull and Bruce McGough, Nicole Cooley, David Crane,

Niki Cunningham, Barbara Epler, Irene Gustafson, Barbara Hall, Arlo Hastie, Chris Holmlund, Sally Hood, Deborah Jaramillo, Sheila Jaswal, Lynne Joyrich, Jonathan Kahana, Bette Kanner, Ben Lieber, Kate Lilley, Karen Lury, Anna McCarthy, Kathleen McHugh, Pat Mellencamp, Marti Noxon, Jan Olsson, Gretchen Papazian, Lisa Parks, Dana Polan, Pooja Rangan, Matt Roberson, Marta Rudolf, Geoff Sanborn, Jeff Sconce, Sarah Sharpe, Shawn Shimpach, Randall Smith, Donovan Smith, Jackie Stacey, Claudia Steinberg, Linda Tropp, Wendy West, and Mark Williams. With extra thanks and many hugs to Tara McPherson for her long friendship and for her generous offerings of food and housing during my various trips to Los Angeles. And special thanks, too, to Patty White for her remote writing companionship as I completed the book. I am also grateful to the anonymous readers for Duke who read my proposal, my complete manuscript, and my revision with careful attention and who therefore helped me shape a better book.

Various archivists and industry professionals have shared their knowledge and expertise with me over the years. With thanks to David Black, Robert Butler, Nancy Meyer, Alexandra Seros, and especially Chris Levinson; a myriad of amazing staff at the Paley Center for Media in New York (where I began my research in earnest) and Martin Gostanian at the Paley Center for Media in Los Angeles; Hilary Swett of the Writers Guild Foundation and Barbara Hall for the initial discovery of *Columbo* scripts there; Mike Pepin at the library of the American Film Institute; Shannon Kelley and Mark Quigley of the UCLA Film and Television Archive; and Nancy Robinson and Melissa Byers of the Television Academy.

At Amherst College, I would like to thank a few key friends and colleagues: the wonderful Betsy Cannon-Smith, who, at our very first meeting when I came to the college, asked what she could do for me and, when I told her about my work on *Columbo*, proceeded to connect me with television writer and producer David Black, who in turn connected me with Mr. Link; Kathy Whittemore for her profile on "Team Columbo" (and Jiayi Liu for the great photos!); Kim Roeder for the invitation to speak about *Columbo* at the college's 2019 Family Weekend; Darryl Harper for his warmth and welcoming as the Director of the Center for Humanistic Inquiry; Dave Moran and John Kunhardt for their kindhearted interest in my work (and Dave for endlessly digitizing episodes of the series); Christian Rogowski for his collegiality, signature kindness, and friendship, which have sustained me since coming to the college to develop the Film and Media Studies Program; Joe Trapani for musical camaraderie and good cheer; and, most of all, Pete Marvin, a fellow *Columbo* aficionado who never failed to inquire about my work on this book over the years and who cheered me on to the end, whether he knew it or not.

A number of speaking engagements propelled my work at various points throughout my research and writing. For extending invitations to me, many thanks to Lynn Spigel to speak at Northwestern University for the Medium to Medium symposium; to Mary Desjardins to speak to her class at Dartmouth College; to Mark Williams to speak to his seminar at New York University; and to Mark Quigley for hosting our conversation after "*Chevy Mystery Show*: 'Enough Rope,'" as part of the UCLA Film and Television Archive screening series. A very special thanks to the bright star Kristi McKim for her invitation to be a Murphy Fellow at Hendrix College and for hosting my visit with such care, and an extra hats off to the amazing staff at Hendrix who won a national award for their design of the reception and dinner surrounding my talk. And finally let me thank Melissa Hardie, whose reading of my first book has forever buoyed me and whose organization of a series of talks at the University of Sydney, including a public conversation with her about *Columbo*, helped me complete the book; Melissa is as kind as she is brilliant (and that is saying something!), which made my visit equally an honor and a pleasure.

There are several stars behind this book, who swooped in at key moments or who continuously supported and propelled my work. First and foremost, I must thank my editor, Ken Wissoker, who invited me to pitch the project to Duke and who then let me write the book I wanted to write, who read drafts in progress, and who simply offered patience, kindness, care, and enthusiastic support throughout these long years. I also want to offer my appreciation to Chon Noriega, who read two chapters in progress and who lent attention to detail as well as a keen understanding of the broader project of the work, as he continuously encouraged the development of my voice therein. My profound thanks go to Mary Desjardins, who has long been a key mentor to me. I am grateful for her deep insights into television studies and television history, but even more than that I am grateful for her truly life-sustaining friendship. She also read a chapter in progress, and she and Michael DeAngelis invited me to submit an essay on *Columbo* for a special issue of *Celebrity Studies*, which became chapter 5 of this book. Were it not for Jenny Horne, I don't think I could have finished this book. I found myself at a crossroads in the spring and summer of 2015, when I knew I had to finally fish or cut bait. After a visit in Santa Cruz, Jenny and I wrote together remotely for weeks that summer, which was one of the happiest periods of writing that I have ever experienced. As icing on the cake, she and her partner, the beloved Jonathan Kahana, watched episodes of the series both so that they had a sense of what my work was about and also to enable Jenny to chime in with ideas and insights during our writing days. Even with hundreds of miles between us, rarely have I felt such companionship in my work. Thank you, dear Jenny, for those halcyon days. Among this embarrassment of riches, however, there is still one person whom I will forever think of as the central hero behind this book: Mark Quigley. As the John H. Mitchell Television Archivist at UCLA, he led me to sources that shaped many of my analytic methods and most certainly my understanding of the history undergirding this series. He brought me to the made-for-television movies by Richard Levinson and William Link, archived at UCLA, as well as another phenomenal television series they produced in the 1970s, *Tenafly*. He introduced me to the great television director Robert Butler, he happily talked with me about John Cassavetes and Peter Falk, and he answered all the major and minor questions I put to him. Every visit to the UCLA archives was a delight, both because I could revel in all things *Columbo* and because I had access to Mark's great mind and his astounding encyclopedic knowledge of television. I wish I had the words to adequately thank him here.

If I have forgotten anyone, please imagine me scratching my head and rummaging around in my pockets for a pen, and forgive me.

Prologue

If there's one thing worse than a television lady who thinks she knows
everything, it's a television lady who knows everything.
—The "Technical Director" in "Make Me a Perfect Murder"

Columbo essentially premiered on television three times. Given the
eponymous detective's signature line, "just one more thing," these repeated returns seem oddly appropriate. Its first iteration was a 1960
"live" teleplay written by Richard Levinson and William Link entitled
"Enough Rope," which appeared as part of *The Chevy Mystery Show*
(July 31, 1960).[1] It starred Burt Freed as the detective Lt. Columbo, a
New York City working-class police officer up against a wealthy psychologist who has killed his wife. The plot goes as follows: Dr. Roy Flemming (Richard Carlson) and his wife, Claire (played to shrill effect by
Barbara Stuart), are preparing to embark on a vacation to Canada, but
the doctor strangles his wife and stages a robbery to cover his crime. He
enlists one of his patients, who is also his paramour, to play the role of his
wife at the airport and on the plane; they stage a fight before the flight
takes off, and she leaves in a huff, to ensure that the "wife" is witnessed
as having returned home when the husband is already on his way to
Canada. Thus, the alibi and timing of the wife's murder appear to be
established, and the doctor disposes of the "stolen" property from their
New York apartment while away in order to maintain the ruse. When

he returns home, Lt. Columbo is on the scene, and the episode proceeds as the detective attempts to prove how the psychiatrist covered his crime. This structure—whereby the crime is committed at the beginning, and the detective needs only to prove what we, the audience, and seemingly he already know—is the model that (nearly) all future iterations will follow.

Levinson and Link rewrote "Enough Rope" to become a theatrical play called *Prescription: Murder*. It premiered in San Francisco on January 20, 1962, with Joseph Cotten as the murderer, Agnes Moorehead as his victim, and Thomas Mitchell as Lieutenant Columbo. After a successful run, Levinson and Link adapted the play in turn as a made-for-television movie on NBC in 1968 now starring Peter Falk in the lead role and with the same title as the play. In this iteration, *Prescription: Murder* (0:0; Feb. 20, 1968), the setting had moved to Los Angeles, with the vacation/alibi now pertaining to Mexico.[2] Aside from the change in locales, the plot was basically the same as the original teleplay, but the character of the detective himself was further developed in both the play and the subsequent adaptation into a made-for-television movie. Indeed, the context of the murderer's profession—psychiatry—enables this development, as both the detective and the murderer comment on his personality, fleshing him out into the character we will come to know over the run of the series.[3]

After the successful airing of *Prescription: Murder*, NBC invited creators Levinson and Link to produce a regular television series, but, at the time, Peter Falk was uninterested in headlining another TV show; he not only had recently played the titular character in *Trials of O'Brien* for a single season in 1965–66, but also had begun a collaborative relationship with John Cassavetes after working with him in the film *Husbands* (released in 1970). NBC thus developed a "wheel" series to accommodate the creators and the actor, as it was a format that rotated between different regular programs, each appearing for varying numbers of episodes. The network based the format on similar successes such as *The Name of the Game* (running from 1968 to 1971, it rotated between characters who all worked in the same publishing house), *The Bold Ones* (running from 1969 to 1973, it had four subseries in rotation, each focused on a different occupation), and *Four in One* (running from 1970 to 1971, it was even more varied than its precursors by occupation and genre). The network's new incarnation was *The NBC Mystery Movie*, which aired Sunday nights and included the additional mystery series *McMillan & Wife* and *McCloud* (the latter of which had previously been part of *Four in One*) and later expanded to another iteration on Wednesday nights.

Columbo thus premiered, yet again, in March 1971 with the now-pilot episode "Ransom for a Dead Man" (0:1; March 1, 1971; written and produced by Dean Hargrove); it then began its regular season as part of *The NBC Mystery Movie* in September of the same year with the episode "Murder by the Book" (1:1; Sept. 15, 1971). It ran as part of the NBC lineup for seven seasons. The most successful of all the series in rotation, it regularly made the no. 1 spot in ratings, earning Falk three Emmy Awards (in 1972, 1975, and 1976) and the writing team one (for "Death Lends a Hand" [1:2; Oct. 6, 1971]).[4] It also won a series of other Emmy Awards for cinematography, editing, and guest appearances, as well as the award for Outstanding Limited Series in 1974, and it received a regular slew of nominations for its entire original run. The series won a Golden Globe for Best Drama in 1973, and Falk won the Golden Globe for Best TV Actor the same year.[5] During this highly successful run, between three and eight original episodes were broadcast each year of its seven seasons, with a total of forty-four episodes overall.

During the first few years on the air, the series helped to launch and foster the careers of a number of significant television writers and directors. Before going on to create his own successful crime and legal series like *Hill Street Blues*, *LA Law*, *Murder One*, and *NYPD Blue*, Steven Bochco penned seven episodes, including "Murder by the Book," which was directed by Steven Spielberg, a Universal regular at the time; Bochco was also employed as the story editor for the first season. Stephen J. Cannell worked on the series early on before he created his own series (*The Rockford Files*, featuring another charming 1970s detective), as did Dean Hargrove (the showrunner for several seasons, who later created US cozies like *Father Dowling Mysteries* and *Matlock*), Roland Kibbee (who executive-produced alongside Hargrove for most of seasons 3 and 4), and Peter S. Fischer (who cocreated *Murder, She Wrote* with Levinson and Link and went on to executive-produce the Angela Lansbury series).[6] Some of the writers were already television veterans, such as Hargrove, Kibbee, and Jackson Gillis, the latter of whom was also a longtime writer of *Perry Mason*. Many of the formative writers of the first several years had moved on to various other projects by the final two seasons, though the series did showcase the directorial work of semiregular Patrick McGoohan in the fifth season and future filmmaker Jonathan Demme in the last season.[7] These final two seasons demonstrate, then, both another beginning and its multiple endings. In fact, the chaotic "Last Salute to the Commodore" (5:6; May 2, 1976), directed by McGoohan in the fifth season, was originally slated to be the last episode, concluding with the lieutenant in a small boat in the Los Angeles harbor, rowing away from the scene of both the crime and his solution. The actual final episode of its original run, "The Conspirators" (7:5; May 13, 1978), reorients that previous ending in grander scope: here the detective remains on land while hailing a ship through the Coast Guard before it can disappear with the murder weapon on board.

Complicating its beginnings and its endings, *Columbo* and "Columbo" have reappeared in various forms since the original series. In 1989 *Columbo* was back on television, this time on ABC, as an ongoing but irregular two-hour movie series; between its first showing in 1989 and 2003, twenty-four new episodes ran, with Falk as a primary producer. Richard Levinson had passed away in 1987, and William Link was a supervising producer only for nine episodes, until 1990, when Falk largely took the reins. While five episodes of this reboot were penned by original writers for the series, overall the production team of the original was not intact; therefore, while it followed the basic formula, it was largely driven by the character rather than the narrative and visual style, with much of the authority on set coming from Falk himself. Two final reappearances of the detective as a crime solver followed: in 2010, Link published a collection of stories of new mysteries for the detective at the same time that the original play, *Prescription: Murder*, enjoyed a revival. And in countless other television series—such as *Monk*, when a character played by Gena Rowlands compares Adrian Monk to the lieutenant, or Hallmark's *Flower Shop Mysteries*, when the amateur sleuth Abby Knight (Brooke Shields) makes a brief distinction between bingeing *Columbo* and *Murder, She Wrote* (two series that regularly reran on the Hallmark Movies & Mysteries Channel, after all)—the character is invoked time and time again. In 2023, the series *Pokerface* was introduced, and was widely recognized as an homage to *Columbo* and other 1970s series. And Columbo's influence has spread beyond television: the "Columbo technique" became a mode of police and psychiatric training.[8]

Given the local networks that have broadcast it over time, in syndication both in the United States and throughout the globe, the series has appeared on more channels than one can count. It was the first US series to air in China after an embargo on importation of American television was lifted, and it was said to be Queen Elizabeth's favorite series in the 1970s. Since the 1990s, it has also been a staple of cable channels such as A&E, Bravo, COZI, the Hallmark Movies & Mysteries Channel, ME, and Sundance. In the twenty-first century, it has appeared on various streaming platforms from Netflix to IMDb/Amazon/Freevee to YouTube to NBC's Peacock channel. Attesting to the series' and the star's international popularity, upon Peter Falk's death in 2011, obituaries were printed all over the world.[9] In 2021, marking the fiftieth anniversary of the first full season, *Columbo* appeared again in the news in the form of tributes and nostalgic references.[10]

The very nature of *Columbo*'s run between 1960 and 2003 signals not just its popularity but also its tenacity; through its repeated returns to television, the series itself operated not unlike its own lead. As the detective invariably uttered "just one more thing" to the murderers at the precise moment they thought they were rid of him, this phrase could also describe the series' unwillingness to go away. But not that we would want it to: the rumpled detective and the easygoing narrative format—revealing to the audience the killer from the start, so that our own work is mainly to *watch*, reveling in the solution that we already know is coming—offer us a level of both comfort and satisfaction as viewers. In fact, essentially knowing the outcome from the beginning enables one to watch each episode over and again, as we are never just watching for the "whodunit." The series, like its lead character, makes for easy company, and opportunities to view it across cable television and streaming platforms make for easy access.

More than perhaps any other television series in my life—and, believe me, there have been many—*Columbo* has proved to be my most steadfast companion. When I was a young kid in the 1970s, my family regularly watched three television series as a unit: *The Mary Tyler Moore Show* and *The Bob Newhart Show* on Saturday nights and, on Sundays, *The NBC Mystery Movie*. As with the majority of American viewers of the program, *Columbo* was my favorite. Taking a page from the detective himself, I am dogged in my returns to the series. As a viewer over decades, my experience with the series is a means of telling my own history (where I lived, with whom, and even what couch I owned), and it's also a means of telling a history of changing televisual access and technological forms. Thus, when I moved to New York City after college, my roommate and I happily discovered it in syndication on Sunday afternoons on the local WWOR station. As a graduate student in Milwaukee, Wisconsin, I watched it regularly on the A&E cable network, sometimes daily. When I moved to Santa Cruz, California, I would look for it on Bravo and the Hallmark Channel in the first decade of the twentieth century. And when I went east to Massachusetts ten years later, I found it on the streaming platforms Netflix, YouTube, IMDb, and Peacock. Even more specific instances and devices—old and new—are linked to this series for me. The episode entitled "A Stitch in Crime" (2:6; Feb. 11, 1973) was one of the first two recordings I made when I got TiVo in November 2004. I bought my first video iPod principally to transfer episodes of the series to take with me to Paris in 2008 (where I also found DVDs of its various seasons at the Les Halles media library in 2009). Driving across the country in the summer of 2013, I landed in a motel in Columbia, Missouri: after a particularly arduous day, I found an episode waiting for me on the ME network when I flipped on the television. The persistent appearance of a series like *Columbo* across both new and old media is itself suggestive of the ways in which the medium has and hasn't entirely transformed, even if, increasingly, new devices and new means of viewing enable viewers to deny that they are, in fact, watching "television."

Inevitably, when I first learned about the opportunity to write an academic book on the series, I was eager to put all of my own viewing history to work. But "*Columbo* and work" also seems a funny sort of combination, given the love I've had for the show since I was so very young. At the same time, I am the first to insist that we write about those things that move us—those things that we care deeply about—while also maintaining an investigatory eye. Not uncoincidentally, for me the very ability to analyze the series and television as an intertextual system comes from *Columbo* itself. And this is, perhaps, partly why I love it.

Introduction

I thought of a labyrinth of labyrinths, of one sinuous spreading
labyrinth that would encompass the past and the future and would
somehow involve the stars.
—Jorge Luis Borges, "The Garden of Forking Paths"

Reading Columbo

In "Make Me a Perfect Murder" (7:3; Feb. 25, 1978), our eponymous hero
is investigating the murder of a television network executive. His work
brings him to the production facilities, where he is trained in, among
other instruments, the technical director's console. When he sits down
at the board with the technician to discuss the production of live
television, the techie first asks after the neck brace that he is wearing at
the time; that conversational strategy—not getting directly to the point,
rather like the spinning of a wheel—is a specialty of the lieutenant's, of
course, and he responds in kind, detailing what a number of medical
professionals have suggested is the cause of his neck problem. Then,
looking at the series of monitors in front of him, he asks, "All these
screens—for just one show?" Turning on one screen, the technician announces, "That's a line monitor; that's what's going on the air." He turns
on another: "The preview monitor is what the director wants up next."
And, as he turns on the four screens below at once, he says, "And those
are what the four cameras see."

The detective marvels at what he sees: "All these beautiful machines, all these buttons to push. I know it costs millions and I know everybody works very hard. But . . . to me it looks like fun." The technician confesses that it is fun and then, in response to Columbo's question, confirms that Miss Freestone (the killer and Columbo's primary suspect) does indeed understand the technology. At that, the technician leaves Columbo alone at the board, and thus begins a two-minute sequence in which the detective plays with the machines. Rather than working with the images available from the four cameras, however, he plays abstract shapes that dance to musical accompaniment—starting with a simple rendition of his signature tune "This Old Man," which becomes increasingly symphonic. Like the discussion of the neck brace, this is another tangent, if a purely audiovisual one. It's a scene, too, that demonstrates the detective's attention and delight. And it invokes attention and delight in the viewer: patience in light of a visual tangent which becomes another sort of amusement, a multiplied focus on simultaneous elements, and an affection for the detective's own simple pleasure.

This scene, with its multiple screens that the detective looks across, its demand for patient attention, and its invitation to delight in what we see as well, also functions for me as a model for reading the series itself and television overall. As a kind of microcosm of this interpretative method, the original format of *Columbo* is itself indicative of the ways in which the series—and television as a whole, whether in the heyday of the broadcast era or in the increasingly digital universe of exhibition and reception—presents plentitude and possibility, logic and serendipity as part of its structural design. Those multiple screens before Columbo's very eyes might stand in for a series of texts (a range of episodes of *Columbo* itself; or perhaps *Columbo* alongside other series during its original airing on Sunday nights; or maybe the Sunday night schedule on NBC: what's on now and what's coming up next; or, five decades later, a subheading of suggestions on a subscription platform). Set alongside one another, they invite intertextual analysis. And as representative of a practice of interpreting the series itself, I'd argue that *Columbo*, too, invites us to read between various texts: various episodes of the series, this and other series, the series and various films, the series and memoirs or board games or tie-in novels, and so on. At

I.1. "All these buttons to push" ("Make Me a Perfect Murder," 7:3; Feb. 25, 1978)

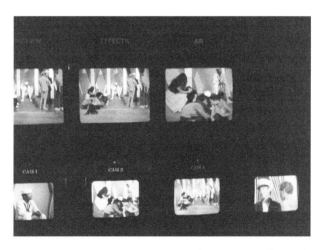

I.2. This is what the camera sees ("Make Me a Perfect Murder," 7:3; Feb. 25, 1978)

the same time, while the detective sits in the director's chair, learning about the production of live broadcast television, I'd suggest that this sequence invites us to recognize that an intertextual reading is also a *con*textual reading—that is, it enables us to understand *Columbo* within the historical moment during which it was made, across a range of contexts that informs its production.

And, in fact, the multiple monitors, or squares, of the scene in "Make Me a Perfect Murder" visually mark a form of reading that is also part of the design of the original broadcast context of the series as a whole, as part of its weekly mystery "wheel series," a mode of programming that rotates between regular series within the same time slot. The wheel itself is a neat mechanism. Individual spokes are connected to a larger whole: spin it, and you'll likely land in a different place time after time. Such a process enables us to find serendipitous connections between things. In fact, it's not unlike watching television in real time: "change the channel" at any time of day, and it's like a spin of a wheel. Hence, as one turns a dial, hits a button, or scans a touchscreen, almost instantaneously a viewer can make connections across series, networks, even historical periods: one instance, or one television text, inevitably informs another. For me, watching *Columbo* is always an invitation to look across many screens at once: even as I attend to this singular text, I am making a series of connections to others, much like the lieutenant's own process of detection. Circles and squares. Serendipity and logic. Their coexistence is possible in the plentitude of television itself and the complex mode of viewing that it demands.

Reading Television, Intertextually

The premise of this book might seem quite simple: the television series *Columbo* trains us as detectives of television. However, as Umberto Eco, himself a fan of *Columbo*, claims, "If you want to use television for teaching somebody something, you have first to teach somebody how to use television."[1] After all, television itself is not that simple, and to learn either about it or from it, "detecting" television requires a particular kind of attention.[2] Such attentiveness is born out of what we might also understand as distraction, for one's attention to television is always an attention to more than one thing at once: for instance, we multiply rather than divide our attention to both form and content together, but we are also always exposed, and perhaps even predisposed, to the range of simultaneous possibilities that television offers, whether from the multitude of viewing options at any one moment to the movement between different kinds of successive segments from moment to moment. Though one could claim that US commercial broadcast or cable television—of which the series was and still is a part—can be easily broken down into its central modus operandi *to sell*, I'd like here to imagine television also as a form that is full of narrative, epistemological, and temporal possibilities through its literal simultaneous play of texts at any and every hour and its accumulation of content (as well as form) over several decades. It offers, in effect, a complex technology of reading for its viewers and its analysts: that is, television—no matter what sort of screen or platform we use to watch it today—provides a mechanism for continuously reading across and between the variety of content that we see before us. Imagine for a moment turning on the television set and a "set-top box" such as Roku or AppleTV: what we see is an amalgam of series and films we have watched across channels and streaming platforms, alongside others that are recommended to us based on prior viewing habits. Here, then, algorithms read viewers themselves, reaffirming and expanding the reach of an intertextual system.[3]

Much foundational work in television studies in the 1970s and 1980s sought to define television as an ideological and textual system. Based on analyses of commercial broadcast television—the dominant delivery system of this period in the United States—critical work emerging at this time considered the complex textual rhythms of television and its economic, psychic, and ideological effects on its viewers. Structurally, critics focused both on the ubiquitous "flow" of television, which integrated disparate segments over blocks of time (narrative or news programs, ads, network announcements, and so on), and on the very segmentation of television textuality.[4] For instance, published alongside one another in the same pages of the Summer 1984 issue of *Quarterly Review of Film Studies*, key contributions to the field by Nick Browne and Beverle Houston centered, respectively, on the demarcation of television textuality and its promise of plentitude—two sides of the same coin. In "The Political Economy of the Television (Super) Text," Browne defines three elements of televisual textuality: the text, supertext, and megatext. The text is a singular entity, such as a program like *Columbo*. The supertext "consists of the particular program and all the introductory and interstitial materials—chiefly announcements and ads—considered in its specific position in the schedule."[5] The megatext, then, "consists of everything that has appeared on television."[6] Houston's "Viewing Television: The Metapsychology of Endless Consumption" is a psychoanalytically grounded investigation of television's basic contradiction: the promise of endless textual flow, blocked by interruptions that leave viewers in a state of endless desire and an endless lack of satisfaction. Describing these complex rhythms of desire, Houston writes, "Of television we say: I always want it as I have never had it."[7] Columbo himself and *Columbo* fans might identify this desire as that for "just one more thing."

My study of *Columbo* is in great part grounded in its "supertext" and "megatext," yet rather than connecting it to "everything that has appeared on television," I'm interested in tracing a constellation of textual relations with the series at the center. This approach links my work to critics like Browne, Houston, and many others who employed intertextual methods of analysis that were at once capacious and focused as they drew on the plentitude of both television's supertext and megatext. As Mimi White argues in "Crossing Wavelengths: The Diegetic and Referential Imaginary of American Commercial Television," televisual structure demands such an interpretive method. Her essay thus begins: "The continuity and multiplicity of texts that comprise the medium of American television present the critic-analyst with a complex, multiform body of material. To analyze requires an operation of segmentation, fragmentation isolating a discrete sequence from the course of the flow of television programming according to a critical principle of pertinence."[8] Homing in on particular sequences of flow, such as an hour of morning or prime-time television, critics delineated this concept through examples gathered from television "supertext" sequences—themselves indicative of the tension between "flow" and "segment"—in order to explore the effects of television's intertextuality.[9] In her book-length study of children's media, *Playing with Power in Movies, Television, and Video Games*, Marsha Kinder defines this approach: "In contemporary media studies, intertextuality has come to mean that any individual text (whether an artwork like a movie or novel, or a more commonplace text like a newspaper article, billboard, or casual verbal remark) is part of a larger cultural discourse and therefore must be read in relationship to other texts and their diverse textual strategies and ideological assumptions."[10] Such potential relationships abound in *Columbo.* One simple example is apparent in the season 2 episode "A Stitch in Crime," which stars Leonard Nimoy as the murderer, Dr. Mayfield; Will Geer as his would-be victim, Dr. Hiedeman; and Anne Francis as one of his actual victims. Nimoy and Geer play characters consistent with their roles in *Star Trek* and *The Waltons*, respectively. Drawing on his turn as the Vulcan Spock, who doesn't experience human emotion, Nimoy plays a seemingly emotionless surgeon (albeit more calculating than Spock), while Geer plays a kindlier doctor, akin to his contemporaneous role on *The Waltons.* In short, the cold and logical Mr. Spock is up against the warm and loving Grandpa. And the nurse who initially investigates Dr. Mayfield's murderous scheme is played by Francis, who helmed *Honey West* as a private detective. Here the intertextual connections serve as a kind of continuity of our understanding of each of the actors' roles, rewarding the attentive viewer for what might at first just seem to be a practice of "endless consumption."

But that consumption is not always, nor need it be, the only aim of viewing television. Following White and others, Hamid Naficy sees intertextual analysis as an essential analytical means of responding to the complexity of television textuality. As he notes, "Defining the television text . . . has proven to be a problem largely because it is such a multipurpose, polyvalent, and amorphous text."[11] Employing a similar method of analysis to White and Kinder, Naficy attempts to "problematize flow" as a parallel to his critique of television's production of normative social values. At the same time, he considers how resonances running across textual segments within a larger television sequence can produce readings that subvert the dominant paradigms that singular texts might attempt to reinforce. Like Houston, Naficy also recognizes tensions that emerge through an intertextual format, noting that complementary and contradictory resonances may occur simultaneously—erecting and dismantling central cultural beliefs.[12] Such is the approach of scholar Herman Gray, whose essay "Television, Black Americans, and the American Dream" was published the same year as Naficy's work. Employing a similar method in his critical interpretation of examples of television's "supertext," Gray argues that "representations make sense in terms of their intertextuality between and within programs"; hence, in his analysis of fictional and nonfictional programming, Gray suggests that "television representations of black life in the late 1980s cannot be read in isolation but rather should be read in terms of their relationship to other television texts."[13] Simply put, the relationship Gray describes here between television texts reveals television as both a textual and a historical-cultural system; understanding television texts, therefore, yields an understanding beyond their narrative purviews.

As the above cases demonstrate, again and again scholars considered television as a polyvalent system, which was formally organized, at once divided and multiplied by time and segments. Drawing on Eco's claims above, I contend that television's organizing principles teach us how to use television, and, arguably, our "use"—whether we are critics, scholars, students, or everyday viewers—is itself a kind of understanding. Watching television, in other words, is replete with acts of recognition, whether that incites tension or builds continuity. And that recognition—with its attendant tension and continuity—is not only of different texts or performances, but also of television as a textual, technological, economic, and ideological system. In "Crossing Wavelengths," White emphasizes that televisual structure is a self-referential system, as it embraces its "self-perpetuation as a medium."[14] Considering a series of examples of the "cross-pollination" of television in which characters from one program appear on others, either directly in a nightly lineup, across nights on a specific network, or simply within singular cameo appearances, White argues that the "all-encompassing self-referentiality of commercial television as the world of television's fictions is brought together as parts of a larger, continuous imaginary world."[15] Arguably, the form of intertextual "reading" White and others describe has become so naturalized that most viewers are barely conscious of it. Take another example that bears its own connection to the last I offered, also evident of the ways in which television stars seemingly glide between personas on our screens yet leave traces behind in their wake. That is, when William Shatner appears in a commercial for Priceline in the twenty-first century—or as a "bad" actor on *Columbo* in the mid-1970s—we likely still see *Star Trek*'s Captain Kirk of the 1960s (who, of course, returned again and again in the *Star Trek* movie franchise), so that our perception of this "character" he now plays is forever informed by his signature role. And even if we don't know him as Kirk, the logic of television still inscribes the character that Shatner has become through a series of embedded references: the neatness of his attire, the clarity of his voice, the command of his manner, the barely disguised mirth on his face. Whether we "know" him or not, we likely know we are supposed to. The rhetorical question television implicitly and continuously asks, after all, is "Aren't you clever?" The "you" it addresses and the "we" who watch forever occupy this position as knowing viewers.

Taking an example even closer to home, Peter Falk appears in comedic detective films in the late 1970s, and we think of him simultaneously as "Sam Diamond" or "Lou Peckinpaugh" and as Lieutenant Columbo. He returns to the small screen a decade later in the reboot of *Columbo* and he carries some of the traces of this parody with him, so that now "Columbo" plays Columbo.[16] Television depends on this multivalent element of actors to keep viewers watching over time, attentive. Of course, such an observation is hardly new in thinking about film or television or celebrity stardom. Still, not merely bound to character or actor crossovers, these kinds of interconnections are enabled by the very form of television, perhaps even more so than they are by film. This possibility doesn't go away as people increasingly watch "television" off the set itself; in fact, it's almost infinitely multiplied as we toggle between platforms and, within platforms, between a multitude of texts (some potentially "live," others dropped on schedule, and most recorded long ago). After all, as Sheila Murphy argues in *How Television Invented New Media*, "television establishes our expectations about media and technology, and it is through television that many people have learned how to be media users and individuals."[17] In its simultaneous "broadcast" and reception of multiple texts at once, I'd argue—that is, in the nearly unlimited access we have to television texts on cable, on DVD, and streaming online—television invites its viewers to always participate in a form of networked thinking. We are not simply watching detectives on-screen but potentially becoming detectives of the medium itself.

Television's Infinite Dimensions

Kinder, Naficy, and White, along with others such as John Fiske, drew on Bulgarian-French literary theorist Julia Kristeva's definition of intertextuality, which—implicitly demonstrating the very practice of this theory itself—was drawn from the work of Mikhail Bakhtin. I want briefly to turn to Kristeva here, not merely as a (quasi) originating site of theoretical production but also for some neat coincidental references she and Bakhtin include in their work. Given her structuralist-linguistic roots, Kristeva develops an understanding by first boiling language down to its basic elements, starting with the word *intertextuality*, which she saw as the "intersection of textual surfaces."[18] To read intertextually, furthered Kristeva, is to read "at least double."[19] Two key notions of such double, or "ambivalent," readings are embedded in this concept. For one, "the writer can use another's word, giving it a new meaning while retaining the meaning it already had. The result is a word with two significations: it becomes *ambivalent*."[20] In her emphasis on the practice of language ("discourse"), Kristeva points to another central issue: "The term *ambivalence* implies the insertion of history (society) into a text and of this text into history; for the writer they are one and the same."[21] In other words, the nascence of intertextuality as a system and method for reading is necessarily linked to social, cultural, and historical contexts. This understanding is vital to a study of television, in which not only is the "text" never only one thing, but it is also always delivered through formal, institutional, ideological, and cultural contexts. Such textual multiplicity is also multidimensional, Kristeva argued, drawing on Bakhtin's key terms. Defining his notion of the "carnivalesque," which itself drew on Fyodor Dostoyevsky's novel *Crime and Punishment* (one of the sources for *Columbo*), she notes that it is where "language escapes linearity (law) to live as drama in three dimensions."[22] Such simultaneity and multidimensionality give way to the "potential infinity" of carnivalesque discourse.[23] Indeed, as she concludes her essay, Kristeva argues, "If there is a model for poetic language, it no longer involves lines or surfaces, but rather, *space* and *infinity*."[24]

Twenty-five years before Kristeva's definition of intertextuality and only seven years before the emergence of US television in 1948, Jorge Luis Borges penned "The Garden of Forking Paths." The narrator of this short story describes his ancestor Ts'ui Pên's dual obsession: the production of a novel with nearly countless characters and "a maze in which all men would become lost."[25] Amid his own byzantine journey of treachery, the narrator comes upon Dr. Stephen Albert, who reveals his ancestor's secret: the novel and the maze were one and the same. Explains Albert, "He believed in an infinite series of times, in a growing, dizzying net of divergent, convergent and parallel times. This network of times which approached one another, forked, broke off, or were unaware of one another for centuries, embraces all possibilities of time."[26] Borges might well have imagined libraries as his labyrinths; and though the one he oversaw, the National Library of Argentina, had a finite number of books during his tenure—numbering about 900,000, which, as Borges wrote, "perhaps . . . seems more than a million"—one might suggest that the works housed together were a model for "space and infinity."[27] Taking this notion a step further, I'd like to imagine that Borges describes and demonstrates, in works such as "The Garden of Forking Paths," textual forms that seem like models for television—or at least for reading television: "a labyrinth of labyrinths."

As other scholars have also declared, I recognize that the design of television—with its own growing "networks" that are divergent, convergent, and parallel—makes for a challenging object of study, demanding that we define carefully our parameters of study, our objects of analysis. Whereas, as I've noted, foundational work in the field of television studies frequently focused on television as a textual *system*, much of the work that has followed in its wake over the past twenty-odd years has turned to singular texts, or series, whether in individual volumes such as those in the very series of which this book is a part, in chapters of anthologies devoted to particular programs, or in collections that showcase multiple series through essays dedicated to individual examples.[28] My own approach is to bridge these critical tendencies and eras—albeit with some additions, distinctions, and permutations—in order to see *Columbo* as a series that enables us to understand television as both a textual and historical system that, no matter what form of delivery or reception, is at heart intertextual. Indeed, my intention here is to narrow the focus (on the series *Columbo*) in order to enable an intertextual analysis and perform a process of interconnected thinking.

To further define my particular practice of intertextual analysis, let me first return to the image of a wheel. *Columbo* remains at the center, and from it I am mapping relations outward, like various parallel and at times overlapping spokes. Such spokes include, for example, the work of actors (not only Falk but also various guest stars); the work of the creators Levinson and Link; and a sampling of other television series and films. Other vectors that stretch beyond the series are enabled by the historical context of the series' production, emerging media forms, and television as a medium, then and now. As I've said, as a medium, television itself is inherently intertextual, which is in part based on its temporal structure, characterized by present, past, and future. In other words, its temporal makeup includes simultaneity of access to multiple texts at once as well as its coexistence with viewers, or what Jane Feuer terms its "liveness" and what Vivian Sobchack would call its "presence"; its role as an archive of television and film history, which is particularly prevalent in streaming platforms but was already in place via rerun culture; and its state of anticipation, articulated through announcements of what's on next, whether flowing through a chronological schedule on cable television or in the near-instant playing of sequential episodes on streaming platforms like Netflix or YouTube.[29] Of course, television's intertextual organization is also a result of its operating machinery; just take a glance at a device like an iPad with a series of streaming apps set alongside one another in their own individual frames. These various subscription services are not so unlike broadcast networks or cable channels, and indeed some of the apps are invariably based on networks and channels (PBS, Paramount+, Max, and so on). Further, the fact that viewers so frequently have multiple devices on which to watch television, even if they deny that it is, in fact, "television" that they're viewing, is a reproduction of television's already "polyvalent" textuality.[30] Viewers may even use these devices simultaneously, whether as a mechanism to "make any room your TV room," and therefore to ensure that "the television" is always on no matter where they are, or to glance between texts in a state of distracted yet interwoven attention.[31]

Ultimately, I believe looking at *Columbo* opens, rather than fore-closes, investigative possibilities. That opening, which at times during my work has felt infinite, is possible through a broad accumulation of research, which links the *Columbo* movies, series, and reboot to a "diz-zying net of divergent, convergent and parallel times," which I begin to summarize in the section to follow. And I would argue that, in his predilection for tangents, Columbo's own investigative process is not unlike Borges's byzantine vision, modeling imaginative processes of as-sociation, processes that I follow in turn.

Learning with the Lieutenant

As I've suggested, *Columbo* is a series that provides delight in knowing—whether that's the knowledge of the crime itself as well as the fact that our detective will always catch the killer, or the cultural knowledge that Lt. Columbo accrues in each episode and therefore shares with us. I shall now trace some preoccupations through the series' narrative struc-ture and by what elements it's commonly known, further developing its place in the context of television as a medium. First and foremost, its narrative form sets up the audience's own knowledge of events be-fore the detective himself comes to know them. The plot structure of each episode is based loosely on *Crime and Punishment*, Dostoyevsky's nineteenth-century novel that begins with the criminal and the crime—the arrogant Raskolnikov who commits murder largely to see if he can get away with it—well before the detective, Porfiry Petrovich, comes on the scene to solve it. In the case of the novel, of course, Petrovich's appearance at the crime scene is the reader's first meeting with the offi-cer, so we don't know immediately what he knows; moreover, we don't know at first that Petrovich's seeming ignorance is merely a guise.[32] In the case of *Columbo*, the audience catches on to this trick of the lieu-tenant's through the repeated televisual episodic formula, so, in essence, it's the murderer who is the last to know how clever our detective really is. Having witnessed the murder ourselves, as an audience we are already presented with the evidence of the crime; what follows is our observa-tion of how the detective uncovers the evidence to match what we (and, apparently, he) already know.

Indeed, as part of the series' formula, Columbo appears to know who the killer is almost immediately upon meeting them. In "Troubled Waters" (4:4; Feb. 9, 1975), he seems to recognize the murderer even before the crime is committed; in a twist on the usual structure, the first person we see on-screen is the detective, running to get on a vacation cruise ship, and he nearly bumps into the man who will shortly thereafter kill his blackmailing former lover. "Candidate for Crime" (3:3; Nov. 4, 1973) begins the same way, with Columbo seeing the murderer, a senatorial candidate, as he walks through the police station. And at the end of "Murder under Glass" (7:2; Jan. 30, 1978), an episode from the final season whose function appears to be to remark implicitly on the conventions of the series, the murderer and food critic Paul Gerard (Louis Jourdan) asks, "When did you first suspect me?" The lieutenant answers, "As it happens, sir, about two minutes after I met you." Sometimes it's even sooner (but otherwise never as soon as in "Troubled Waters") and sometimes a bit later, but it's never too long; after all, the murderer in this series is almost always the most arrogant person on the scene, the one who is certain they have gotten away with it, the one who has answers to all of the detective's questions. In fact, this element of the formula is also based in *Crime and Punishment*'s Raskolnikov, whose belief in his own superiority over others enables him to commit murder. Though this belief is usually not explicitly stated by the killers of *Columbo*, it is an implicit motivation for their crimes.

The first regular episode of *Columbo*, "Murder by the Book," is, in many ways, a blueprint for the faithful audience's own preoccupations with the series to come and the series' preoccupations and narrative conventions that ultimately fascinate all of us. Most obviously, it is the story of a partnership in crime: the murderer and his victim are together the cowriters of a series of mystery novels featuring "Mrs. Melville," an older woman not unlike Agatha Christie's Miss Marple. But it also begets our own partnership with a series—and its eponymous detective—that will last seven years in its initial run and decades beyond in both its syndication and its reboot. An instance of the creation of the prolific writing team Richard Levinson and William Link, starring three-time guest star Jack Cassidy, scripted by television producer-to-be Steven Bochco, and directed by future Hollywood magnate Steven Spielberg, this episode is at once rife with self-reflexive references and with elements that predict its historical significance to come. With its nods and winks—one of the first cowritten Mrs. Melville novels is entitled *Prescription: Murder*, the very title of the *Columbo* stage play and pilot—it's no wonder that many viewers facetiously asked which of Link or Levinson was the murderer and which was the murdered.[33]

In essence, the episode goes like this: as one writer, Jim Ferris (Martin Milner), wishes to dissolve the partnership, the other, Ken Franklin (Jack Cassidy), plots his murder.[34] After all, Franklin can't afford to lose the wealth he's garnered as part of a best-selling team. He takes Ferris to his vacation house by a lake, where he suggests Ferris call his wife to claim he's still at the office. While Ferris is on the phone, Franklin shoots him, essentially establishing his own alibi, as Ferris has told his wife he is still in Los Angeles. Shortly thereafter, Columbo first encounters Franklin at the duo's writing office, where he is investigating the disappearance of Ferris, particularly because his wife reported hearing the sounds of the gunshot over the phone. At the office, Franklin offers the detective a stack of mystery novels by the team to peruse, suggesting the detective might learn from their Mrs. Melville. Columbo also travels to Franklin's lake house, where he wonders about the cost of vacation living. He travels, too, to the widow's home, where he spontaneously whips up an omelet (the secret is not to add milk, he reveals) and keeps her company as he questions her about her husband's writing habits.[35] Thus, this episode establishes several conventions that will come to preoccupy the series as a whole: the implication that the killer's intelligence is superior to the lieutenant's, an ongoing emphasis on class difference, the role of communications technology as alibi, an implicit and sometimes self-reflexive obsession with plotting, and the demonstration of the detective's character traits we come to know with affection.

Key to the detective's traits is his own fascination with learning. The detective's expertise is superficially humbler than that of the killers he tracks. Not only do these killers, then, repeatedly not recognize his investigative prowess, but nearly every episode also requires that the detective educate himself about something, particularly in relation to the killer's own field of expertise (such as a cultural commodity like wine or a technological gadget like a VCR) or in relation to money matters (the cost of a tailored suit or a new pair of shoes). An episode in season 5, "A Matter of Honor" (5:4; Feb. 1, 1976), explicitly spells out the logic of the series. The setting is Mexico, and the detective's field of study becomes bullfighting, as the killer is a famous matador (played by Ricardo Montalbán) who murders his best friend rather than being exposed as a coward.[36] Around halfway through the episode, the police chief, Commandante Sanchez (played by Pedro Armendáriz Jr.), with whom Columbo has been working, greets the detective as he's reading up on bullfighting. "Learning anything?" he asks. Answers the lieutenant: "I have to learn something, since I didn't know anything to start with."[37] This is a definitive moment for the series, for, as I've suggested, *Columbo* is a series that is about *knowing*—or the process of coming-to-know—whether about crime detection, television, or cultural forms. But it is also a series that was and is *known*. It is known, first and foremost, for its eponymous character and for its narrative format, which gives way to a particular pace, dialogue style, and aesthetic. And it's certainly known, as I'll come to discuss, for its class consciousness—the class conflict designated between the killer and the working-class cop, set within Los Angeles and its cultural environs.

Central to its plot structure and dialogue, the detective confirms what he knows in part through conversations with the killers.[38] These conversations set the pace—the "plodding" of the plot—for each episode. The lieutenant offers the killers those questions about the case he cannot seem to answer himself, and it's the murderers who hypothesize, usually offering an alternate scenario than that which they plotted. (The innocents almost never have an answer to such conundrums.) In part, this hypothesizing certainly makes sense, as several cases involve people in the business of murder or of manipulation (the latter involving both mind and body). These killers include plotters of fictional murders, like writers or publishers of detective fiction, a television producer, and a television actor who plays a detective, as well as a pop psychologist, a body-building expert, a makeup maven, and even a magician. Indeed, the very first murderer, recall, is a psychologist, to whom the first Columbo (Burt Freed) queries whether he should pursue therapy: "I think I'm too suspicious. I don't trust people." And he goes on to offer the particular case in point to demonstrate his mistrust. In all these situations, when Columbo brings a dilemma to one of these suspects, he's speaking with an "expert": thus, in "Try and Catch Me" (7:1; Nov. 21, 1977), after the popular mystery writer Abigail Mitchell (Ruth Gordon) catches her breath after "learning" of her nephew's murder, she tells her assistant she doesn't have time to rest because she has "work to do with Lieutenant Columbo."[39]

The conversational formula of the series and its eponymous detective applies to all the suspects, not just the "experts." Indeed, the conversations might appear to function as a "talking cure"; surely, they do ultimately induce the guilt of the criminal. The killers want to speak—either in an attempt, presumably, to throw attention off of themselves in offering an alternate scenario or, more than likely, in order to flaunt what they believe is their superior intelligence over the hapless detective. By season 6, "The Bye-Bye Sky High I.Q. Murder Case" (6:3; May 22, 1977) is an episode explicitly about intelligence and analysis, in which one Mensa-like club member has killed another in order to cover up his crimes of embezzlement. In the final scene, as the detective reels in the killer, Oliver Brandt (Theodore Bikel), Columbo offers a pretense of his own misunderstanding of the crime. When he explains his solution of how the killer covered his crime with an alibi, creating a highly complex mechanism to fake a series of gunshots, he emphasizes that "the killer is a very intelligent man." Since Columbo gets the setup for the mechanism "wrong," Brandt grows insistent upon proving his own superior intelligence both over the detective and his fellow members of the Mensa-like club. He corrects Columbo suddenly in order to demonstrate the exact process by which he created the shots that designed his alibi, shouting "The man who conceived all this—you've made him out to be a bumbling ass!" while the image cuts to reveal Columbo slyly smiling. The image cuts again to Brandt moving quickly around the room to restore the conditions of the alibi: "No, this is what he would have done!" We watch in slow motion as the mechanism works to fire the shots. He victoriously repeats "There!" as Columbo again smiles, having caught him not in the actual act, of course, but in the perfect reenactment.

Though key, these conversational games, which often spell out the motive, are only part of the detective's investigative process. The crime is

I.3. A murderer's hubris ("The Bye-Bye Sky High I.Q. Murder Case," 6:3; May 22, 1977)

I.4. The detective's "gotcha" ("The Bye-Bye Sky High I.Q. Murder Case," 6:3; May 22, 1977)

I.5. A murderer's realization ("The Bye-Bye Sky High I.Q. Murder Case," 6:3; May 22, 1977)

ultimately solved when Columbo can detect the "means" (which hinges on the ultimate clue) or when he can reveal the "opportunity" (which inevitably hinges on time) for the crime.[40] Those are the questions, after all, that most beg proof and that are mostly varied over the course of the series' run, for the motive, too, is part of the show's formula. Tracing a clue is not unlike the performance of a magic trick—or the unveiling of one—and it's certainly what the climax of the plot depends on. Indeed, the series was known as much for the originality of these clues as for the novelty of its form; the audience might have guessed at what would trip up the murderer in the commission of the crime, but more often than not the detective's eventual solution comes as a neat trick. The case of "Suitable for Framing" (1:4; Nov. 17, 1971) is definitive of the lieutenant's own sleight of hand: hence, the reveal that the fingerprints on a pair of stolen Degas etchings are not the killer's (for the killer wore gloves to cover his crime) but rather those of Columbo himself. He further remarks on this sort of handiwork in "Murder under Glass," when he stops the murderer, Gerard, from drinking a poisoned glass of wine meant for the detective: "You switched the openers again, but I switched the glasses." And as he takes the poisoned glass back from Gerard, he announces, "That's what they call proof."

Up Next, on Columbo

The form as well as the content of this book is driven by *Columbo* as a complex if repetitive text and by the context of its original production, reception, and exhibition. Perhaps mirroring syndication, rerun, and algorithmic structures, certain favorite episodes of mine will pop up again and again, whereas others may merely play a supporting role. My turn to particular episodes also aids me in considering the series' roots, its circulation and proliferation, and its branches that spread into what at first glance might seem to be insignificant connections but which reveal both the complexity and even dependability of television's intertextual nature. In other words, to understand television in both its new and old permutations is to recognize the connections that it produces and allows: through programming structures, nightly lineups, or home pages of subscription streaming services; through stars and guest stars;

through the series' creators and teams of writers; and most certainly through the world it reflected time and again over the course of its run. Along with an analysis of these textual and intertextual associations, this book is also a contextual study, however humble, of some key historical developments in television production and reception technologies. But the roots of these analytical and historical inquiries, of course, are ever grounded in *Columbo* itself.

To aid in my intertextual analysis of the text and context of the series, my work is informed by academic fields based in film and media studies, ranging from research in television studies, production studies, and star studies, as well as by affect theory and other arenas of cultural and textual studies. At times I draw explicitly on popular intellectual and analytical models of the era in which the series originally aired, including studies of psychology, media, and even paranoia. Finally, my intertextual investigation also builds from a range of archival materials, including memoirs, interviews, oral histories, original and revised scripts, and contemporaneous reviews and critiques. But, like other Spin-Offs volumes, my study is primarily driven by the central series itself. As I've suggested, this drive entails setting *Columbo* in conversation with other television series and films that I see as part of its substantial textual orbit. Furthermore, based on the interconnectedness and even the repetition of the figure of the series' detective, the organization of this volume also speaks to the very structure of television itself. After all, television is organized by both repetition and interruption; and interruptions themselves, whether subplots or commercials, are as central to the mission of television as its narrative programming.

The chapters that follow alternate between two points of focus. The odd-numbered chapters trace the history of Peter Falk's work, including the development of the most famous and most long-term character he played. Given the detective's persistent returns, one chapter will not be sufficient attention to him; instead, he will repeatedly return in the odd-numbered shorter chapters throughout the book, allowing me to pivot to "just one more thing" regarding Falk's long career and the ways in which it was forever bound to the lieutenant. These chapters are also largely structured chronologically, which enables me to interweave a historical narrative with intertextual analysis. The even-numbered chapters, therefore, trace other key figures and key thematics of the series, which also allow for an intertwining of historical context and analytic speculation.

Chapter 1 begins with Falk's work that preceded his tenure on *Columbo*. Attending to his appearances in both film and television, I draw out some of those characteristics that became the foundation of his performance as the detective. The chapter that follows focuses in a parallel way on the two cocreators of the series, Richard Levinson and William Link. Here, too, I consider their roots as writers that lend themselves to the development of arguably their most well-known production, though I primarily focus on their writing for made-for-television and theatrical films during the initial run of the series, as much of that work depended on a similar logic present in *Columbo*. Together, grounded in origins and subsequent histories, these first two chapters set up the focus of chapter 3 on the main character himself, particularly attending to his (and the series') concerns with class and the distinctions that emerge between the detective and the killers he investigates. Chapter 4 shifts to the actors who played the detective's foils, especially those who made multiple appearances through the series' original run. My focus on guest stars is a particularly intertextual one, for it is grounded in part in the field of star studies and in part through the linkages between 1970s television and various eras of US film production (namely, classical Hollywood, particularly of the 1940s and 1950s, and "New Hollywood," which roughly spanned 1968 to 1975). Subsequently, as a companion to the chapter on guest stars, chapter 5 centers on Falk's involvement with New American Cinema writer/director/actor John Cassavetes, which largely took place during the run of the series. My approach in this chapter is not only to design an intertextual study of their work together but also to sketch a biography of the friendship between them and with costar Ben Gazzara. The remaining chapters attend to technological forms within the series and the primary technological form that made the series possible in the first place: television itself. Hence, chapter 6 is largely a textual study of the series via its own obsession with new technologies; though *Columbo* was by no means the only television series to explore changing technologies, it is one of the only to highlight these technologies through a quasi-pedagogical lens, as the detective himself

I.6. Evidence of time ("Negative Reaction," 4:2; Oct. 6, 1974)

is repeatedly schooled in them. Chapter 7 considers Falk's final years on television and in film in relation to the eponymous character he played, with an emphasis on the modifications of the original character and series. My epilogue is offered, briefly, as a means to reflect on the life and afterlife of Lt. Columbo and the series that made him.

As this structure shows, I am driven by the methods of decipherment displayed by the series itself, based on tangents, associations, and quotidian details. If television has taught me one primary method of analysis, it's one that is based on association. In his essay "Clues: Roots of an Evidential Paradigm," Carlo Ginzburg traces serendipitous parallels between historical contemporaries, which are themselves parallel to my own work here: an art historian (Giovanni Morelli), psychoanalyst (Sigmund Freud), and detective (Sherlock Holmes). Relaying these historical coincidences, Ginzburg makes a case for the reading of "discarded information" and "marginal data."[41] Such is the stock-in-trade of the psychoanalyst and the detective; it is also the method of the television viewer and scholar. In Ginzburg's words, I am designing an evidentiary and conjectural paradigm: like the detective before me, my own method of analysis entails the "systematic gathering" of "small insights."[42] Employing the "flexible rigor" such paradigms allow, I am reading through signs and associations, linking up texts and contexts, and interweaving figures and feelings.[43]

Indeed, in order to define my approach to *Columbo* and to television as a medium, I can't help but think of a seemingly incidental detail in "Negative Reaction" (4:2; Oct. 6, 1974), where these various elements converge. Columbo appears at the scene of the murder, which had previously been staged for a photograph to document a kidnapping. He stands at the fireplace, traces his finger over an object atop the mantle, and stares at the dust that's been transferred to his finger. He then stares at an electric clock, runs his finger over it, and finds it's clean. Dust and no dust, both linked to time: this moment is definitive of *Columbo*'s quotidian detection and of television's simultaneous temporalities. Evidence is all around us, it seems to say. In the case of television, we just need to know how to see it.

1 Mapping the Detective

> I'd kill to play that cop.
> —Peter Falk

Falk's Route

At the end of "Death Lends a Hand," which was originally intended as the first episode of season 1 of the series, the lieutenant confides in the widower Arthur Kennicutt (Ray Milland) that he and his friends learned how to disable a car without harming it by putting a potato in the exhaust pipe (intimating that he has done the same to the killer in order to get his car to a mechanic's garage). In his last line of the episode, he remarks, "And I got a feeling that the reason I became a cop was to make up for all those jokes I played when I was a kid." In a sense, the detective's statement seems like a potential commentary on much of Falk's work as an actor up to this point. The same could be said for his statement to Levinson and Link when he called them after seeing a copy of the script for *Prescription: Murder*: "I'd kill to play that cop." After all, while Falk was surely best known for his role as Columbo, it's hardly fair to say that he was *merely* Columbo, for better and worse. And those "jokes he played"—for which his role as the lieutenant "makes up"—could be understood as part of a series of patterns that emerge across his work, whether before, during, or after his titular role as the detective, for these are patterns that involve crime. While this book is, admittedly, *not* a study of the actor Peter Falk or his overarching career, Falk is certainly one of the central spokes of the wheel that drives my study of *Columbo* as a text. And as such, I'm interested in those connections—and, at times, disconnections—between his role as the lieutenant and various roles that he played across his career. Here I want to go back in time, in order to sketch the route that the actor took to his signature role, allowing for differences as well as continuities in his work to coexist—ultimately landing on those elements of his performance and the series that neatly remark on the drive toward *Columbo* itself.

Falk's very first appearances on-screen were fairly minor and for largely forgettable productions, but his accolades increased quickly and steadily in the early and mid-1960s. His debut on television was an appearance on the anthology series *Robert Montgomery Presents*, followed by *Studio One* and a range of others, including a series headlined by film star Barbara Stanwyck, as well as gigs for various other anthology and episodic series, such as *Naked City*, *The Untouchables*, *The Twilight Zone*, and *Alfred Hitchcock Presents*. In many of these early appearances, Falk was cast as a low-level thug and, in his more successful outings, as a working-class man. In *The Twilight Zone* ("The Mirror," 1961), he is even a working-class peasant, Ramos Clemente, who becomes a dictator of a fictional South American country. As "The Mirror" attests, in many of these cases he played a "type" defined not just by class or crime but also by ethnicity. By various turns, he is Greek, Italian, even Latino. Like the shirts Columbo wears as time goes on, Falk is not quite "white" across many of his roles. The characters he plays are also not usually Jewish, in spite of the fact that Falk himself was. But it may be that his unrecognized (or misrecognized) Jewish identity was precisely that which incited a kind of ethnic ambiguity across the parts he played as a whole. And then, in circular fashion, ethnic ambiguity bound him often to class and crime, in one way or another.

As an actor, Falk is also increasingly known through another orbit: during this time, he became a *star*. In fact, the year 1961 was a watershed one for him. As Dick Powell described him before his appearance in the *Dick Powell Show* teleplay "The Price of Tomatoes," he was the kind of "newcomer" *The Dick Powell Show* liked to help "on the way to stardom." Powell goes on to say that this newcomer "not only took

Hollywood by storm—he was a one-man hurricane." After all, Falk had been nominated for both an Academy Award and an Emmy Award in the previous year. Said Powell, "It was the first time in our history that an actor was nominated for both awards in one year. I'm speaking of course of Peter Falk." And, in fact, Falk would continue to set a record, as he garnered the same nominations for 1962, ultimately winning for "The Price of Tomatoes" itself.

In "The Price of Tomatoes," Falk played Aristede Fresco, a Greek truck driver from Ohio, who has just started his own business with his father. Again an ethnic type, he's simultaneously a working-class man (a truck driver by trade) who aspires to work his way up in rank (he and his father have put their savings into their own business). In order to keep his business afloat, he's eager to get a truckload of tomatoes from Mexico back to his home state ahead of his competition and his former employer, the Sindells, whom he repeatedly refers to as "the Romanians." Though he's running against the clock, as time and tomatoes are money, he takes on a passenger at his first stop—a pregnant woman named Anna, who is eager to have her child in the United States in order to gain citizenship. After all, as she tells him, she is Romanian, too, and she's fled her country. Almost constantly shouting and kvetching about this extra load, Fresco also repeatedly saves Anna from various perils: the "immigration cops" who are "looking for some dame," a quack doctor, and, of course, her imminent labor outside of a hospital. After chastising her for not knowing how close she is to her due date, he becomes sympathetic to her tale of escape from Fascism again and again, the loss of her parents back home, and the death of her husband after they arrived in Mexico on their way to the States. Perhaps this particular story appealed to the actor, since his parents were themselves Eastern Europeans who came to the United States (though, unlike the fictional Anna, their arrival was well before Nazi occupation).

As Fresco, Falk veers between a tough and a softie, an angry and a compassionate man. In this way Fresco is much more akin to the parts Falk played in the late 1960s and 1970s with John Cassavetes than he is to the eponymous detective, but the figure of Fresco also seems to encompass Falk's overall run in the 1960s and 1970s in film and television. Two moments in particular offer clues to who he will become as an actor and a character. In one, Fresco's truck becomes stuck on a bridge under construction. Perilously close to cracking the structure and falling through, he ushers Anna across the bridge on foot and returns to the truck to guide it very slowly and patiently. This pause in his passion signals the possibility of introspection and care—a mode he certainly brings to Columbo (however much his sense of reflection may often be played as forgetfulness), as well as to various talk-show appearances over the course of his career. And then, after Fresco has brought Anna safely to a hospital where she delivers her baby, he relents on his vow to hit the road and instead visits her so that he can see the infant. As she draws the blanket back from her tiny son's face, Fresco smiles so widely that we can't help but see Peter Falk himself emerge. With such charm and joy on his face, this character and this actor are at once so likable that it's no surprise he would be awarded for this outing.[1]

But this appearance sets another, more thematic path for Falk as well, which is realized in two of his next films in that decade: *It's a Mad, Mad, Mad, Mad World* (Stanley Kramer, 1963) and *The Great Race* (Blake Edwards, 1965). Both films are madcap comedies in which several drivers compete for financial reward. As in "The Price of Tomatoes," the drivers meet setbacks time and again, though in the service of comedy more than dramatic tension. Falk had supporting roles in both films, as he did in those for which he was nominated for Oscars in 1961 and 1962: *Murder, Inc.* (Burt Balaban and Stuart Rosenberg, 1960) and *Pocketful of Miracles* (Frank Capra, 1961). Surely those nominations, as well as his Emmy for "Tomatoes," spurred him to get the parts, but so must have his fictional role as a driver. Over and over he is behind the wheel meeting and defeating various obstacles. Is it any wonder that his signature car in *Columbo*—a car the actor himself chose from the Universal lot—is a 1960s model that looks like it's had its share of off-road travel?

In spite of his early honors, Falk declared that he didn't see himself as a Hollywood actor until his roles in these two films. Describing *The Great Race*, he writes in his memoir, "Keep in mind that this was the early 1960s, and I still saw myself as an off-Broadway theater actor who had stumbled into the Hollywood dreamworld."[2] Granted, though his pay was slight, his work in theater included prestigious plays like

1.1. Falk as cabdriver (*It's a Mad, Mad, Mad, Mad World*, Stanley Kramer, 1963)

Molière's *Don Juan* and Eugene O'Neill's *The Iceman Cometh*. This early success on stage, which led to his first television performance, also led to what was apparently a precipitous attempt by his agent to introduce him to Harry Cohn, the head of Columbia Pictures. In the midst of their meeting, Falk recalls, Cohn announced that he was "concerned" with the actor's "deficiency"—his glass eye. According to Falk, after some heated debate about the difference between the small and big screens of television and film and whether or not the artificial eye would be visible, Cohn notoriously announced, "Young man, for the same price I'll get an actor with two eyes."[3] Hence, the actor's return back to Broadway (and, occasionally, the small screen) before the long-term successful run that began with the two films for which he was nominated for Oscars, in both of which he played a small-time hood.[4]

As Dick Powell's 1962 introduction to Falk's leading role on "The Price of Tomatoes" shows, his reputation was steadily building. By 1965, this meant that he had his own television series, *The Trials of O'Brien*, which at once placed him between criminals and legal officials and skewed him in the direction of an atypical, even misplaced detective. Daniel (Danny) O'Brien was actually a criminal defense attorney, but in order to free his clients, he needed to find the real criminals in their stead. The series ran for just one season, but it maintained this narrative ploy throughout. O'Brien appeared in and out of court as a "detective" as well as a lawyer. His methods, moreover, are sometimes a little devious, as if all the years playing characters on the other side of the law have just been too hard to shake. Still, Falk's work on the series developed his charming persona, even including some of the gestures for which the actor and the character Columbo were known, such as the way he places his right thumb and index finger against his forehead when he's thinking. His energy, moreover, is somewhere between that which he develops as Columbo and the characters, such as Nick Longhetti, he played in Cassavetes's films. In the episode "What Can Go Wrong?," for instance, he's at once focused and frenetic as he announces to the courtroom that he will not only prove the innocence of his client but also name the actual murderer. Responds the judge, "Your performance has left us all quite drained." These performances continue outside the courthouse as, in a secondary plot, O'Brien attempts to break up his ex-wife, Katie (Joanne Barnes), and her new boyfriend, Roger (played by Roger Moore). At once suave, occasionally absent-minded, and a little shady, Falk as O'Brien is hard to resist.

In fact, a mark of his increasing stardom during this period was the actor's appearance as *himself* on television. Like many emerging stars of the day, Falk was a guest on the game show *I've Got a Secret* during the run of *The Trials of O'Brien*. As was the usual case with *Secret*, guests would be revealed to the audience at home while anonymously introduced to the panelists on set and screen. The panelists would then attempt to determine the guest's identity through specific queries or through a brief performance on the part of the guest. The satisfaction for *I've Got a Secret*'s audience at home would be twofold: knowing something that those on television did not know, and watching the process of their investigation. In his case, Falk was introduced as an actor who has "gone on to become one of our most important young actors, whose TV series is acknowledged by the critics and the public to be one of the finest new shows of the season." The introduction was followed by a segment in which Falk was implicitly asked to play a version of that titular role for the on-screen gang by testing them in order to determine what kinds of trial witnesses they would be. In hindsight, this game show is the perfect format for an actor who would become synonymous with investigations of a "secret" already known to the audience, and it's therefore a perfect pivot within his television career; two years after this appearance and the end of *The Trials of*

O'Brien, he debuted as Columbo in the made-for-television movie *Prescription: Murder*.

Falk was thus primed to enter the regular run of *Columbo* as a serious and award-winning actor whose star persona was both playful and warm. Levinson and Link describe certain characteristics of Falk as the same as the detective: "In an uncanny way he was very much like Columbo: clever, reflective, and oblique."[5] When he appeared on *The Tonight Show* with Johnny Carson on September 15, 1972, Carson introduced Falk by announcing that a survey among television viewers revealed that, among high school students, Columbo was more popular than David Cassidy of *The Partridge Family*; among college students, he was more popular than Archie Bunker in *All in the Family*; and overall he remained the most popular character on television, due, as Carson put it, "almost entirely to this gentleman, the Emmy Award winner Peter Falk." Falk himself attempted to describe the popularity of *Columbo* among television audiences: "They like to see the little guy get the big guy. They like Columbo because he's unpretentious. They like him because he's polite. I think he's a polite man, a decent man. I think they like him because he likes his job. He's involved with his job." The kind of decency that Falk describes for the character is as original for a detective as it is for a detective series; whereas so many popular American detectives maintain a reserve at best or a hardened, almost unbreakable persona (except in fits of anger, seemingly the only emotion many hardboiled detectives are capable of expressing), Columbo is kindly, warm, a little bit rumpled, but always and ever tenacious.[6]

Balancing Acts

Over the course of decades, Falk's screen roles continue to veer between opposing sides of the law, sometimes even precariously straddling the line between criminality and legality. This legal contrast is just one of many oppositions that define his roles, and some of his roles embody both sides at once. Such is the case for the eponymous Columbo, in which Falk plays both detective and cop—"white collar" and "blue collar" at once. The character of Columbo balances other traits of the detective in the first iterations that Link and Levinson designed. In "Enough Rope,"

1.2. The debonair Lt. Columbo in *Prescription: Murder* (0:0; Feb. 20, 1968)

Burt Freed's Columbo is a New York cop; eight years later, for *Prescription: Murder*, he is in Los Angeles (though the theatrical play is based in New York). The shift of this locale enables another important shift that defines the hardboiled detective more than it does an austere one such as Hercule Poirot: in Los Angeles, Columbo necessarily navigates the city by car. While certain NYC vestiges carry over into the 1968 adaptation of "Enough Rope," the detective is also a bit more refined in Levinson and Link's made-for-television movie. His suit is neater, his shirt whiter. His hair is lightly slicked into place, and he seems to work to keep his temper in check (which fails him briefly, too). These details of his character are, of course, on the page, but Falk adapts them as well, particularly in the shift from the movie *Prescription: Murder* to the pilot "Ransom for a Dead Man" to the first aired episode, "Murder by the Book." The changes to the cut of his jib—in fashion and in temperament—that take place across these three early versions are linked to another kind of groundedness that the detective represents: his shabby French Peugeot, at once

1.3. Falk is more comfortable on the ground ("Ransom for a Dead Man," 0:1; March 1, 1971)

a European model (as the detective often likes to brag) and a run-down vehicle. In fact, characters in more than one episode remark on his car, alternately, as destined for the junkyard or a Hollywood set or as a sign that the cop is working undercover. It is a kind of automotive manifestation of class consciousness (a topic I return to in chapter 3).

His car, like in noirs of old, keeps Columbo where he is most at home: on the streets. That fact is evident in those episodes where he's taken out of his comfort zone. "Ransom for a Dead Man," for instance, puts Columbo in a small plane piloted by the murderer, where he is physically uneasy—a trope that repeats when he flies with the murderer played by Johnny Cash in "Swan Song" (3:7; March 3, 1974) or when he is aboard a boat or a ship in three other episodes. His physical distress plays in a similar way as does his forgetfulness (indeed, "Ransom" begins the refrain of the detective constantly looking for his pen or pencil): it throws the murderer off guard, as the detective seems weaker than the criminal. But the detective's discomfort on planes and boats also neatly, if only implicitly, further associates him with the car as one of his primary accessories.

Thus, Columbo's mobility—between public officer and private detective—is also at the heart of the detective's navigation through the posh environs of Los Angeles. As an echo of his roles in the early 1960s—whether in "The Price of Tomatoes" or *It's a Mad, Mad, Mad, Mad World*, this movement is quite literally where his car (and the cars of the killers) comes into play. Given LA's notorious car culture, perhaps it's not surprising that automobiles would function significantly in a number of plots and characterizations; in fact, even in "Troubled Waters," an episode that takes place on a cruise ship, cars are part of the plot, for the killer is an owner of a large used-car dealership. But it's not just that cars appear as a part of the story line or part of the geography: cars also signify a neat *connection* between mobility across the city and plotting—of both crime and the mystery narrative—itself. In certain cases, vehicles enable murders, steering the killers' alibis and then ultimately directing clues for the detective to find. The killers in "Publish or Perish" (3:5; Jan. 13, 1974) and "Mind over Mayhem" (3:6; Feb. 10, 1974), for example, both stage car accidents in order to give themselves alibis for the times of the murders (the murderer in the former episode even lands himself in jail for drinking and driving). The killer in "The Greenhouse Jungle" (2:2; Oct. 15, 1972) fakes a kidnapping and a car crash (of the victim's beloved Jaguar) in order to set his nephew's murder plot in motion. In "The Most Crucial Game" (2:3; Nov. 5, 1972), the murderer borrows an ice-cream truck as part of his disguise to kill his victim with a block of ice in a swimming pool, and in "Requiem for a Falling Star" (2:5; Jan. 21, 1973), the killer borrows a car from the movie-studio lot to follow her victim and set the crime in motion. In several episodes, cars or elements of or within them serve as evidence of the crime. We see this trope in "Ransom for a Dead Man," as an officer on the scene notices that the driver's seat is pulled forward whereas the victim was quite tall. And we see it again in season 1: transporting his (unintended) victim in his car in "Death Lends a Hand," the murderer is tricked into believing that the victim lost a contact lens in his trunk. The theme continues even into the final season when the victim in "Make Me a Perfect Murder" has ordered a new car as a kind of consolation prize for his scorned lover in lieu of the job she felt she deserved; the gift of the car and its vanity plate, "Kay#1," confirms for the detective that there was more to the relationship between the two than the suspect originally admitted. Unsurprisingly this thread even appears in the only episode Falk directed himself, "Blueprint for Murder" (1:7; Feb. 9, 1972), in which the fact that the killer snobbishly changed the radio station from country to classical in his victim's car leads Columbo directly to the culprit.

The pattern represented in these episodes is further underscored in those cases when the detective himself traverses the city. Two episodes— season 2's "Étude in Black" (2:1; Sept. 17, 1972) and season 5's "A Case of Immunity" (5:2; Oct. 12, 1975)—use a similar trick for an alibi. In each case, the murderer secretly borrows his own car back from a garage in order to use it in the commission of his crime. And in each case, the detective drives the route each must have taken, checking it against the mileage recorded at the mechanic's, in order to prove their alibis were not as ironclad as they claimed. Driving more than a mile in their cars, so to speak, he inhabits the physical and mental space of the killers, represented by the posh neighborhoods of the Hollywood Hills and Bel-Air. In fact, it's in the act of tracing a killer's route in "Candidate for Crime" that the detective is nearly ticketed for breaking the law himself. He is, in effect, out of place, and this is the point. Becoming briefly lost while driving through an upper-crust neighborhood, Columbo is pulled over by two highway patrol officers, who are apparently (but inexplicably) checking "random" cars for vehicle violations. He tells them he works for the LAPD, offering his identification, and the first highway patrol officer incredulously asks, "This isn't a department car, is it?" He then says he needs to inspect it. Finding that Columbo's right-turn signal is out, his high beam doesn't work, his smog device is leaking, and one of his windshield wipers is missing, the officers ask him to sign a form, explaining that he'll have "two weeks to correct these things." As Columbo signs the form, the officer asks, "You ever, uh, consider getting another car?" "I got another car," Columbo says. "My wife drives it. But that's nothing special. Just transportation."

He makes the exact same statement to another officer of sorts—a guard at a Hollywood studio—in "Requiem for a Falling Star." But in this episode, the detective also, albeit briefly, takes a passenger in his car,

1.4. "You ever, uh, consider getting another car?" ("Candidate for Crime," 3:3; Nov. 4, 1973)

which reverses the effect of who is out of place in LA's stratified class environs. In "Requiem," Hollywood actress Nora Chandler essentially kills her assistant with a car—first flattening her assistant's tire and then setting fire to the car her assistant borrowed from her boyfriend, a Hollywood gossip reporter. Claiming that he needs her to see something at the station, Columbo himself drives Chandler in his own beat-up car. As she steps out of it, brushing who-knows-what off of her stylish ensemble, we see the grimy veneer of the detective's car—seemingly grayer and dustier up close. When Chandler turns, she suddenly gasps, coming into view of the burned-out car from the night before—a car that, after having caught on fire, now looks a lot like the lieutenant's.

These two make a funny pair: a burned-out rich man's car, a still (if barely) functioning police detective's car. The detective and the star are a funny pair, too, both acting in this scene: she pretends shock and sadness, while he uncharacteristically barks orders at his officers to check the other car's tires while he consoles the distraught killer. These

1.5. The star's car ("Requiem for a Falling Star," 2:5; Jan. 21, 1973)

similarities, of course, are also bound to the characters' visible and tacit differences in terms of gender, the law, and class. On the one hand, then, driving through the killer's environs, he's out of place. But on the other, as punctuated when he and Chandler move together here, the point is that the wealthy don't constitute the "citizenship" of Los Angeles, or at least not the primary constitution and not the highest "rank" thereof—a fact made even more clearly in Levinson and Link's one-season series *Tenafly*, which ran the same year as this episode of *Columbo*. The rank and file, after all, are those who flesh out the background of the city. But given that such citizenry remains largely in the backdrop, Columbo is a stand-in for the working and middle class of Los Angeles. In other words, while the comparison between Columbo and the killer repeatedly draws out the class differences between them, it also wipes out that which exists across the city; Columbo therefore stands in lieu of the great denizens of the city.

Falk was never a major romantic lead, and, though he played various toughs in the 1960s and 1970s (even a killer in *Murder, Inc.*), he also didn't play a classic macho hero. Perhaps in lieu of such conventional roles, class identity and, more specifically, class differences comprise a central, defining thread for Falk's work in film and television leading to (and most certainly including) *Columbo*. Put differently, because Falk was a character actor who became a star, his defining characteristic combines both difference and continuity at the same time. He's the "everyman" who is unlike the reigning stars before and after his own rise.

Straddling the two sides of the law—and maintaining his likability in almost all cases—fed into this "everyman" persona. Falk would continue to work across those lines as he simultaneously worked between the borders of film and television during *Columbo*'s original run; in some of his films in the 1970s he also intermixes genres, through his appearances in such crime comedies as *Murder by Death* and *The Cheap Detective*. Moreover, his film work would situate him in John Cassavetes's milieu, with some of that work set on the "wrong" side of the law. Thus, 1976 sees the release of Elaine May's *Mikey and Nicky* (shot in 1973), in which Falk costars with his friend Cassavetes. As Nicky, Cassavetes is a working hood who is hiding from the mob, and Falk plays his longtime gangster pal Mikey, who tries to ease him out of his jam but who is also double-crossing him for the boss. Two years later, Falk is Tony Pino in *The Brink's Job* (William Friedkin, 1978), who helps to organize a major armed bank robbery; Cassavetes's wife, Gena Rowlands, plays Falk's wife in *Brink's Job*, as she does in *A Woman under the Influence* (John Cassavetes, 1974) as well. The character's class status and those connections that spin out of the actor's friendships and professional associations within this series of films will be the driving force of the Falk chapters to come.

2 Best-Selling Mystery Team

Columbo cocreators Richard Levinson and William Link were plotting murders from the time they met in their Pennsylvania junior high school, and they continued to write together for the next four decades, with only a relatively short break in their twenties. Together they wrote a high school musical, and at the University of Pennsylvania they cowrote a television pilot as their undergraduate thesis. After stints in the military, they reunited in New York City in the 1950s and started to work together professionally, penning short fiction and eventually becoming primarily writers for television. Together they moved to Los Angeles, back to New York, and finally to Los Angeles to stay, where they would "go commercial."[1] Their first broadcast cocreation was the episode "Face to Remember," which ran on January 18, 1959, as part of the Canadian anthology series *Encounter* (also known as *General Motors Presents*). That same year they cowrote episodes of *Westinghouse Desilu Playhouse* ("Chain of Command," March 23, 1959) and *The Rebel* ("Gun City," Dec. 27, 1959). "Chain of Command" focused on military recruits, and "Gun City" imagined a town in the nineteenth century in which townspeople gave up their guns; both of these early efforts would echo in later television films. Some of their early work also shows a self-reflexive air, which will return in their 1970s crime series. In their November 1959 episode "The Rain Man" for the Aaron Spelling Western *Johnny Ringo*, the first characters they described on the page were "two old men, seated by the blacksmith shop. Their chairs are tilted back—they fan their withered faces, almost in unison."[2] At this point in their careers, Levinson and Link are barely thirty, so this pair is hardly a stand-in for them. But the "unison" of the characters' actions stands out to me, over half a century later, as a neat remark on the writers' work together.

In fact, twenty-five years after *Johnny Ringo*, wiser if not withered, the two of them together described their writing collaboration at a workshop held at the Writers Guild Foundation (WGF). As Link emphasized, "It's like a marriage. You must respect your partner. You must respect your wife, and if you don't, forget it." Levinson interrupts: "It doesn't hurt to be friends." Link chimes back in: "When you have a partnership, I'm always testing things on Dick, and he's always testing things on me." Levinson points out that they don't write anything that they don't *both* like, but he also jokes that they are "a very bad example of what one would assume a psychologically balanced collaboration should be," as they largely agree with one another and, moreover, they "tend to be lethargic at the same time."[3] They may jest a bit here (though I don't think they're kidding about the shared lethargy!), but indeed they did write together almost all of their lives, until the early death of Richard Levinson in 1987. "And I've missed him every day since," Mr. Link told me during one of our conversations over the years.

As the first iteration of Detective Columbo in the 1960 "Enough Rope" would show, detective writing was their primary modus operandi. They wrote mystery stories together from a young age, repeatedly submitting them to magazines, collecting a series of rejection letters over time, and their first story was accepted in *Ellery Queen's Mystery Magazine* when they were in college.[4] Though evidence of that genre infects even those films that wouldn't be classified as such, in the television industry their long-running interest in mystery and crime was most central in the various series they worked on. Extremely prolific writers, even before developing *Columbo*, they contributed episodes to series such as *Alfred Hitchcock Presents* and *The Alfred Hitchcock Hour, Honey West*, and *Burke's Law*, and they created *Mannix* in 1967 with Bruce Geller. They subsequently wrote single episodes for two of the NBC *Mystery Movie* series—*McCloud* and *Banacek*—and, of course, they also created *Tenafly* for the 1973–74 season of the Wednesday night edition of the mystery wheel series. In the prime of *Columbo*, they additionally adapted the 1970s version of *Ellery Queen* (lasting only one season), and in the years following they cocreated with Peter S. Fischer both the popular series *Murder, She Wrote* and the short-lived *Blacke's Magic*.[5] Their major works of the 1970s exhibited liberal (and sometimes more progressive) political concerns, and they occasionally engaged with the act of writing itself as a central narrative element.

To plot is the mystery writer's stock-in-trade. After all, the verb is defined both by developing secret (and often illegal) plans and by creating a story. Levinson and Link's primary creations—those episodes and films they wrote as a singular team and those series that they developed and often over which they maintained creative control—emphasized character and plot over the conventional "action" associated with detective and police shows of the same era. Plotting itself of both the crime and its solution took on a particularly central role in their various television series. Certainly this is the case with *Columbo*, known for its reversal of the form (with the murder committed on-screen at the beginning) and the cleverness of the final clue the detective discovered, and it was also the case with *Ellery Queen*, a franchise already known for its self-conscious narrative structure. Coauthors Frederic Dannay and Manfred Bennington Lee created the character of Ellery Queen in 1929, even writing under the character's name as their pseudonym. Their novels were known for pauses in the narration for Queen to ask his readers if they had yet solved the crime themselves. Levinson and Link revived this structure in their 1970s television series, so that, in their adaptation, *Ellery Queen* maintained its meta qualities. First and foremost, Queen was a writer of detective fiction himself, whose police detective father often called in for support on cases, and many plots (either primary or secondary) revolve around the production of a new novel. Moreover, because of Queen's occupation, a number of episodes are set within entertainment industries and contexts—from radio soap operas to comic books to a film crew adapting a Queen novel. Every episode also began self-reflexively, with an image of a character and the following announcement: "Soon this woman/man will be dead." Finally, of course, there was Queen's trademark question to his audience; on Levinson and Link's show, just before solving the case, he would pause to address the camera directly in order to ask the viewers if they had already guessed

2.1. Ellery Queen solves the case (1975–76)

the answer. In some ways *Ellery Queen* was, structurally speaking, something of an anti-*Columbo* (though someone was soon to be dead, we wouldn't see the killer commit the act), but in its emphasis on plotting, it was actually the other side of the same coin.[6]

Success in the Seventies

Though arguably best known for *Columbo*, Levinson and Link left the daily workings of the series after its first season in order to pursue other work.[7] After they stepped away from producing the series themselves, *Columbo* would cycle through four different executive producers; Levinson and Link continued to be involved through conversation with the producers and with Falk, sometimes supplying clues, story ideas, or other elements, but of course the primary constant in the production of the show was Falk himself. With their break from the day-to-day of the series, the two collaborators focused on made-for-television movies, which

I'll discuss as the chapter continues. But let me begin here with their theatrical screenplay for *Rollercoaster* (James Goldstone, 1977), a film that rode the wave of disaster films and theatrical effects of the era. While it might seem like an outlier in their oeuvre of the era, *Rollercoaster*, like their other productions of this period, shares both a sensibility and a structure with *Columbo*. Reading these works in tandem with one another—taking a cue from the overlap, intersection, and circularity of a ride like a roller coaster—is a means of following the investigatory process, or their preoccupations, which informed the detective series.

Master-of-disaster Irwin Allen created a genre that put a crowd of characters—usually played by a crowd of contemporary and classical Hollywood stars—in peril. Several entries in this set of films involved the premise that personal and corporate greed has created a state of potential peril: in the case of *The Towering Inferno* (John Guillermin, 1974), for instance, subpar wiring used in the construction of a giant skyscraper initiates a fire that ultimately endangers the stability of the entire building. Two primary characters—the architect played by Paul Newman and the fire chief played by Steve McQueen—fight the fire and attempt to free those trapped in the building (played by actors running the gamut from Faye Dunaway to O. J. Simpson to Fred Astaire). *Rollercoaster* plays off these conventions but also recasts the disaster genre, in part doing so through the very structure of *Columbo*. Thus, like their television series, *Rollercoaster* opens with a violent act: a man plants a bomb on a small theme-park roller coaster, and several cars of riders are plunged to their deaths. The rest of the film follows one central character, amusement-ride inspector Harry Calder (George Segal), as he works to track the killer, both with the aid and against the impediment of FBI officials.[8]

Structurally and narratively, this film, unlike other disaster films of the era, is more of an investigation than it is a series of thrilling or horrifying scenes of danger and death. As the *New York Times* reported in its description of the PG rating at the time of its release, "*Rollercoaster . . .* treats its mayhem so discreetly that, indeed, one has to look fast on a couple of occasions to know exactly what dreadful event has taken place. The fun is not in the violence, which is almost nonexistent, but in its possibility."[9] The reviewer, Vincent Canby, was likely referring in part to the terrorist's death: running from the FBI after being shot by Harry, he comes to the tracks of the ride he has tried to sabotage. Looking directly into the eyes of his captor, Calder, the killer pauses; the film cuts to the impending roller coaster on the tracks above; and the film cuts again to the killer's body against the fence, killed by the very object he attempted to blow up. Harry then bums a cigarette from a passerby (he's been trying to quit since the beginning of the film), pulls it out of his mouth, and tosses it away. The film stops here.[10] Although this ending is even more anticlimactic than an episode of *Columbo*, the narrative structure resembles Levinson and Link's television series through the "cat-and-mouse game" between the central protagonists, with the inspector attempting to solve the crime and catch the criminal.

Starting and ending in roughly the same place, the film's circumscribed terror also resembles an amusement-park ride. In fact, its scenes that take place on the roller coaster are a perfect metonym for narrative structure: building suspense and anxiety as we follow the car up (positioned as if we are in the first car), we hit the top, speed down, and even out again. This ride remains ever contained: we topple out of a car, a little dizzier but essentially the same as we began. Obviously, the terror underlying the film is that such experiences are threatened: the carefully constructed fear of an amusement ride could extend well beyond its promises. *Rollercoaster* threatens the design of the disaster film, too; but, rather than extending its violent boundaries, it contains them, and, in the process, it turns the disaster film into mystery and melodrama. In fact, it shares its melodramatic impulses with *Jaws*, the blockbuster that was also built on disaster films but which cannot fit squarely into that genre. (This likeness is ironic, given that Spielberg invited Levinson and Link to write *Jaws*, but they declined because they were already committed to *Rollercoaster*.)[11] In effect, Levinson and Link appeared to recognize the central elements of the disaster-film formula, and then they resituated those components in a more measured, investigative form. This approach makes *Rollercoaster* akin to *Ellery Queen*, *Tenafly*, and *Columbo*, which share a restrained pace, tied, of course, to character and plot. Compared to twenty-first-century models (and to those that followed *Columbo* in the late 1970s and beyond), the detective himself moves slowly, and so indeed does each episode. Driven more by intellect than by conventional "action," the series repeatedly represents the very process of thought itself, whether the murderer's or the detective's.

Their thoughtful approach to plot and character often demonstrates the writers' liberal politics, which play out, for instance, in their concern with gun violence on and off *Columbo*. They designed rules of nonviolence for the series (only occasionally broken by the approach of directors, other writers, and/or studio representatives). One of Columbo's most pertinently defining characteristics, alongside his trench coat and his rusty French car, was that he did not carry a weapon. This decision was in opposition to a series like *Mannix*, which, though initially cocreated by Levinson and Link, took such a violent direction from what they intended that they never wrote for it themselves.[12] In turn, this decision is also explicitly followed in a 1974 made-for-television movie that Levinson and Link wrote, based on a pitch by Jay Benson, a friend and associate producer at Universal, which stands as a noteworthy companion to the weaponless detective: *The Gun*.[13] As the title suggests, the film is the story of a single gun and its effects on its owners over a three-year period. With this weapon as the titular character, the film opens with its "birth" of sorts: its construction in a factory and its ensuing arrival at a gun shop, where it becomes inventoried. From here on, the movie is made up of several vignettes, each of which is constructed similarly. First the date is announced on-screen, as if the opening of a chapter, so that every story appears to begin anew, although each is also parallel to the next. Every "chapter," therefore, unfolds as follows: the cost of the gun is declared (including when it's "free"), a new person takes ownership, danger appears to be imminent, danger is averted, and the story starts over again. For instance, after the gun is inventoried, the date is spelled out as March 3, 1971: an older white man, Mr. Hilliard, enters the gun shop and asks the clerk for the recommendation of a weapon "for the protection of [his] home." The clerk recommends the 38 Special for $68.50 plus tax. After his wife pleads that they remove the gun from their home, Mr. Hilliard asks a security guard to take care of it for him, but rather than getting rid of it, he sells it to a pawnshop and profits from it. The gun goes through four subsequent owners. The next owner plans a killing rampage with it (thankfully aborted); another owner's aging father nearly kills himself after he's lost his best friend; and the next owner is involved in the trafficking of guns in order to pay for his daughter's wedding (and is ultimately arrested, with his cache clearly discovered). In each case a character is overwhelmed by emotion of some sort—anger, grief, love for a child—and the film suggests, in a more compassionate than preachy means, that throwing a gun into the mix can lead to disastrous and tragic consequences for their owners and for those around them.

At this point in the film, the gun becomes part of a "news story" covering the destruction of firearms. Thus, on "September 20, 1974," we see a stock of guns removed from a police evidence room in order to be turned into scrap metal. In a reversal from the opening scene is a powerful image in which hundreds of guns are lifted en masse by a giant magnet. A local news reporter announces that it's been a "lethal twelve months" as the guns are crushed behind him. But we see that the 38 Special has survived, only to be picked up by one of the workers at the site. In its final role, the gun joins the worker's small family where, less than two months later, we watch the worker's child snoop around in his parents' room as his mother is getting supper ready. The view of the film is on a window when the sound of the gun explodes, thus ending the story. With anxiety continuously attached to the weapon, this outcome is dramatically predictable, particularly as guns are classically objects of narrative economy, beginning with the very early days of narrative film.[14] But even while the film resembles a lengthy PSA (for instance, we learn various facts, including that there is a five-day waiting period to take ownership of a legally purchased gun), its structure also produces an important argument. While bookended with scenes of industrial machinery, *The Gun* functions as an investigation of the social and economic mechanics that engineer violent personal crises across economic and racial lines.

In such creations beyond *Columbo* and other crime television, investigation remained Levinson and Link's primary mode. As I've suggested, this investigative mode is born of the writers' careful plotting, whether in the made-for-television movie in which the main character is a gun with five lives or in the first sequence of "Murder by the Book," the first main episode of the series. As the episode opens, the link between writing and murder is most overtly drawn through the parallel editing between two objects: a typewriter and a gun. As the show begins, the primary sound is the tapping of typewriter keys, rhythmically integrating two scenes of action: a writer at his desk and a driver on the streets of LA. When the driver parks and pulls a gun out of his glovebox, writing and murder become locked together as interwoven plots. And less than ten years later, such interlocking became the central subject of a Levinson and Link production again, in their made-for-television film called *The Storyteller*. This film is the tale of a young boy who commits crimes potentially based on a fiction writer's work. In other words, criminal plots follow narrative plots: the two meanings of the term itself converge.

The inquiries and associations—about plots and the role of guns within them—were evidence not purely of a nonviolent ethos (after all, the writing team of Levinson and Link was regularly plotting murders for the screen) but of a humanism that undergirded everything they originated together. This liberal humanism was spelled out most explicitly across their made-for-television movies of the 1970s, like *The Gun* and *The Storyteller*, but those progressive politics are part of the foundation of their famous series nevertheless. Appearing during the series' original run, the films underscore the progressivism of *Columbo*, while the investigatory nature of the series bears even on those films that are not about criminal investigations. Three of Levinson and Link's most significant made-for-television movies in the early 1970s—*My Sweet Charlie* (produced in 1969, aired January 1970), *That Certain Summer* (1972), and *The Execution of Private Slovik* (1974)—do not fit squarely into the detective genre by a long shot. But the writing team's investigative training, and, in turn, that which they cultivated in their viewers, is central to an understanding of each of them.

Reading for Answers

I realize now that I have watched these films as Columbo himself might have. In other words, I have watched them as *Columbo* trained me to, which also means I see them as Levinson and Link have taught me to see. Like their mystery series, the pacing and structure of both *That Certain Summer* and *The Execution of Private Slovik* invite introspection. But whereas the murder mystery is all about the solving of a crime, in the case of these made-for-television movies their dramas don't enable an easy resolution. Each work takes on, after all, incredibly complicated topics and stories for their time period: *That Certain Summer* concerns a fourteen-year-old boy who comes to realize his divorced father is gay, and *The Execution of Private Slovik* narrates the true story of the first US soldier to be executed for desertion since the Civil War.

The structure of *The Execution of Private Slovik*, which aired in 1974, shares some features with *The Gun*, though it also complicates that narrative structure. Whereas *The Gun* tells multiple stories about the same instrument, *Private Slovik* investigates an incident from multiple points of view. Moreover, opposed to *The Gun*'s linear, chronological structure, *Private Slovik* instead resembles feature films like Orson Welles's *Citizen Kane* or Akira Kurosawa's *Rashomon*. In its exploration of his execution, its implicit question is not necessarily focused on whether Private Slovik was "guilty" of desertion during World War II but rather on who is accountable for his execution. In its exploration of this central question, it integrates conversation and investigation into the narrative itself, starting with the soldiers who are commanded to kill him. Their sergeant specifically asks, "Is there much talk about this among the men? . . . How do they feel about it?" And shortly thereafter the chaplain gives the "boys" who are charged with shooting Slovik the chance to talk about how they feel.[15] Such questions concerning both the ramifications of the command to kill another soldier and the emotions involved in this act set the stage for the viewer's response to the events as well.

The film continues to pose these questions through following a series of flashbacks that tell the story of the minor criminal misdeeds of Eddie Slovik (played by Martin Sheen), his attempts to set his life straight, and his romance with the woman whom he eventually marries (played by Mariclare Costello, who also appears as the mother in the final sequence of *The Gun*). Rather than the chronological sequence of something like *The Gun* (or an episode of *Columbo*), *Slovik* moves back and forth in time—via both flashbacks and, implicitly, flash-forwards. When the film comes to Slovik's experience in the army, based in Europe during the war, we watch as he and one other soldier are separated from their platoon, surviving a dangerous shelling by the enemy when they hide

2.2. Private Slovik turns over his weapon (*The Execution of Private Slovik*, Lamont Johnson, 1974)

overnight in a cave. That experience rattles Eddie considerably; a man who already seemed a little off-kilter (not unlike Kit Carruthers, whom Sheen played at roughly the same time in Terrence Malick's 1973 *Badlands*, but without the murderous proclivities), Eddie is now undone, and he ultimately refuses to return to combat. In his court hearing, Eddie admits to his actions and accepts his fate. But the film itself refuses to accept it so easily. In its own search for responsibility for his death, the film suggests instead that the accountability for Eddie's loss of life is a shared one.

This film, like the broader series of which *Columbo* was a part, is to some extent like a wheel. There are many narrative pivots or spokes that are not entirely conjoined. At the same time, these "spokes" bear with them a durational quality, enabling a sense of "real time" (what the film theorist André Bazin would call, in the context of *Nanook of the North*, the "actual" time of "the waiting period").[16] Bearing with

Slovik, with his wife, Antoinette, and with his army comrades and superiors, we experience the extended time necessary for contemplation. In other words, in the time the film itself spends with him, his death comes to mean something to the film's audience. Its final scene is harrowing: the first round of shots does not kill the soldier immediately, so that his very death lingers. And it is harrowing not just because of the chaplain's impassioned pleas over whether he must be shot again and again (a monologue demanded by the network), but, in a sense, in spite of them, for the film demands that we effectively accompany Eddie while he dies. Does Slovik's death resolve the narrative? I would argue that it does not. Nor does it absolve those agents involved in his death. Rather, we are left with the sense that Slovik was not independently to blame for his desertion and even did not deserve execution. Contemporary reviewers remarked on the fact that the film included "no villains," and the writers heard from viewers who took the same position, including from a man who had also been found guilty of desertion during the war but whose sentence was ultimately commuted. Detailing the dehumanization that he and other accused soldiers faced, he wrote, "Of the two of us to be shot (Slovik or I) it should have been I. Slovik was thoroughly courageous and stuck to his stand right to The Firing Squad. I didn't have the guts to do this, and though I was accused, tried and judged by a kangaroo courts-martial and sentenced to death I knew that they wanted to hear the cop-out."[17]

That Certain Summer doesn't involve the explicit multiple points of view that *The Execution of Private Slovik* does, but it still works through diverse positions. The film opens with what looks and sounds like an image from a home movie. We watch as a woman walks toward a house carrying groceries; she enters, calling out to someone, and then we watch as she dances about and plays with a baby, clearly happy. No sound but the whir of a projector accompanies this image, and ultimately another camera—not that which originally captured the woman, but that which frames the screen on which she now moves—pulls back first to reveal the screen in a room, then to show a man sitting alongside the running projector, watching the images before him. As the images continue to play, we might recognize him in the film he watches: he and a young boy together blow a dandelion. From here we cut to another scene entirely: a mother and son prepare to pack for what seems like a summer vacation. We return fairly quickly to the home movies, where the viewing father (played by Hal Holbrook) appears to be searching for something in the image itself, in which the mother stands aside him while he holds the child. Now the film cuts again to the mother and teenaged son, who are in a convertible on a highway. "I'm going to miss you," she tells him. And the son, Nick (played by Scott Jacoby), responds, "I'm not going to Vietnam." It is, after all, 1972: home movies are shot on Super 8 film, and sons are still heading to war, the latter fact embedded almost mundanely into the backdrop of this scene. The film continues to alternate between these two settings; stitching them together, we begin to understand a divided domestic stage. The teenaged boy appears to be the child from the home movies, shuttling between the mother and father.

Watching the film more than forty years later, I wonder how and when its cues were recognized. Would those viewers who did not read the advance publicity or attend to the warnings that preceded it be able to follow the film's signs more quickly than the child himself? Or, given the inevitability of its publicity and its historical status as the first mainstream sympathetic portrait of a gay male relationship in a television movie, should we read it as Columbo—or a *Columbo* viewer—would, knowing the facts of the case from the beginning? Following the credits, after all, the signs pick up. The father, Doug, an architect, is at a domestic construction site, where his client, a middle-aged divorcée, repeatedly expresses her "love" for him while he responds in a friendly but disinterested way. He then gets a call from home at the job; on his end we, and the divorcée, hear, "Dinner? Anything—he's got a cast-iron stomach. . . . I'll just introduce you. It shouldn't be a problem." Cut to a young man standing by an unmade bed, looking for something in the sheets. The young man is played by Martin Sheen, a seeming favorite in Levinson and Link productions; since the film premiered more than forty years before the television show *Grace and Frankie*, perhaps few viewers in the twenty-first century realize that the Netflix comedy was not Sheen's first role as a gay character.

Shortly after the phone call, Doug picks Nick up at the airport, where they greet one another with lines from *The Maltese Falcon*; as they drive into town, the setting is confirmed: San Francisco. After a drive through the iconic sites of the town iconically known as a safer haven for queer folk, Nick and Doug arrive home, where the man from the earlier scene, Gary, has baked a cake to finish off their supper. Gary's presence and his offering create a sense of unease for Nick, as does the shared language between Doug and Gary, for their conversations about a bottle of wine or eight-track cassettes clearly hinge on accumulated prior experiences together. By the end of the evening, after an emergency call to the divorcée's house, Nick snoops in his father's bathroom, uncovering shaving cream, which can't be his dad's since Doug uses an electric razor. At this point his suspicions, however, remain under cover, which is where his father tells him to put his "tail" after he chastises him for said snooping. But in the scene that follows, the film lays its own position bare, out in the open for direct debate.

During Nick's stay, Gary has dispatched himself over to his sister's house. It's clear they are relative strangers to one another—loving enough, but not entirely familiar. Over breakfast, his beefy brother-in-law Phil asks Gary about Doug, inviting Gary to bring him—or any of his "friends"—over to meet them. This scene is an awkward one. Gary becomes increasingly hostile, and his sister grows more and more tense watching her husband and brother as they talk. Part of the awkwardness may well be on account of its origin: besides working with ABC's Department of Standards and Practices, who gave notes on the script, the network insisted that two professors on retainer to ABC would also review the script. As Levinson and Link recall in *Stay Tuned*, these advisers (psychology professor Melvin Heller and law professor Samuel Polsky) were concerned that the script was "prohomosexual" and therefore needed "balance."[18] As a compromise, the writers agreed that the brother-in-law could function as a kind of foil for Gary, with the following caveat: "We refused to have him openly condemn the gay lifestyle. Instead, we'd make him solicitous and ponderously broad-minded, an ersatz liberal whose attempts to be reasonable about his brother-in-law's sexual preferences are patronizing and ultimately a greater condemnation than naked disapproval."[19] This compromise may well be why he does not read as naturally as so much of the rest of the film and why Gary does not initially respond well to him.[20] At the same time, the writers' resolution of the problem that the network presented them comes with one of the more astounding statements of the film. When Phil states, not disingenuously, "I believe everyone has the right to live their lives any way they want to," Gary accuses him of being patronizing. When Phil questions this response, Gary stands up and exclaims: "I've been getting it all my life—if not from the militant straights, then it's from the well-intentioned liberals." While in conversation with me, Mr. Link himself referred to Levinson and him as "so liberal back then," I read this brief monologue as far more radical than liberal; indeed, its critique of the "well-intentioned liberal" and its naming of "straights" denormalize heterosexuality.[21] The two characters superficially resolve the situation as Gary goes out the door, but Gary's sister still apologizes for him to her husband: "It's just that he gets a little sensitive sometimes." Once the two are alone, we can better understand his "sensitivity," as Phil says to his wife, "I was just trying to be friendly. [*pause*] I mean some guys wouldn't even let him in the house."

Such debates continue throughout the made-for-television movie as the plot slowly unwinds. In the context of their shared interest in music, Doug encourages Nick and Gary to work on a session together. When Nick backs off the idea, Gary gently responds, "You're absolutely right. Nobody should force you into doing anything you don't want to do." At the same time, Gary is more insistent with Doug about being open about their mutual affection for one another. At Golden Gate Park, Nick witnesses a couple of young (male) lovers holding hands, and Doug announces to Gary, out of the range of Nick, "I don't like public displays." Gary asks if he's ashamed; it's a question about the closet, he says. Interestingly, an object that represents at once their intimacy and Doug's guardedness is the final clue of Nick's father's sexuality—the planting, or *plotting*, of which seems almost out of a *Columbo* episode. At a party Doug gives in order to introduce Nick to his pals, Nick unearths his dad's watch, which bears the following inscription on the other side of the face: "TO DOUG / WITH LOVE GARY." And when he then glances over the banister to see his father put his arm around Gary, Nick finally puts two and two together. The next day he takes off, in a fit of anger and confusion.

The final act of the film cuts between Nick riding a streetcar up and down for much of the day while his parents and Gary worry over him.

Nick's mom, Janet, flies up to San Francisco to join the search, and she arrives at the house before Doug returns. What follows is a frank conversation between the two, with Janet open about her own confusion and loss, while Gary maintains a critical stance about the different rights ascribed to straight and gay partnerships. Upon her implicit questioning over what he's doing there, Doug responds, "I happen to live here, too." And the conversation proceeds:

Janet: You've established your credentials.
Gary: Have I? I don't think so. You'd need a ring or a marriage certificate for that. If I were a woman, everything would be acceptable, wouldn't it?
Janet: If you were a woman, I'd know how to compete with you.

Shifting their focus away from one another, they begin to talk about Doug, about whom they obviously agree and disagree.

Gary: Doug is a very decent man.
Janet: I know he's a decent man. I was married to him!
Gary: He never lied to you, did he? You knew how he was before you were married?
Janet: I knew. Like any woman in that situation, I thought I could change him.

Meanwhile the conductor, Mr. Hurley (played by James McEachin, another regular in Levinson and Link productions), who had been running the cable car while Nick mulled and moped, ends his shift and asks the kid to join him. He takes Nick for a walk, shows him the master cable for the cars, lets him work a practice car. Indeed, McEachin plays a similar role in his instruction on how to run a projector in "Make Me a Perfect Murder." Taking things at a slow pace, Mr. Hurley eventually asks Nick why he ran away from home; when he invites him to talk about it, Nick agrees. Rather than seeing the content of their conversation, however, the film cuts back to the threesome of Gary, Doug, and Janet—self-conscious about the arrangement together, but united in their concern over the child.

There is much that is remarkable about this film, but what I find most compelling is that it's a portrait of a group of people who are trying to do the best they can, with honesty and understanding, under complex personal—and historical—circumstances. Personalizing this contemporary moment within four years after the Stonewall Riots, Levinson and Link developed a film that literally brings home not just same-sex love, but also a revised conception of marriage and, ultimately, of the traditional nuclear family. After Mr. Hurley takes Nick home and the split scenes reconverge, father and son take a walk. Doug asks, "You ran away this morning. Do you know why?" And he goes on to answer his own question: "You ran away because something was happening that you didn't understand. That was my fault." From here on comes explicit evidence that Levinson and Link are participating in the cultural work that helped to bring about social and legal change in the twenty-first century, culminating with the full-scale recognition in the United States in 2015 of gay marriage. He begins by asking Nick if he knows what the word *homosexual* means, insisting, "Look at me. Keep the door open." Surely this plea is directed to the television audience as well—one that ultimately wasn't entirely prepared for this film on a number of scales. For one, what Doug goes on to say is decades ahead of its time: "Gary and I have a kind of a marriage." When Nick insists that he doesn't want to talk about it, Doug gently presses on: "We love each other. . . . Does that change me so much? I'm still your father! . . . I've lied to myself for a long time. Why should I lie to you? I never talked about this to my own father. I should have. . . . The hardest time I've ever had was accepting it myself. Can you at least try to understand it?"[22]

In the film's focus on the father rather than the son, *That Certain Summer* suggests that gay identity isn't one of the "future" generation: rather, the film implicitly says instead, "We're queer and we're *already* here." And in Gary's brief outburst to his brother-in-law, the film also announces that being straight is not a given: naming straights *as* such in his reference to "militant straights" is a demand not to see gay identity in terms simply as difference, as the only identity that need be named because it diverges from the "norm." That said, it's a film that, through its conversational style and patient pace, also keeps the door open for understanding, if not for easy resolution. In fact, in spite of its title, the film is left largely *un*certain. Nick runs from his father, crying. Shortly thereafter he leaves with his mother to return to Los Angeles. And while Gary goes back to his sister's home to retrieve his things, Doug sits alone on the stairs in his house, weeping. The film ends with a shot of the home movie, young Nick staring back from the screen. Like *Rollercoaster, That Certain Summer* concludes in the space in which it began but with a potentially changed viewer looking back at it.

The contemporaneous critical acclaim for *That Certain Summer* in the *New York Times* and in *TV Guide* was matched by its honors at the time: Scott Jacoby received an Emmy for his performance as Nick, and the film was nominated for several other Emmys, including Outstanding Writing. It also received the Golden Globe award for Best Television Movie, and director Lamont Johnston received a Directors Guild Award for his work as well.[23] But these honors themselves are not matched by a documented place in history, either on-screen or in scholarly work. Like the film's ending, it is left unresolved in other ways as well, particularly in its lack of a return to television in syndication. Furthermore, though it was indeed the first network television film exploring gay male identity, receiving substantial awards, *That Certain Summer* has been largely absent from academic histories of either television or queer representations in moving-image media.

Writing around Race

While the writers' liberal humanism was spelled out most explicitly in their made-for-television movies of the 1970s, those progressive politics are also present within their famous series. Whether or not the original intention of the creators, these politics are most apparent in *Columbo*'s emphasis on class structures, given that in almost every episode the lieutenant is pitted against a rich denizen of Los Angeles. Even the exceptions prove the rule. That is, interestingly, some episodes in the fifth and seventh seasons are set outside of the Los Angeles class and caste system by focusing on other national arenas: one takes place in Mexico when the lieutenant is on vacation, whereas two take place in LA but concern, in one case, a fictional Middle Eastern nation and, in the final episode of the original series, Ireland. An earlier such example, "Dagger of the Mind" (2:4; Nov. 26, 1972), even takes place in London, where Columbo battles wits with two Shakespearean actors; in this case, however, the setting is both akin to that of Hollywood star culture and situates the lieutenant in the land of arguably the most famous fictional detective in history, Sherlock Holmes. But these episodes, too, include murderers driven either by their class position or by a need for money or both.

I would argue that class difference is also functionally a complex catchall for this series that premiered in the latter stage of the civil rights era and in the midst of the women's liberation movement. Some episodes over the course of the series do feature women murderers, some of whom are compelled to murder precisely because of their experience with the glass ceiling (in fact, almost every single case of a murder by a woman is business-related). But, quite intentionally, no murderers—or victims—are African Americans, for the cocreators wanted to dispel the link between Black Americans and violent crime.[24] In effect, they sought to resist what scholar Herman Gray would later describe as the "gerrymandered framework" of media representation.[25] Moreover, while Gayle Wald writes that "television and civil rights are deeply implicated in each other's histories," in *Columbo* these histories coexist through absence, metonym, and seemingly marginal characters.[26] For instance, Black actors play other cops, security guards, television production employees, occasional witnesses, and, in one particular case, the right-hand man.[27] The characters are never called explicitly to represent Black identity, but their presence certainly signals the ways in which the series is implicitly entrenched in issues of race and ethnicity. Moreover, though if taken out of the context of Levinson and Link's broader oeuvre it may not seem so significant, this concern was exactly that of Levinson and Link's first made-for-television movie, *My Sweet Charlie*. Adapted from a theatrical play, which was itself adapted from a novel, this movie was not an original Levinson and Link creation. Yet its politics seemed to appeal to the writing team, with its "common humanity of two individuals from alien cultures."[28] The film is the story of a Black civil rights lawyer who is accused of murder while in Texas; he takes shelter with a pregnant, undereducated racist white woman in an abandoned house, and the two eventually develop a romantic relationship. While Levinson and Link's approach was perhaps more idealistic than explicitly progressive, they fought against entrenched racism at the network in their insistence on telling an interracial love story.[29]

They brought a similar sensibility to casting and, ultimately, to writing their other series for the mystery wheel. James McEachin, the

2.3. Opening credit of *Tenafly* (1973–74), starring James McEachin

friendly conductor in *That Certain Summer* and an African American character actor on NBC during this era, appeared in two episodes of *Columbo*: as the Maestro's primary assistant, Billy Jones, in "Étude in Black" and as the projectionist Walter Mearhead in "Make Me a Perfect Murder." Each role positioned him in relation to television technology, whether he was instructing Columbo on reel changes in the seventh season or speaking into the camera (and appearing on the screens of the director's console) in the second. Importantly, these *Columbo* episodes bookended his stint as star of his own series, *Tenafly*, which was the only other series Levinson and Link created for the NBC *Mystery Movie* wheel. When the pilot for *Tenafly* premiered on February 12, 1973, it was the first television drama with a male Black actor/character in the singular (and eponymous) lead.[30] Moreover, it was one of the only series during this era to include a Black writer, which Levinson and Link negotiated when they made their deal with NBC. Albeit, the network demanded that the producers find a Black writer themselves, which they did: Booker Bradshaw cowrote the episodes "Joyride to Nowhere" and "Man Running" with television veteran David P. Lewis, and he went on to write for television for the next ten years, including one episode of *Columbo*.[31]

As Harry Tenafly, McEachin played a former cop who shifted to work as a detective for an insurance agency, and each episode balances an investigative case with a personal issue. Like Columbo, Tenafly gets around town, but his venues include a wider range. Interestingly, two episodes of McEachin's *Tenafly* focus squarely on moving vehicles in Los Angeles. And in so doing they underscore not just class differences within and between the two Levinson and Link series but also enable a broader analysis of race in 1970s Los Angeles. The episode entitled "Joyride to Nowhere" (1:1; Oct. 10, 1973) focuses on a robber of cabdrivers who eventually commits murder, whereas the following episode, entitled "The Window That Wasn't" (1:3; Dec. 5, 1973), offers a subtler representation of a moving vehicle.

While both the detective's actual family and overt mentions of race are absent from *Columbo*, in *Tenafly* each are woven into the narrative of every episode of the series. For instance, Tenafly's wife, Ruth (Lillian Lehman), is frequently a visible presence; whenever she calls her husband on the phone, we see a cross-cut sequence that alternates between the two of them as they speak. Moreover, as was an element of the very plan of the series by Levinson and Link—a departure from *Columbo*—parts of each episode also take place at Herb Tenafly's home. These details are central to both episodes in question. When in "Joyride" Tenafly goes undercover as a cabbie, his first night out is bookended by family business; before he goes, his wife calls to alert him to a scheduled dinner with family friends, and while he is on the job he realizes he's running late for dinner and must rush back. As Herb hightails it home, he sees a Black man on the side of the street hailing a cab. When he pulls over, the man says, "Two cabs have passed me up already. . . . Will you take me to Watts? If *you* don't take me, who will?"[32] Moreover, the subplot of the episode more explicitly includes family "business," for Herb's friend asks him to look into his daughter's boyfriend. When Herb goes to speak with the young lovers, they are both styled for the day in hip clothes and natural hair. Eschewing the middle-class lingo of Herb and Ruth, they take him into their confidence over their marriage plans. A minor detail, perhaps, but it's also one that depicts generational differences in politics through style.

"The Window That Wasn't" doesn't have the overt setting of Los Angeles auto transportation as does "Joyride," but the wheels of the plot are predicated on mobile machinery, both big and small. The story is that a young girl runs away from home, only to witness, through the window of a house, a man kill a woman. She calls her mom for a ride back home, and her mother, Mrs. Lenox (played by the great Ruby Dee), reports the incident to the police, who don't believe her. So instead Mrs. Lenox seeks a private detective to get to the bottom of it. When Mrs. Lenox first opens the door at her home for Tenafly, she asks, "Did their computer match us up?" "Beg your pardon?" returns the detective. "I mean a Black woman with a case; they send a Black detective. I guess that's to be expected," she explains. Tenafly brushes it off with "Kind of a coincidence, that's all," though throughout the short-lived series he makes similar observations himself (and usually more trenchant ones). Such fleeting statements—about Watts-bound taxi passengers, about race-based matchups—form a pattern in the series that enables an acknowledgment of the pattern, in turn, of racist discrimination in the United States on the heels of the civil rights era. Thus the "machines" of mobility in this episode are also telling: the house where Mrs. Lenox's daughter witnessed the murder turns out to have been a mobile home; an errant roller skate is a recurring object; and the Tenaflys get a flat tire on the way to a wedding that falls flat itself when the groom doesn't show.

Certainly the series is an imagining of the lasting presence of African American life in Los Angeles that *Columbo*—and almost every other drama on television in this era—does not reveal. On *Tenafly*, we see what Columbo doesn't see in the midst of his usual cases, and we go where his criminals don't normally take him: into the larger space of Los Angeles and into the middle-class homes of Black families. Hence, both "Joyride to Nowhere" and "The Window That Wasn't" tell stories of seemingly aimless movement and lost homes: cabs that circle the vast city, passengers that take taxis to "nowhere," and homes that slip away, almost undetected. In contrast, both episodes also include scenes of Herb Tenafly and his family at home, over the dinner table with friends, or in the living room taking care of their guests. I find these scenes not just significant but also deeply moving. In her study of the PBS variety show *Soul!*, which ran just prior to *Tenafly*, Gayle Wald describes the relation between the host Ellis Haizlip and his audience as an "affective compact." This relationship is based on mutual recognition, and it both designs and illuminates Black communities on- and off-screen. Looking at *Tenafly* forty years later, much like my experience of seeing *That Certain Summer* more than four decades after it first ran, produces for me an almost ineffable sensation, but surely one that is defined by an affective—or emotional—one: the thrill of looking at a screen that holds *only* Black Americans together at home. Not unlike the Diahann Carroll vehicle *Julia*, *Tenafly* enables a sense of intimacy with its characters that is otherwise largely unrepresented on television.

Of course, we also see models of the "affective compact" between the community of characters across episodes, such as in the scene in "Joyride" when Harry picks up his Watts-bound passenger. Such community and even intimacy are, moreover, extended to a sense of solidarity between Tenafly and women characters, from his wife, Ruth, to his secretary, Lorrie, to the various guest characters of each episode. Moments between Tenafly and various white women are marked by brief exchanges of dialogue that present parallel experiences. In "The Cash and Carry Caper," he's paired with a white detective at a department store where robberies are taking place; when she meets Harry she admits she checked him out in advance, as he did with her. In their mutual suspicion is also a mutual understanding. (Granted, he's missed some key details in his initial check, as she turns out to be one of the crooks.) In "Joyride," he meets with a lawyer, Leslie Storm (Ellen Corby), who previously oversaw a case related to the cabbie murders; in the midst of her description of the case, Storm announces to Tenafly, "I could practice law, but I just couldn't vote." Harry responds: "You know something? That happened to my grandfather, too." And "Window That Wasn't" ends with a scene between Tenafly and his white secretary, Lorrie, on the heels of her abandoned wedding. On her way out of the office, Lorrie warns Harry, "I'm having lunch with the girls—we might even open a branch of women's lib, so watch out."

James McEachin's Walter in "Make Me a Perfect Murder" experiences a more implicit camaraderie with the killer, Kay Freestone, for the two of them never acknowledge their shared struggles in the television industry. But McEachin's turn as Walter is actually indicative of this struggle, given that *Tenafly* lasted merely one season, with just five episodes completed; in other words, he may have needed the work that *Columbo* offered, and eventually he became a regular on *Columbo* producer Dean Hargrove's *Perry Mason* reboot. *Tenafly* also met a fate in history parallel to that of *That Certain Summer*. It did not return to television after its original run, it does not exist in any circulating collections (it's housed only at Universal and in the UCLA Film and Television Archive), and it has not been a central subject of discussion of any television scholarship prior to this volume. Both of these works and, arguably, their cocreators Levinson and Link, were seemingly ahead of their time, even as they were central to the social and political experience of the era. *Columbo* and class, it seems, was an easier sell to the network and to its audience.

Mysteries of Television Authorship

While Levinson and Link's work is shaped by their camaraderie as a team, they do and don't represent the collaborative structure of television production. Thus, while it may not be as complicated as murder (or certainly as finite), television authorship is not so easy to plot. Individual writers at work on television series have many other forces to deal with: creators, producers, stars, and, of course, network or studio executives. Writing an episode, or a made-for-television film, is inevitably an act of collaboration—and likely tension—with other creative and regulatory forces. With two writer-producers behind its creation, *Columbo* obviously can't claim a single author. Most importantly, while Levinson and Link speak in a form of unison, Falk's role as star—and reputed improvisational and directorial force (even if he took the role of credited director only once)—disputes a singular creative force behind each episode. Falk was himself the only constant force within the series, but he, too, was playing a creation by the dual writers.

To borrow a usage from scholar Miranda Banks, the creative *labor* of multiple figures was responsible for the production of the original forty-four episodes. At the same time, the consistency of tone is arguably due to the cocreators in tandem with the show's star. The other hired writers for the series had to become, in Banks's terms, "mimics" of Levinson and Link, whose words would then be brought to life by

Falk's performance.[33] Or, as Julia Kristeva asserts in her explication of intertextuality, "The writer's interlocutor, then, is the writer himself, but as reader of another text."[34] To further complicate things, this mimetic language was part of later creations, which in turn informed later iterations of *Columbo* itself. After all, the original series functioned as a training ground for significant writers as well as directors. The eventual creator of series such as *Hill Street Blues* and *LA Law*, Steven Bochco, in particular saw Levinson as a mentor when he worked as writer and story editor in its original incarnation. Bochco himself was just a part of a stable of writers, who were each responsible for one or multiple scripts, over the course of its seven-year run on NBC.[35] Other key figures in this group would go on to develop their own series that drew from their experience on *Columbo*. And that experience would sometimes return to the later remaking of *Columbo*. For instance, writer and producer Dean Hargrove created *Matlock*, and he also developed the *Perry Mason* reboot movies that ran from 1985 into the 1990s—which themselves may well have been the inspiration for the reboot of *Columbo*, ultimately falling prey to parody in some cases.

I'll come back to issues of parody and the reboot in my final chapter, but for now I want to consider the intricate details of the opening of that first official *Columbo* episode, "Murder by the Book," in order to illustrate the complexity of the authorship of the original. Lacking dialogue and any outward exposition, it seems nearly experimental in form. Almost before we perceive the image of a silent luxury car driving along a city street, we hear the sound of typewriter keys, and in the sequence that commences, this is the only sound we will hear for a full two minutes. Shot from above, the car fades into the distance, as the camera pulls into the interior of an office, revealing a bookcase full of mystery novels, ultimately panning right to show the man behind the typewriter, responsible for the sound. Pulling back again, the camera reveals a set of artifacts on the desk, including a large and small skull, seemingly the habitus of the mystery writer (indeed, a similar prop appears on Ellery Queen's desk). That this is a mystery writer's lair is confirmed with a cut to a framed cover of *Newsweek* that announces a "best-selling mystery team" before heading back to the typist himself

2.4. The writer's lair in "Murder by the Book" (1:1; Sept. 15, 1971)

(whom we now recognize as one of the best-selling duo), then forward to the words on the page as the keys hit the paper. And from the office we move back out the window, where we continue to track the luxury car on the streets far below, with the camera moving in and out of the vehicle, ultimately witnessing the driver's hands remove a gun from the glove box. The driver steps out of the car, and the camera's skewed perspective shows him looming above the building behind him before we return to the typist inside. The rapid tap-tap-tap of the typewriter keys is now cut short by a knock at the door. The writer opens it, and the driver of the car faces him with a gun. But rather than terror, the writer meets his would-be killer with a laugh.[36] This opening sequence doesn't follow what we might think of as conventional narrative rules. However, it implicitly plots the rest of the episode to come, as the man with the gun is the murderer-to-be, at first staging a failed crime only as a cover for that which will become successful in an imminent scene. In this way, "Murder by the Book" suggests alternative forms for narrative information and narrative structure as it begins. In its audiovisual track, it patiently re-plots the detective genre. And for those who are watching closely—those who have adopted its pace—*Columbo* begins its design of a thinking viewer.

The remarkable nature of this sequence is its patient tenacity, which ultimately matched both the detective and what he demands of us as viewers.[37] This sensibility also defines Levinson and Link as a writing team. Yet, even as we may recognize that the "best-selling" team of the episode reflects the team of Levinson and Link (generally speaking only, of course), the facts of the production of this episode also map the complexity of television authorship. That is, while the episode's credits include "story by" Levinson and Link, the screenplay was written by future television great Bochco and directed by then-prodigy Steven Spielberg.[38] Especially with these names involved, it's tempting to tease out the signature of each individual "author" involved in each episode's production. Such is the frustration and delight of knowing television: every episode of a series like *Columbo* comprises so many working parts that it may seem ultimately impossible to fix its origins. Hence, even with future luminaries Bochco and Spielberg as writer and director, "Murder by the Book" was still also a Levinson and Link creation, given the cocreators' original design and, subsequently, their propensity to continually rework the script.[39] Moreover, these moving parts continually change. Spielberg never directed another episode, for instance, and, though Bochco was the story editor for the first season, he was one of many writers over the years of this series that employed a stable of ongoing and one-off scribes.

In closing this chapter, I hope to strike a balance between historical accuracy and theoretical inquiry. Because television texts—whether "text" is defined by episode, season, or series—are multiply authored, it's nearly impossible to locate a singular voice of creation as their author. We might then choose to look at one specific text (again: episode, season, or series) in order to seek the emergence of a dominant voice of creation, but I would suggest—after philosophers like Roland Barthes—that the voice which emerges is of the text itself. Moreover, that "voice" emerges in the act of "reading," or in the case of *Columbo*, watching. Watching *Columbo* becomes, in so many ways, an act of recognition. To tease out these ideas toward a conclusion of this chapter, I will turn now to a set of scripts produced for the series, three examples of which offer both conventions of and exceptions to the rule.

Paper Trails

"The Most Dangerous Match" (2:7; March 4, 1973) was written by regular scriptwriter Jackson Gillis (and produced by Dean Hargrove), focusing on the murder of one chess champion by another. The WGF holds three versions of the script, and each iteration is increasingly tailored to become a more typical episode of the series. Three elements particularly mark the script's eventual adherence both to narrative economy and to the conventions of the series. First is the clarification of the relationship between the murderer, Emmett Clayton, and the victim Tomlin Dudek's personal assistant, Linda Robinson (Heidi Brühl). In the first iteration of Gillis's script, Dudek's assistant is named Sonja Robinson, and she appears to have had no previous interaction with Clayton. This lack of a relationship seems to enable her to share Dudek's medical information with Clayton without suspicion (this knowledge will ultimately allow him to finish off the master chess player), and it also leads to an extended scene following Dudek's surgery during which the two of them go out for a drink. But subsequent drafts eventually both elaborate on their prior relationship and intensify Linda's disdain for Clayton, even as their scenes together are trimmed back. In the second version of the script, Linda still does not have a previous relationship with Clayton, but she is suspicious; stage directions state, "Angle to Linda . . . They have never met—but she already doesn't like him. She is brittle."[40] Ultimately, the final script version includes the information that the two of them had once been engaged, and Linda was apparently spurned by Clayton. In the episode that aired, this detail is a little confusing, largely because it's so condensed. It is thus a vestige of multiple drafts, but one that is largely legible only through those drafts that did not make it to the screen. That is, the detail of Linda and Clayton's prior relationship becomes fairly rare background information; it concerns, in particular, a character (Linda) who is not central to the plot but who still plays a role in our understanding of the two men. Through the details of their relationship, Clayton is, of course, visible as not only a murderer but a scamp, too, and Dudek is even more apparent as a caring paternal figure. Hence in the early scenes of the produced episode, Dudek repeatedly shows concern for Linda, which also dilutes his own suspicion of Clayton as he attempts to mollify her concerns. In fact, Dudek's protective role is another similarity both to that which Columbo at times plays toward surviving spouses or lovers and to that which Will Geer's would-be victim, Dr. Hiedeman, plays in the preceding episode toward his medical assistant Nurse Martin, who ultimately becomes an actual victim of the murderous Dr. Mayfield. These changes therefore tease out affective relationships between characters rather than clarify elements of the central plot.

A second alteration occurs across the revisions of scripts; it concerns the lieutenant's dog, and it furthers an understanding of the plot. In the first draft of the script, when we initially encounter Columbo, he is playing checkers over a bowl of chili. In subsequent drafts, he is playing checkers with a veterinarian while his dog is resting after a procedure. The dog is introduced into the episode for reasons largely of narrative economy, for he becomes invoked at two distinct moments in subsequent scripts: first when Columbo receives a phone call in front of Clayton and then when the dog almost falls into the giant trash compactor where Clayton had pushed Dudek in his first attempt to kill him. In the former, Columbo responds to the news that "he" will survive, so that he is able to observe Clayton's reaction to the news (who clearly believes it concerns Dudek): at first, Clayton appears worried but relaxes upon learning Columbo is referring to his dog. But the dog's appearance has an even more important narrative function, for his near tragedy helps Columbo solve the case when he learns the specifics about the compactor's operation (it is programmed to stop if someone falls in), thus clarifying why Clayton would not have realized that Dudek didn't originally perish; his hearing disability meant that he could not register the sound of the machine turning off.

A third alteration to the original script concerns the title and focus of the episode itself. Its original title, "Fool's Mate," refers to the move that bests Clayton in the final scene—a move in which a checkmate is delivered in the fewest possible moves from the start of the game. While

2.5. "Just a foolish blunder" ("The Most Dangerous Match," 2:7; March 4, 1973)

this strategy is explicitly delivered by a chess opponent, it also comes, of course, from the lieutenant himself. I can only speculate on the title changes—most titles of original scripts held at the WGF did change, after all—but my sense is that it was too specific of a reference, which only chess aficionados would understand. Interestingly, the naming of the move throughout the episode is also eliminated in subsequent drafts, though Columbo's eagerness to learn more about the game of chess remains. But even that element of the episode—Columbo's trademark attempt to learn about a cultural object—is largely pared down from the original.

The reasons for these various changes are not outwardly legible in the scripts held at the WGF; the scripts contain no marginalia and no notes from the creators, story editor, or the studio. I therefore read them at once for their narrative purpose (such as enabling Columbo to recognize a key clue), their relational clarity (Dudek's "fathering" of both Linda and Clayton), and their revelation of the sensibility and the logic of the series. However, the changes to the script are evidence of a larger issue concerning the multiple forces at work in television production: Gillis is one of many creative laborers working in tandem with other creative and authorial leads, and his changes would have been required by these multiple forces in order to best represent the broader sensibility or logic of the series.

Another script by Gillis held at the WGF poses a tension between a myriad of voices—writer, director, cocreators, star—because it stands as an exception to the general narrative and performative rules. "Last Salute to the Commodore" was initially designed as the last episode of the series' run; it appeared as the final episode in season 5 (ultimately two more relatively short seasons would follow). Written by Gillis and directed by Falk favorite Patrick McGoohan, it defies the conventions of the series on a number of levels: the audience is misled over the identity of the murderer, and the final solution appears in a scene far more akin to an Agatha Christie novel than to an episode of *Columbo*, as the detective gathers the suspects together in a room in order to offer the big reveal. Structurally, then, this episode works against the series' formula. The initial drafts of scripts were even more defiant of the series' rules than the episode that ran. For instance, in the first script, our initial encounter with Columbo occurs at an amusement park where Columbo is on a ride with a kid named Lawrence, described by Gillis as "an owl-eyed drippy nosed brat of a kid." Not only would this scene be a rare visual intrusion of Columbo's personal life into the scenery of an episode, but the description of Lawrence is actively mean-spirited, defying the voice of the detective, certainly, but also the tenor of the series itself.

Before reading Gillis's scripts, I had put the blame for the odiousness of this episode in the hands of McGoohan, particularly given that he directed another episode from the same season, "Identity Crisis" (5:3; Nov. 2, 1975), in which he also appeared as the murderer. "Identity Crisis" includes scenes that appear to function as spoofs of the series or at least as revisions of its sensibility. In one instance that borders on parody, a conversation between the lieutenant and the murderer, Nelson Brenner (McGoohan), is strung out for a nearly unbearable duration, with pauses and tangents seemingly encouraged by character Brenner as a stand-in for director McGoohan. Another brief yet remarkable scene occurs at a belly-dancing club, in which the audience is privy to the detective happily ogling a dancer (rather than, say, looking away as he otherwise did in similar scenarios elsewhere in the original series). With McGoohan at the director's helm, both episodes appear to have an identity crisis indeed—and they certainly presage the reboot fifteen years later, for which he occasionally served as writer, director, and actor.

But if McGoohan, Gillis, and presumably Falk would stretch the limits of what would appear as part of the series, an episode that was never produced draws a line for what is acceptable. Theodore J. Flicker's 1973 draft of "Dead Swan"/"Dead as a Duck" was originally intended as a *McMillan & Wife* episode, but, as indicated on the first page of the script at the WGF, Flicker then adapted it for *Columbo*.[41] The script opens at the Hollywood Bowl, where Columbo is seated with another unlikable kid, watching a puppet show, for which one of the characters is described as follows: "an anal-compulsive stork. [He is] Mr. neat-and-clean, and everything in its proper place. He wears glasses, and has a mean piercing voice. He thinks Furry is stupid, but is somehow saddled with having to be his best friend. He is Abbott to Furry's Costello."[42] Shortly after a scene between the puppets, a clown named Ding-Dong is murdered right before Columbo's eyes when a plastic bomb explodes inside the performer's mask. Indeed, neither such plot points nor subsequent descriptions of characters (especially women) are consistent with the conventions of the series; "Dead as a Duck" is so off-form that, on the surface, it's obvious why it was never actually produced, and as such it proves the rule of the series in its narrative conventions and its sensibilities. But then "Dead as a Duck" was written two years before "Identity Crisis," which might suggest it was too early to push the conventions guarding the series and the detective himself.

Either way, the tone and the narrative details stand outside of that circularity that defines the original *Columbo* text. Initially describing a practice of reading invoked by Marcel Proust's work, Roland Barthes declares he reads with "a circular memory."[43] But this practice most certainly, as Barthes himself surprisingly suggests, could pertain to television. After all, such is the "inter-text": "the impossibility of living outside the infinite text—whether this text be Proust or the daily newspaper or the television screen: the book creates the meaning, the meaning creates life."[44] The "meaning" that emerges from the text—particularly the "meaning" of the text's author—is based in its continuities recognized by its viewers. Thus, the fixation of an authorial voice is a result of reading/viewing practices, but those continuities that develop this voice are also already forged in the texts themselves by their creators, who collaborate together, even in tension. Such an interpretive practice, as Barthes would say, is indeed circular, but it's also another form of collaboration: between text and viewer, between the makers of the works and their audiences. After all, writes Kristeva, "The one who writes is the same as the one who reads."[45]

Granted, this circularity inevitably produces both limits on and liberties of interpretation. A little more than a decade after the close of the original *Columbo*, scholar and novelist Umberto Eco draws on the series in order to define, as his title suggests, the "limits of interpretation" of serial fiction. He concludes his chapter "Interpreting Serials" with the following hypothetical case: "Let us imagine a society in the year A.D. 3000, in which ninety percent of all our present cultural production had been destroyed and of all of our television serials only *one* episode of *Columbo* had survived."[46] As he goes on, he wonders how we would "read" this work: "How would we read a piece of a series if the whole of a series remained unknown to us?"[47] In the early twenty-first century, this question is not one we need to ask about *Columbo*: it exists in DVD sets, it plays regularly in syndication, and it has had a place, however irregular, through online streaming sites. But I could pose this question to other works that Falk starred in (such as *The Trials of O'Brien* or many of his early television appearances) or, certainly, to "the whole" of the work composed by Richard Levinson and William Link. Though much of their work has survived, in one form or another, that which remains most known is, of course, *Columbo*. Can we "read" the series without *That Certain Summer*, *The Gun*, or *Tenafly*? Sure we can. But to do so is to limit both our understanding of television as an intertextual system and our comprehension of a broader history of production. In particular, I imagine that a version of Eco's scenario—to read *Columbo* without these other works—would likely write Levinson and Link themselves out of television history, given Peter Falk's inevitable association with the role and his control over its ongoing creation. Happily, however, the detective would never allow for such a selective reading. In order to make sense of a murder plot, he has to take into account everything at the scene—and even those elements that were explicitly absent from the scene. He has to look at the murder and beyond the murder. In my own mapping—or *plotting*—of Levinson and Link's work, I'm looking beyond murder as well. At the same time, I know that my interpretation, even with its own limits, is driven by detection.

3 "I'm Fascinated by Money"

The Detective's Place

Lieutenant Columbo is forever set between classifications; most notably, he is a police officer who is a detective. But it's also more complicated than that: in terms of traditional detective and police fictions, Columbo plays both roles and neither role. While Lieutenant Columbo self-presents as a working-class cop, this status is and isn't the whole truth, like much of what he reveals (and doesn't reveal). After all, he isn't just a cop who is walking the beat. He has risen to the rank of lieutenant, which is one rank below captain. Notably, the very origin of the word *lieutenant* from the French means to "hold a place in the absence of a superior," and this indeed is the common role of a lieutenant in police bureaus and the military today. This position—to be "in place of," or, more literally, "in lieu of"—is partly what enables Columbo to work solo as an investigator, for he is standing in for an absent presence of another authority. The very fact that he largely is on his own suggests that he has also likely reached lieutenant second grade.[1] Moreover, he has also been promoted to detective, of a similarly top grade, enabling him to work homicide cases. Surely this man, as the audience well knows but as the murderers often fail to grasp, is a highly accomplished professional.

As both cop *and* detective, the role of "Columbo" also underscores a difference in genre (the detective series, the cop show) and in type (the figure of hardboiled detective fiction and the "cozy" sleuth), which means, in turn, he is unlike his contemporaries on television. He's not a private investigator such as Jim Rockford (James Garner) of *The Rockford Files*, nor is he a hardboiled police detective working both in and out of a precinct like Telly Savalas's eponymous *Kojak*; though he may depend on inaccurate assumptions on the part of murderers, he's hardly an undercover cop, like Pepper Anderson (Angie Dickinson) of *Police Woman*; he doesn't work with a team of assistants like the wheelchair-bound detective Ironside in Raymond Burr's later televisual turn, nor does he have a sidekick in either a family member or an underling as does Rock Hudson's police commissioner McMillan of the often madcap *McMillan & Wife*.[2] He also differs from these and other iconic 1970s television detectives in terms of temperament and investigative approach. He's not sexualized—nor, in turn, are the vast majority of the female characters in the original series—as are the titular characters of *Banacek* or *Quincy, M.E.*, which each appeared as part of the NBC *Mystery Movie* wheel, or, of course, as are Charlie's "Angels."[3] Barring a scene like one in "The Greenhouse Jungle" (2:2; Oct. 15, 1972), when he stumbles down a hillside in order to investigate an automobile crash, Columbo neither thrives on nor battles chaos, as does the charming Jim Rockford. He doesn't revel in violence, like the cops of *Baretta*, *Starsky & Hutch*, or *Kojak*. And he's not an amateur, as are *The Snoop Sisters* or even *Ellery Queen*. But perhaps most importantly, time and again Lt. Columbo already appears to know who the criminal is from nearly the start of every episode; in that way, he is parallel to the viewer who has witnessed the crime. That knowledge, in turn, enables him to pursue other parallel investigations of cultural and technological phenomena, as I will later discuss in this and ensuing chapters.

The distinctions between Lt. Columbo and other contemporary television detectives of the early to mid-1970s may have much to do with his own textual origins and inspirations, which are drawn less from hardboiled detectives of noir or even screwball comedy than his counterparts. The literary critic Helmut Heissenbüttel describes different detective types as "a classic pair of opposites." He delineates them as follows: "the one who, roughly or even brutally, thrashes his opponents (and naturally is himself also thrashed on occasion) until he has found out who done it; and the other who, by a mixture of investigation of facts and combinatory puzzle solving, brings what was at first confused and opaque into plausible connections and makes it transparent."[4] Indeed, the analysis of detective fiction—its own complex form of detection— often turns to the ways in which detective novels, as Roger Caillois notes, are "not a tale but a game, not a story but a problem."[5] Moreover, writes Caillois, "The pleasure one gets from a detective novel is not that of listening to a story, but rather that of watching a 'magic' trick which the magician immediately explains."[6] Through games, problems, even "magic," we watch the detective as he detects. We watch him, in other words, as he thinks.[7]

While the formula of *Columbo* means that the detective doesn't work with "what was at first confused," for the viewer has seen the murder itself take place, the work of the detective is dependent, as Heissen- büttel notes, on "logical thought."[8] Columbo thus fits into the legacy formed by fictional characters such as Edgar Allan Poe's analytic Au- guste Dupin and Dostoyevsky's Petrovich, as well as Agatha Christie's Hercule Poirot and Georges Simenon's Commissioner Maigret; indeed, Dostoyevsky's and Simenon's creations were two important influences for Levinson and Link. After all, writes Heissenbüttel, Poirot was de- scribed as "a laughable little man, whom no one took seriously," and the same could be applied to a first meeting of Petrovich.[9] The fact that Columbo himself is not taken seriously by the murderers often stems from the fact that they seem to confuse class and intelligence, each of which are the focus of the series and of this chapter. To some degree, he better resembles the circumspect Maigret, who was known for his "human and psychological sympathy."[10] Like Maigret, Lt. Columbo is both circumspect and humane. Indeed, the kindness that emanates from him and which transforms into viewers' affection for him in turn makes one almost forget that his specialty is homicide. And arguably the series really isn't about death at all; though, of course, every plot is propelled by murder, the affective dimensions of the show have very little to do with the intensity of grief and the pain of loss. In the detective's work to stop killers who believe they are above the law—and who, quite simply, lack respect for human life—Lt. Columbo also reveals a care for life itself, as his circumspection and humanity are often linked through his interest in and references to quotidian details regarding the living and the dead.

The fascination of the detective and on the part of the series for everyday details is further suggestive of an important difference between Lt. Columbo and both Christie's and Simenon's creations, in that the latter are, in Heissenbüttel's words, "urban petty bourgeois." Or, put a little more bluntly by producer-writer Dean Hargrove, "He looks like a bum, but he's really Sherlock Holmes."[11] Hence, Columbo doesn't fit into the world of the wealthy murderers he investigates or even into the middle class, as do Levinson and Link's other detectives: Harry Tenafly and Ellery Queen. Instead he seems to spring from the community of small-time or professional hoods that the actor Peter Falk played before and after his role as the detective. Such oppositions structured through class and legality define our detective. While I'll come to the heady games the detective plays with his suspects later in this chapter, for now I want to consider the ways he wears those differences of class and legality if not on his sleeves, then on his feet.

Footwork

In his memoir, *Just One More Thing*, Peter Falk tells a story about the detective's shoes in "The Most Crucial Game." The crime in this episode takes place at a swimming pool: Robert Culp plays the murderer, Paul Hanlon, who kills the victim, Eric Wagner (Dean Stockwell), with a block of ice as he lounges in the water. Wandering through the crime scene, the detective gets his shoes wet, which begets a thread in the episode. In the course of the investigation later that day, a number of characters have gathered in the victim's living room: Hanlon, Hanlon's assistant, Wagner's attorney, and a group of police officers. In his habit of offering dialogue in the form of a screenplay, Falk writes:

> During an important speech by Culp detailing his whereabouts at the estimated time of death, Columbo taps the defense attorney on the shoulder and very quietly, unobtrusively whispering, asks the attorney a question—
>
> COLUMBO
> Excuse me, sir, how much did you pay for those shoes?[12]

3.1. The gumshoe is all wet ("The Most Crucial Game," 2:3; Nov. 5, 1972)

3.2. "How much did you pay for those shoes?" ("The Most Crucial Game," 2:3; Nov. 5, 1972)

The question wasn't scripted but was rather an ad-lib that Falk contributed, and it became a running joke for the actor himself. As he reveals in his memoir, "I'd be walking down the street and people would come up and ask me regarding not only my shoes but anything I might be wearing—my tie, my pants, anything—How much did you pay for them?"[13]

Shoes are a running joke in the series, too, or at least an ongoing point of reference, whether they belong to the detective, the victims, or innocent bystanders. In fact, though Falk doesn't mention it, they are briefly even a running joke in "The Most Crucial Game" itself. That is, later in the episode, the lieutenant also asks a side character, a scout watching a pickup basketball game that the murderer is also scouting, where *he* got his shoes, too.[14] The cost of shoes comes up in other episodes; for instance, when a television repairman in "Make Me a Perfect Murder" suggests the detective buy a new TV, Columbo tells him he has other expenses, like the future purchase of a new pair of shoes. Footwear also presents clues regarding both the victims and their killers in various other episodes: in "Candidate for Crime," the detective climbs into the hearse with the victim's body to check out his shoes, suit, and watch; in "Playback" (4:5; March 2, 1975), a clue centers on the lack of a footprint in the garden, in spite of the fact that the crime scene is staged to appear as if an intruder entered through a window; and in "An Exercise in Fatality" (4:1; Sept. 15, 1974), shoes pose both one of the first and one of the last of the major clues in solving the case.[15] In the latter episode, when he investigates a room outside the scene of the crime (an exercise facility at a gym franchise), Columbo notices scuff marks on what was supposed to be a freshly waxed floor. Following up, he wanders through the investigation area, repeatedly asking all the officers on scene if the soles of their shoes are brown. He later reveals the final clue to the killer by way of demonstration: taking a pair of sneakers, he shows the different direction the laces take when tied by the person whose feet they are on, as opposed to when they are tied by someone other than the wearer. To visually punctuate this preoccupation with footwear in the middle of the episode, Columbo attends to his own shoes after having been forced to run on the beach alongside the killer, an exercise maven. He takes a breath as the suspect, Milo Janus, throws himself in the pool for a quick lap, practices with a punching bag, and jumps rope. During this spectacle of hyperbolic manliness, the detective walks over to the garden and removes a shoe, pouring sand from it behind his back into the bushes, with a sense of childlike shame.

The disparity between the detective and his suspect couldn't be clearer in this scene: Janus shows off his physical prowess, accentuated by his near-naked body, as part of his own power game with the lieutenant while the detective, covered in his own sweat, barely catches his breath. Though not always marked by physical strength, of course, in

3.3. Columbo completes a run ("An Exercise in Fatality," 4:1; Sept. 15, 1974)

episode after episode, the killer's motive, too, frequently concerns a question of power, often having to do with financial control and sometimes the loss thereof. Murderers kill to make money, to save money, to keep that which they consider to be theirs; in "An Exercise in Fatality," Janus has killed off a gym-franchise owner who discovered his financial scams. The arrogance and vanity of the murderers, moreover, is often tied to their wealth; indeed, the least vain of the series' killers are those who seem to have humbler origins or have a more tenuous grasp on what they own, such as country singer Tommy Brown (Johnny Cash) in "Swan Song" or vintner Adrian Carsini (Donald Pleasence) in "Any Old Port in a Storm" (3:2; Oct. 7, 1973). And, of course, every single episode includes some reference to Columbo's own self-presented working-class status, whether via repeated references to the cost of shoes, his run-down car, or his unkempt appearance. "Some men . . . do not want to look like an unmade bed," Helen Stewart (Suzanne Pleshette) says in "Dead Weight" (1:3; Oct. 17, 1971). Is it any wonder that the detective is so frequently described, on-screen and off-screen, as either "bumbling" or "rumpled"?

After all, each word (like the word *humble*) nearly rhymes with the very name "Columbo."

The economic disparity between the detective and his prey is perhaps most neatly spelled out in the first episode of season 2, "Étude in Black," when Columbo appears unannounced at the killer's house about a third of the way through the episode. Played by Falk's friend and collaborator John Cassavetes, Alex "the Maestro" Benedict invites the lieutenant into the living room. Columbo refuses the comfort: "I'm not going in there, I'm not messing up the room," he says. Claiming that he's there because "I never got to ask you last night what I wanted to ask you," Columbo then pauses to compliment the Maestro on the "terrific place" he has, ultimately asking permission to "take a look in there." Our eyes only on the detective, we don't see the room he stares at as he exclaims, "Gotta be a forty-foot living room. Forty by twenty. Dining room's fifteen feet deep. I can't see the rest. Windows, windows, windows. Ideal. This is a dream house."

"I'm glad you like it," the Maestro responds. After a brief discussion of New York versus Los Angeles, which seems as much about the actors as the characters, Columbo inquires, "Can I ask you a personal question?" His question is what Benedict pays in taxes on his house. "Eighteen thousand dollars a year," the Maestro responds. Then the detective mumbles a quick set of calculations: "Three times eighteen, carry the twenty-four. Seven down. Bring down the zero. The place cost you 720,000." "Seven-hundred-and-fifty thousand," corrects the Maestro. Columbo wanders toward the room on the other side of the staircase where Benedict soon perches. "Can I look in there?" he asks, while Benedict inquires how he came to his figure. "It's a real estate rule of thumb. It's a trick. No magic. I'm not an appraiser or anything like that." The differences between tricks, magic, and appraisal brushed aside, Columbo goes on to ask how much the conductor has in furniture, and the Maestro responds by querying if he's going to get to what he came to ask him. "I'm going to get to that, but I'm fascinated by money, aren't you?"

"Fascinated by money." That phrase could define the series as a whole. In this particular case, Columbo pushes further. Hence, as the Maestro concurs in response, the detective continues, "What I was going to ask you is this: How much do you make?" Benedict becomes increasingly uncomfortable, even a little peeved, suggesting that the question is "very impertinent." Columbo persists, and when he gets nothing, he then works through a second set of calculations to figure out how he might be able to swing the place on his annual salary of $11,000: "That's ninety years of work for me to live here, without eating." But then even this wasn't the real point; what he actually came for, he claims, is the conductor's autograph to bring home to his wife. He hands him an envelope, and the Maestro glares at him as he takes it. "What do you want me to say?" "Just put your name; that would be good enough." The Maestro signs and glowers some more.

The detective's fascination with money is so prevalent that we see it explicitly spelled out in the very next episode, "The Greenhouse Jungle," in which Columbo tracks the mastermind behind his nephew's fake kidnapping and subsequent very real murder. In one scene he arrives in the killer's solarium to surprise the murderer, Jarvis Goodland (played by Ray Milland, who also played the would-be killer of his wife in Hitchcock's *Dial M for Murder* and who was in the second episode of season 1, "Death Lends a Hand," as the husband of the murder victim).[16] Admiring the "flowers"—"orchids," corrects the killer—Columbo suggests his wife would love to see him come home with one. "That specimen happens to be called a Moth Orchid. Its value is approximately $1,200," says Goodland.[17]

Playing one after another, these episodes are representative of the series as a whole, which pitted the working-class cop against the well-heeled killers of Los Angeles. In fact, almost all the murderers across the series were either already rich, attempting to recover money they felt was owed to them, or immersed in cultural capital. The Maestro kills his mistress because she is going to expose their affair and therefore ruin his marriage, which bankrolls not just his lifestyle but also his living as an orchestral conductor; and Goodland kills his nephew in order to have access to the $300,000 of an otherwise unbreakable trust fund, since, as Columbo says of the uncle's orchid habit, "A fella could go broke with a hobby like this." Such links between death and lifestyle are typical in the murder plots of the series, as a smattering of references easily shows: in "Old Fashioned Murder" (6:2; Nov. 28, 1976), the ownership of a family museum is at stake; in "Swan Song," a singer (Cash) is being manipulated by his wife (Ida Lupino) in order to build a giant cathedral; in "Lovely but Lethal" (3:1; Sept. 23, 1973), the crime hinges around ownership of the formula for an antiwrinkle cream, which could make or break the bank; in "A Friend in Deed" (3:8; May 5, 1974), the deputy police commissioner kills his wife for her inheritance, which he believes should be his, as it can support his avocations as a gambler and philanderer; and the list goes on and on. As Jeff Greenfield wrote in the *New York Times* in 1973, "This is, perhaps, the most thoroughgoing satisfaction 'Columbo' offers us: the assurance that those who dwell in marble and satin, those whose clothes, food, care and mates are the very best, *do not deserve it*."[18] Hence, given that the killers' motives are inevitably bound to questions of power, control, and greed, part of what the series allows us to "know" on a regular basis is class structure and class difference.[19]

Of course, the shoes are one of Columbo's accoutrements—like his rickety Peugeot, his woebegone basset hound, his overworn raincoat, his forever half-smoked cigar, and even his disheveled hair—that mark the detective's singularity, as well as both his cultural and his financial status. As Falk himself said in an interview with Terry Gross on *Fresh Air*, his shoes set him apart from the killers who were "God's Chosen." He declared, "They all could buy suits off the rack, and they fitted them, and they looked good, and their teeth were white, and they had dough, and they spoke well. And so clunky shoes were a good contrast."[20] He is forever somewhere in between: blue collar and white collar, a flat foot and a gumshoe, everyman and a solo show.

That is, while Lt. Columbo's class position is always set in opposition to the killers he tracks, his professional position confuses the categories and distinctions of class and rank. Hence, several episodes concern professional matters that are explicitly related both to financial gain and to "rank." These episodes continue to emphasize the class difference between the detective and the criminals, but they also enable a distinction between class and "rank." For instance, both "Mind over Mayhem" and "A Matter of Honor" include murders that cover up actions that would upend a professional's standing. The former pits the detective against a particularly arrogant murderer at a "think tank," whereas the latter has him working alongside a peer in Mexico to take down a national hero. "Make Me a Perfect Murder" narrates as much the murderer's revenge for her lack of a promotion as an attempt at eliminating the competition for a job. And "Candidate for Crime" includes a murder committed for professional status, as well as one that demonstrates an act of "pulling rank." In this case, a well-heeled senatorial candidate, Nelson Hayward (played by Jackie Cooper), kills his campaign manager, Harry Stone (played by Ken Swofford), both to ensure that he wins a senatorial race and because the manager—officially Hayward's underling—is too bossy, as he has demanded that the candidate dump his mistress in order to better ensure his wholesome reputation.

This classy "candidate for crime" lives in a plush house, complete with a swimming pool on-site and a beach house across town. But class difference is also his undoing. The first piece of evidence that allows Columbo to prove he planned the murder is directly connected to his lifestyle and vanity. Noticing a beautiful new camel hair jacket delivered to his office—the mirror image of the one that the victim Harry had swapped with him and thus was wearing when he was murdered—Columbo asks him how much it cost. "Two hundred dollars," Hayward answers, and, without thinking, adds the name of his tailor. The lieutenant shortly thereafter visits the tailor under the pretense that he needs a new jacket for a special event (a bowling party with his wife!), and there he learns that the candidate ordered the second jacket several days before Harry was murdered. Whereas Hayward attempts to explain this seemingly murderous intent away by claiming that the other jacket had become too ragged, for Columbo it clearly suggests a sense of forethought.

The second instance of class distinction appears in two related sequences, which are as much about the detective himself as the suspect he's trailing. After having been pulled over by two highway patrol officers and given citations for a series of automotive infractions, Columbo next appears driving another vehicle entirely, a tow truck, checking a stopwatch as he drives. When he pulls into a garage, we see a mechanic spinning the wheels on the lieutenant's car. The mechanic announces his car is ready, and Columbo thanks him for the use of his truck, handing him a tip for the loan—which he seems to regret after he gets the bill for $65.25. Awkwardly staring at the mechanic, he asks if he might take a check. The mechanic wavers: "You haven't got a credit card?" And Columbo

3.4. Evidence on time ("Candidate for Crime," 3:3; Nov. 4, 1973)

3.5. A more fitting watch ("Candidate for Crime," 3:3; Nov. 4, 1973)

responds, "I'm from the police. Lt. Columbo." As the mechanic looks at his ID, he asks, "You undercover or something?" "I'm under*paid*," the detective responds. (And then he borrows a counter check to pay his bill.) In the midst of this interlude about Columbo's beloved car—and his cop's salary—we learn two more pieces of information toward the solution of the case as well: the drive from the candidate's beach house to the nearest gas station (where Columbo has just had his car repaired) is seven minutes away, and the station closed early the night of the murder because it ran out of gas. Thus, the time of the murder, for which the candidate had an alibi, and the location of the phone call that led to the discovery of the body are both put into question.

To begin to wrap things up in his investigation, Columbo returns to sartorial matters. Visiting the candidate and his wife out by the pool, he brings a box of Harry's own clothes from the night of his murder. As Hayward is busy filming a campaign spot, Columbo enlists Mrs. Hayward in solving his puzzle: Why doesn't Harry's watch match his coat and shoes? Harry's own jacket, after all, was designed to be durable, and so were his shoes. But the watch he was wearing, which was smashed presumably upon the impact of his body when he was shot, was a slight instrument, with a leather band and a thin face (fitting, it seems, more as an accessory to the cashmere jacket he'd swapped with Hayward). Columbo explains that he took the jacket and the shoes to a jeweler and asked him to match a watch to the outfit; what he was given was a watch whose face wouldn't break. The episode doesn't end here; these clues, after all, are circumstantial. But they plant seeds of doubt in the candidate's wife's mind, and they lead the candidate himself to take a risk that ultimately proves his guilt. More to the point, they suggest a mismatch between class and innocence that is a definitive claim of the series. That is, the rich aren't "classy"; they're killers.

Battle of Wits

As I have said, one of the mistakes nearly every killer makes is to equate wealth with intelligence. Therefore, if they see the detective as a lower rank in class than that which they occupy, they also assume he is a rung below them in smarts. At once a study of class difference and a study of the detective's intelligence, the series portrays again and again the myriad ways he mobilizes his intelligence (including, of course, pretending that he is lacking in it). Several episodes, including the original "Enough Rope" and its remake, *Prescription: Murder*, employ psychiatry to analyze both his character traits and his intelligence. After all, during the era of the run of the original series, popular psychiatry was itself afoot. Such a cultural presence of psychiatry and psychoanalysis reveals itself in those episodes in which the killer is a psychiatrist: *Prescription:*

Murder, of course, as well as "A Deadly State of Mind" (4:6; April 27, 1975), in which the killer first murders his patient's husband and then his patient herself, eventually identified by a blind earwitness. But popular psychiatry also serves as a kind of heuristic for the series, particularly in the ways that the episodic formula highlights "not a tale but a game" via the detective's rhetorical pursuits of his suspects.

By the 1970s, neo-Freudian psychoanalysis was well established, but a wide range of alternative therapeutic and self-help approaches emerged, too, that placed personal psychology in a social context, and these were quickly integrated into film and TV narratives. For example, in "The Bye-Bye Sky High I.Q. Murder Case," a scene takes place in a singles bar, where the killer's secretary, George, meets up with a woman who offers the following pickup line: "Hi. I'm Susie. I've tried Esalen, Primal Scream, Pyramid Power, Synanon [. . .], Open Marriage, EST, TA, TM, I'm-Okay-You're-Okay, and I'm still a target."[21] Within this quick catalogue are telling references to Transactional Analysis ("TA" and "I'm-Okay-You're-Okay"), a field of therapy pioneered by psychiatrist Eric Berne.[22] As this albeit superficial reference shows, elements of Berne's theories and his lexicon were integrated into US culture in the 1970s, largely based on his 1964 best-seller *Games People Play*; such references speak to a generalized pervasiveness of Berne's work—and certainly of an emerging therapeutic culture—in the United States at the time of the series.[23] In the case of *Columbo*, it narrates games the characters play with one another and invites games that the spectators play with the series. Certainly, such play is part of the fun of the series—the pleasure for the detective and for his fans. My turn to Berne here is bound to a slight detail in one particular episode, but it's a serendipitous one, as it is also evidence of a series of parallels—historical, cultural, conceptual—that provide a mechanism of analyzing the detective's intelligence and the refusal of his nemeses to recognize it.

Berne himself was trained psychoanalytically and he was influenced by Freud, but that's not the primary basis of my interest in his work here. Rather, I'm interested in the brief trace his work left on the series—a kind of cultural dust that the detective himself might find at a crime scene—to which I can turn to understand a narrative device of the series. Specifically, the gist of Berne's theory further helps to articulate what's commonly referred to as the cat-and-mouse game of *Columbo*, the "game" that elucidates the murderer's desire to make his or her crime known to the detective, such as the killer, Oliver Brandt, displays in "Sky High." Such a desire may well be bound to guilt, which is obviously a central concept in any crime show. In *Columbo*, "guilt" is established at the beginning of every episode, so that, legally speaking, it is not the question to be resolved. But then guilt isn't merely a *legal* question; it's also a matter of emotions and ethics. To be guilty is to be legally responsible for something; to *feel* guilty is to experience remorse and, one hopes, accountability. In fact, it's exactly that kind of guilt that Columbo impresses upon low-rung accomplice George in "Sky High" when he follows him to the singles bar.[24] Yet while that ploy works on poor George, the vast majority of *Columbo*'s murderers are without remorse, though they would hardly quibble over legal responsibility (or, at least, that latter process is not what the series is about). Their desire to speak to the detective about the crime—that is, to offer alternate scenarios and then, sometimes, to reveal the actual particulars when Columbo gets it "wrong"—rarely seems a result of a guilty conscience, even to a dyed-in-the-wool Freudian. They speak not to prove guilt-as-remorse but rather to enact guilt-as-responsibility; they speak to prove their superiority to the detective, to show they are intellectually responsible for the brilliance of the crime they have committed.

In this way, the "cat-and-mouse" game of *Columbo* entails what Berne calls a "con." In *What Do You Say after You Say Hello?*, a work published posthumously in 1972, Berne summarized the analytic theories he developed over the past decade in order to develop a highly complex idea into a much more accessible one for the popular reader. His definition of con games neatly describes much of Columbo's work with the killers. Noting that "games are sets of ulterior transactions, repetitive in nature, with a well-defined psychological payoff," Berne asserts that "since an ulterior transaction means that the agent pretends to be doing one thing while he is really doing something else, all games involve a con. But a con only works if there is a weakness it can hook into, a handle or gimmick to get hold of in the respondent, such as fear, greed, sentimentality or irritability."[25] In *Columbo*, many of these weaknesses are those of the killers he tracks, and they are almost always also tied to arrogance (and to financial capital). Their weakness means they don't see what's coming. As Berne continues, "After the 'mark' is hooked, the player pulls some sort of switch in order to get his payoff. The switch is followed by a moment of confusion or crossup while the mark tries to figure out what has happened to him. Then both players collect their payoff as the game ends. The payoff, which is mutual, consists of feelings (not necessarily similar), which the game arouses in both the agent and the respondent."[26] Whereas the murderers in *Columbo* are just arrogant enough to think it's their game, the viewer knows that it's actually the detective's. And Columbo's con is nearly always the same, hinging on this very belief: a pretense that he knows less than he does. Ultimately each of the two—the detective and the criminal—experiences a payoff: Columbo solves the case, and the killer's own intelligence for having planned such a brilliant crime becomes known by someone just as smart as her or him. Brandt of the "Sky High" case makes this point quite explicit when he attempts to measure the lieutenant's IQ after Columbo solves the case, suggesting "it must be very high," implying it is comparable even to his own. After all, throughout the episode, the men have been involved in a "battle of wits," what Berne says is descriptive of the childhood game of hide-and-seek, in which, after the appropriate suspense, "being found is the necessary payoff."[27] These battles of wits, which contain both suspense and the ultimate payoff in being found, are key to the plot and the pacing of each episode. They are, in effect, the narrative game of the series, most explicitly marked in two other episodes that are about men who, like Brandt, identify as geniuses.

Well before "Sky High," two oddly similar episodes appeared in a row during season 2, each narrating professional anxieties of highly intelligent men. "A Stitch in Crime" is largely an attempt to eliminate professional competition. And the episode that immediately follows it, "The Most Dangerous Match," is entirely concerned with the matter of rank. "A Stitch in Crime" and "The Most Dangerous Match" share another narrative commonality as well, which is actually so glaring that it almost seems as if the latter one were an attempt, in some form (more likely unconscious than conscious) to re-solve the matters of the first. Both are stories of a younger man (each dark-haired, tall, with sharp features) vying with an older man (each congenial, fleshy, fatherly types).

3.6.
Generational
differences
("A Stitch in
Crime," 2:6;
Feb. 11, 1973)

3.7. Genera-
tional differ-
ences ("The
Most Danger-
ous Match,"
2:7; March 4,
1973)

In both episodes neither of the victims suspects the younger men of
malice; both attempt to mentor them, even soothe their worries. In
"A Stitch in Crime" both men are heart surgeons and researchers; the
older Dr. Hiedeman, played by Will Geer, has been testing the possibility
of heart transplants, and the younger Dr. Mayfield, played by Leonard
Nimoy, is eager to start the transplant surgery before any other surgical
teams. "The Most Dangerous Match" is the story of chess opponents:
an older, amiable Eastern European former world champion, Tomlin

Dudek (Jack Kruschen), has been up-seeded by a younger champion, Emmett Clayton (Laurence Harvey), during the older man's five-year illness, but the two are now preparing to meet for their first match to test their world rankings. Hence, this latter episode is a particularly appropriate one to comment specifically—or at least metonymically—on the issue of rank, class, and intelligence. After all, "rank" is also the term for the horizontal row on the chessboard, while "file" is the term for the vertical row. Indeed, the expression appears before us in many scenes: even if we don't know the game's lexicon, we visually witness "rank" and "file" on the chessboards that appear throughout the episode.

Both episodes are unusually upsetting, perhaps because we get to know the victims and because they are indeed kind and quite vulnerable human beings. For instance, "A Stitch in Crime" begins with Dr. Hiedeman being rushed to his own hospital for an emergency heart treatment; we move from the ambulance into the interior of the hospital where we see, close-up, a range of other patients who are unlike the usual characters (or at least the usual murderers and victims) of the series and whom we might imagine as the patients for whom the doctor cares: first, a middle-aged, professional-looking African American man whose arm is in a sling, with an older Asian couple in the corner behind him, and then a Latino family to the side (the camera pans first past the mother and two children and then lands on the father, whose head is bandaged, with a third young child sitting on his lap). We see, too, that Dr. Hiedeman himself is cared for by his staff, especially Nurse Sharon Martin (Anne Francis, formerly of *Honey West*). And Will Geer, after all, is the same actor who played Grandpa on *The Waltons* during this same period, further enlisting our sympathy. We can add to that sympathy the fact that Geer was blacklisted during the Communist purge around Hollywood in the 1950s, returning to television in a series that highlighted his own "everyman" qualities (and one whose narrative went back in time before those purges took place).

Maybe, too, these episodes are upsetting because the main characters are not unlike our detective: the primary victims are so likable that one might forget that they are at the top of their game, but they are also more benevolent father figures than the generation seemingly represented by the likes of Dr. Mayfield and Mr. Clayton. Characters

3.8. Los Angeles denizens ("A Stitch in Crime," 2:6; Feb. 11, 1973)

like Dr. Hiedeman and Tomlin Dudek parallel the lieutenant through the care they reveal for others. That is, Columbo is not only relatable to his viewers but also relation-able; the care he shows for human life is demonstrated in those relations—however often fleeting—he fosters with other characters, even sometimes with the very criminals he's tracking, and the subsequent "relationship" a viewer might develop toward him. In what might seem like an ironic twist, a viewer's relationship with him may well be possible because of the absence of his familial relations on the series. Absence, as I noted, defines the role of the "lieutenant," who holds a place in the absence of an authority.[28] And it defines Columbo himself as well, as he works largely on his own and, in the running joke of the series, we never see his wife. Because we don't see him at home, we don't experience him as a ruling patriarch, benevolent or otherwise. In fact, through the absence of his wife, we might guess from "The Most Dangerous Match" and other episodes that Mrs. Columbo is his superior at home; when we first encounter him fifteen minutes in, via a cut from a sequence narrating Clayton's chessboard nightmare to a shot of a checkerboard where the detective is playing a game with his dog's vet, he complains: "My wife went to visit her mother for a few days, and it's like everything was waiting for her to leave so it could happen to me. First the kitchen sink and then the pilot light on the stove. I don't even know where the pilot light is."

Whereas his wife forever remains out of sight, what is fascinating about "A Stitch in Crime" is the fact that, like us, Columbo gets to know the original would-be victim (as well as the second and third actual victims). Dr. Mayfield's murder scheme of his mentor is a particularly clever one: in the performance of a surgery to replace a heart valve, he uses dissolving suture thread, so that Dr. Hiedeman will die within a few days rather than instantly. But in his ruthlessness, he kills a series of victims to cover up his first crime: first, Nurse Martin who suspects him and then the man whom he attempts to frame for the nurse's murder. In his interactions with the older doctor, Columbo doesn't appear to identify with him, though perhaps his deep respect for him might be a clue to us that he recognizes some sense of a kindred spirit. At the very least, *we* can't help but see a resemblance between them (in fact, Will "Grandpa" Geer gives Peter Falk a run for the money in the charm department). Notably, however, this episode is one of the very few in which the lieutenant both loses his temper—he actually yells at the murderer, who never appears to lose his equilibrium (drawing on Nimoy's Spock-like cool)—and almost fails to solve the would-be murder. In the final scene Columbo begrudgingly, even angrily, admits to the killer that he appears to have won and leaves the room, offering Dr. Mayfield just enough time to enjoy a moment of smugness, only to have the lieutenant victoriously reappear a moment later after discovering the precise evidence he needed to solve the case.

"A Stitch in Crime" is a little like a murderer's bad dream. Mayfield doesn't actually pull off the primary murder he wanted to achieve, which means he won't get the professional fame he wanted from its results (i.e., the success of a heart transplant), and then, just when he thought he was safe, he gets caught both for the attempted murder and for the actual murders he did commit. In a sense, "The Most Dangerous Match" starts where the previous episode left off: with a murderer's nightmare. Emmett Clayton is wildly traversing a giant psychedelic chessboard, whose fleshy king laughs down on him until he awakes. Next we see

3.9. A killer's nightmare, close up ("The Most Dangerous Match," 2:7; March 4, 1973)

him in the lobby of a hotel, being pursued by a group of reporters who question him about his status and that of the former champion Tomlin Dudek. When Dudek himself appears, he is revealed, of course, to be the "king" of the chessboard in Clayton's dream. Shortly thereafter Clayton tracks Dudek to a small French restaurant, where he joins him for a rich dinner (against Dudek's doctor's orders) and where they proceed to play a game of chess on the checkered tablecloth, improvising with salt and pepper shakers, various bottles of oils and other condiments, as well as shells from Dudek's forbidden escargots. As Dudek is clearly about to win the game, Clayton abandons the play and stomps out of the restaurant. He is, after all, outranked by the older man. Dudek consoles him, and the two return to the hotel, where they ultimately take up another game of chess in Clayton's room. And there Dudek beats his foe handily, even taking on the role of both the black and the white pieces, announcing every play as he does so. Again Dudek consoles his opponent, offering easy rationales for why he would have lost, promising the younger man that he'll do better in the match the next morning.

After Dudek departs, Clayton experiences another nightmare; upon waking, he seemingly cannot control the visions, which we see in split screen, as he covers his ears, eventually grabbing the cord that runs from his earpiece and yanking his hearing aid out of his ear, flinging it at the mirror. To film aficionados, such a performance may come as no surprise. That is, if Dr. Mayfield logically recalls Mr. Spock of Nimoy's well-known role on *Star Trek*, Mr. Clayton, or rather the actor Laurence Harvey, here recalls one of his most famous roles: that of the eponymous character in *The Manchurian Candidate* (John Frankenheimer, 1962). Like the Manchurian Candidate, Clayton is seemingly manipulated by forces beyond his own powers; in this case his trigger is not the Queen of Diamonds playing card, as in Frankenheimer's film, but rather a distorted image of the chessboard king.[29] In order to regain control, he seeks to overthrow the king in his attempt to kill Dudek by throwing him into a trash compactor at the hotel. With Dudek out of the picture, Clayton can maintain his rank—and "class"—as world chess champion.

Coming on the heels of "A Stitch in Crime," "The Most Dangerous Match" offers an interesting commentary both on that preceding episode and on the series' implicit distinctions between class, rank, and intelligence via the character of Lt. Columbo. First of all, as I said, the latter episode takes off, figuratively speaking, where the former left off. The phases of the murders are also similar, if unintentionally so on the part of the murderers themselves. That is, Dr. Hiedeman ostensibly remains in recovery from his surgery in the hospital, whereas, by Dr. Mayfield's plotting, he is eventually going to die when the dissolving sutures from that very surgery give way. In "The Most Dangerous Match," Clayton's first attempt at murder merely lands Dudek in the hospital (though in a coma), as the trash compactor automatically turned off when he landed inside of it. Dr. Hiedeman's death is prevented when Columbo forces a second surgery to restitch the replaced valves; in fact, Columbo joins the surgeon and his team in the operating room as Mayfield performs the new surgery, secretly replacing the dissolving thread with permanent sutures. In the following episode, however, Clayton completes the murder of his chess adversary while he is lying in the hospital and before he is able to name

Clayton as his assailant. It is as if the murderer of the preceding episode were given a second chance, and this time he is able to succeed. But then our detective is given a second chance as well. And this time he doesn't come as close as he does in the previous episode to *not* pinning the murder on the killer. Instead he quite literally beats him at his own game.

Even the final settings are parallel to one another. That is, while Columbo joins Dr. Mayfield in the operating theater in "A Stitch in Crime," he appears in the auditorium where Clayton is playing multiple chess opponents at once in "The Most Dangerous Match." There the detective repeatedly interrupts him to question him about his skills of memorization, as the final murder of Dudek depended on Clayton's quick memorization of his medication list in order for him to ensure an overdose at the hospital. At first Clayton deftly moves from player to player, making quick moves, often narrating the eventual outcomes of their games. The detective follows the game and the players, disclosing more and more information as Clayton makes his moves on the board. When the two come face-to-face, the detective shows his own hand, announcing the various clues are adding up. Clayton arrogantly asks, "Do you really think that the finest chess player in the world would make even half the mistakes that you ascribe to me?" As Clayton pauses to speak to Columbo, the camera shifts to focus on the opponent as he moves toward a resolution of the game. Next the opponent announces, "Mr. Clayton, sir, I'm afraid that's check and mate, sir," as the entire layout of the board comes into view. Clayton realizes his double loss at once: the game is over and the jig is up. In seeming response to the chess game (but also, of course, to the murder), the detective says, "Just a foolish blunder. Could happen to anybody." In that utterance he reveals that he knows more than might appear, but only to a particularly knowing audience in turn: the phrase is a reference to the name of the move, "Fool's Mate," that has just bested Clayton.

4 Special Guest Stars

As I discussed in chapter 3, the second season features two parallel performances by actors known best for other fictional characters they played: Leonard Nimoy, ever yoked to Mr. Spock of the original *Star Trek* franchise, appears as an unfeeling killer in "A Stitch in Crime," while Laurence Harvey, most famous for his role as brainwashed Raymond Shaw in *The Manchurian Candidate*, seems similarly triggered by distorted images of a game piece in "The Most Dangerous Match." Together these two guest stars demonstrate *Columbo*'s links to the histories of the film and television industries; with such actors appearing (and sometimes reappearing) in the series, *Columbo* subtly integrates that history into its mysteries.

Straddling a period of transition for both the film and television industries, *Columbo* inevitably reflects other elements of those histories of each, as well as their contemporaneous intersections—some fraught, some mutually beneficial. For instance, when the series officially premiered in 1971, the mainstream Hollywood film industry was undergoing three significant changes. First, the Motion Picture Association of America (MPAA) ratings code, adopted in 1968, explicitly defined film audiences in terms of age as it also defined films in terms of content. Second, the studio system continued to wane; studios, in fact, had largely become increasingly corporate (many of them even purchased by non-entertainment-based conglomerates), in the business more often of financing and distributing than of actually making films. No longer were contract players or directors confined to one particular film studio like Paramount or Universal. Third, with this shift in studio structure, a new brand of director emerged: the independent "auteur" (who eventually either created his own studio or attached to one of the giants as a financing and distribution body).

A force for film to reckon with, television had increasingly gained popularity and US presence over the two decades prior to the premiere of *The NBC Mystery Movie*. While movie tickets were still roughly on the rise in purchase by sheer number (though not entirely accounting for population growth), color television ownership quadrupled between the year that *Prescription: Murder* first appeared in 1968 (13,700,000) to the year when the first run of the series ended ten years later (56,900,900) and ownership of televisions overall increased by approximately 16 million. Television structure and content also continued to evolve. The 1940s and 1950s were dominated by two kinds of nonserialized programs with new characters and stories each week—repertory series and anthology series. The first case included a continuous set of former film stars in a variety of roles in discrete weekly stories, while the latter featured new casts each week (i.e., a revolving group of guest stars and character actors appearing in original teleplays). Some anthology series maintained continuity through a key figure; Mary Desjardins writes that "many of these included a 'hosted by' or even 'starring' format, providing a framework of stability in what was otherwise a constantly revolving cast."[1] As I've previously noted, Falk himself appeared as a guest on several such series in the 1950s and 1960s before landing his own series *The Trials of O'Brien*.

Following on the heels of three other such shows (*Name of the Game*, *The Bold Ones*, and *Four in One*), *The NBC Mystery Movie* functioned as a new kind of anthology series, one that intersected with the episodic drama. As in the original trio of *Columbo*, *McMillan & Wife*, and *McCloud*, each series shared a stable cast (or, as in the case of *Columbo*, at least a consistent single star) with a revolving set of prestigious guest stars. *Columbo*, like the anthology series *Kraft Theater* or *The Alfred Hitchcock Hour* (both of which Falk also appeared in), attracted a range of guest stars. Indeed, given its popularity and critical acclaim, big names were interested in *Columbo*, with various actors of the time and of past celebrity clambering to guest on the series.[2] Its initial run included appearances by film stars associated with old Hollywood, such as Anne Baxter, Janet Leigh, Myrna Loy, Ida Lupino, Ray Milland, and Vincent Price, as well as contemporary stars associated with Hollywood productions and new independent cinema, like John Cassavetes, Roddy McDowell, Gena Rowlands, Martin Sheen, and Dean Stockwell. This casting strategy was one developed in television's "golden age," which brought Hollywood stars into one-off appearances on television anthology and repertory series, as well as those, like *Four Star Playhouse*, that were built around Hollywood stars. With its regular circulation of classical Hollywood stars in which they play both killers and murder victims, *Columbo* integrates these two industries at a moment of transformation for both, implicitly raising questions about classical Hollywood's life span. That is to say, perhaps the declared death of film in the 1950s was vastly exaggerated.

Similar to the anthology series of past decades, many guests appear more than once, each time as different characters. Ray Milland, for instance, plays the victim's widower in "Death Lends a Hand" and the killer in "The Greenhouse Jungle." Director and star Ida Lupino appears as the victim's widow in "Short Fuse" (1:6; Jan. 19, 1972) and as the victim two years later in "Swan Song." And various character actors appear in multiple episodes as well. For instance, William Windom, who would go on to play the grumpy but affable Dr. Hazlitt on *Murder, She Wrote*, appears in two early episodes of *Columbo*: the original made-for-television movie *Prescription: Murder* and "Short Fuse"; James Gregory (perhaps best known as Inspector Frank Luger on *Barney Miller*) appears also in "Short Fuse" as victim and in "The Most Crucial Game" in a bit part as Coach Rizzo; Leslie Nielsen is the boyfriend of the murderer in "Lady in Waiting" (1:5; Dec. 15, 1971) and the victim in "Identity Crisis" four seasons later; and so on. And, of course, Falk's second wife, Shera Danese, appears in two episodes of the original run ("Fade in to Murder" [6:1; Oct. 10, 1976] and "Murder under Glass") and four of the reboot. By drawing on the casting structure of early television, *Columbo* embodies an element of the history of television production, and in the cast members it includes, it showcases the history of film as well as the future of both film and television. A landing place for former film stars, it also functioned as a training ground for film actors and television writers.

In Neil Simon's penned 1976 film *Murder by Death*, Peter Falk plays an amalgamation of film and television detectives in the persona of "Sam Diamond." Along with Simon's follow-up two years later, *The Cheap Detective*, also starring Falk (this time as "Lou Peckinpaugh"), these films are an homage to and a spoof of the movies, and they also, of course, implicitly refer to Falk's signature television role. But while the wording of the title "murder by death" might play as an affectionate joke, it's also a mark of the association between movies and mortality. This association is evident, too, in "How to Dial a Murder" (7:4; April 5, 1978), which aired two years later. One of the final episodes of the series, the title is a neat nod to Alfred Hitchcock's 1954 *Dial M for Murder* (the costar of which was Ray Milland, one of those actors who appeared in two different episodes on previous seasons, as I note above). Whereas the title suggests that the telephone is the instrument of demise, its reference to Hitchcock's film is a clue that it actually narrates a case in which the killer commits murder with the movies as his unwitting accomplice.

The first scene of this episode opens with the words "Peter Falk as" and "Columbo" laid over a shot of the iconic circle K gate from the opening of the classic *Citizen Kane*. As in Welles's film, the camera then pans through a series of souvenirs belonging to the owner of the house. But rather than the lavish collection of a dying millionaire, this is the collection of a pop psychologist who has made—and spent—a killing on his film fandom. When we see the snow globe and sled that figure so centrally in *Kane*, they don't signify the innocence of childhood or romance gone by as they do in Welles's fictional film. They represent, instead, a material history of film: they are evidence, in other words, of the killer's desire to possess the movies. In this way, the episode refers to and reflects on Welles's canonical work rather than attempts to remake it. It also reflects the usual narrative of *Columbo*: unlike *Kane*, "How to Dial a Murder" is not a mystery about the dead, but one about the killer. It thus begins with a rehearsal of the murder he's plotted: a dummy stuffed with hay hangs in the kitchen, next to a ringing phone. Upon its ring, the two Dobermans of the house—Laurel and Hardy—run to it. When the ringing stops, a speaker inside the dummy issues the infamous last word Kane himself spoke: "Rosebud." The dogs growl. The issuance becomes a command, louder, and the dogs viciously attack. The dummy lies "dead" in the kitchen.

As the scene begins to cut, we hear the words "You're gonna die," and Dr. Eric Mason (Nicol Williamson) comes into focus, where he is giving a lecture to a large crowd on "taking control," especially controlling the power of words. From a booth upstairs where he monitors the response of the seminar participants, Dr. Mason's partner, Charlie, announces that the audience doesn't seem to like the word *death*. Mason retorts: "Food. Money. Boss. Wife. Sex." Words "took the control," he says, announcing that the paying participants will learn how to get this control back, and then he blithely leaves for lunch. Back in his office, working out the logistics of a tennis game, a doctor's appointment, and care for the dogs, our killer sets the scene for the murder of his friend. Thus, when Charlie arrives at Mason's house for their scheduled tennis game, Mason calls during the resting period of his cardiogram and asks his friend to settle a bet: What is the name on the sled in *Citizen Kane*? The dogs have already "answered" the ring of the phone themselves, and they now stand in wait. As Charlie says "Rosebud" aloud, repeating it at an increasingly higher volume at the request of his friend, they attack.

When Mason arrives back home, he finds Columbo playing fetch with the seeming killers, apparently having already figured out the basics of the actual murderer's plot. The detective's work throughout the rest of the episode is to wade through film paraphernalia to find the sites of the rehearsals for the crime scene and to figure out the dogs' control word—two elements of the crime, which, of course, turn out to be neatly related. Thus, at the end of the episode when Columbo announces to Mason, "You killed him with a phone call," he's only telling part of the story. The telephone was the conduit, certainly, but the control word and the tools for the murder, Laurel and Hardy, show instead that Mason killed Charlie with the movies. And then, upon the detective's revelation of his own knowledge, the doctor tries it again with Columbo: "Rosebud," he commands his dogs. They chase the lieutenant onto W. C. Fields's pool table, where they merely kill him with kindness. Columbo then reveals his own plot: he changed the control word for the dogs so that "kill" becomes a "kiss." This, too, is the movies: a happy ending.

4.1. Columbo meets film history ("How to Dial a Murder," 7:4; April 5, 1978)

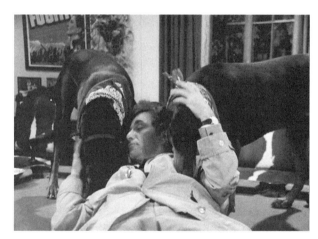

4.2. Laurel, Hardy, Columbo, and W. C. Fields ("How to Dial a Murder," 7:4; April 5, 1978)

Though "Dial" is particularly explicit about the relation between murder and movies—implicitly suggesting that classical Hollywood lends us the tools and the executioners for the act—the series as a whole engages a range of iconic stars from the classical Hollywood era in its mission. This interest in Hollywood also has a diegetic role in the show. For instance, "Ransom for a Dead Man" includes an extended sequence of *Double Indemnity* (Billy Wilder, 1944), which the victim's daughter watches on a small television at the breakfast table. And at various

4.3. Femme fatales ("Ransom for a Dead Man," 0:1; March 1, 1971)

points over the run of the series, we learn that Columbo himself is a bit of a movie fan. In "Publish or Perish," for instance, he complains about not sleeping more than five hours in the past two nights: "Last night it was Bette Davis. Four o'clock in the morning and my wife wants to watch Bette Davis." But, as he puts it, "She was a terrific actress. Forgetaboutit." It's hard not to imagine—maybe even hope—that his late-night viewing included the phenomenal *All about Eve* (Joseph L. Mankiewicz, 1950), one of the masterpieces of Davis's masterful career. Along with *Sunset Boulevard* (Billy Wilder, 1950), *All about Eve* was one of the key films to narrate the coterminous anxieties of the aging of great film actresses and the aging of classical Hollywood as an industry. Both films, after all, appear during television's first "golden age." Though neither are explicitly about television (in fact, *All about Eve* is about the difference between the theater and film), they certainly represent the anxiety prevalent at the time: that television was sounding the death knell of film. The bodies of female stars became the visual manifestation of this impending doom.

This representation of an aging and agonizing female film star is a somewhat common trope in the first decades of television, which, like Hollywood films of the 1950s, marks a concern between the aging actress and the "aging" medium of film. As Desjardins asserts, "The status of the aging female star, as both agent and representation, in television after 1950 was negotiated, in part, within anxieties about feminine survival in the 'new Hollywood.'"[3] Interestingly, Ida Lupino, who appears in two episodes of *Columbo* herself, plays two such characters on other television series: Barbara Trenton in "The Sixteen-Millimeter Shrine" (Oct. 23, 1959), an early episode of *The Twilight Zone*, and Gloria Gibson in an episode of *Charlie's Angels*, entitled "I Will Be Remembered" (March 1977).[4] In the episode of *The Twilight Zone*, Desjardins writes, Barbara Jean "can't get enough of herself."[5] The episode opens as such: "Picture of a woman looking at a picture. Movie great of another time. Once brilliant star in a firmament no longer a part of the sky, eclipsed by the movement of earth and time. Barbara Jean Trenton, whose world is a projection room, whose dreams are made of celluloid." Of course, as Desjardins and Christine Becker also note, this story is not so very different from the film *Sunset Boulevard.* Nor is it so different, in a sense, from Bette Davis's film *All about Eve*, which, like *Sunset*, wrestles with the experience of the aging actress.[6] Jodi Brooks contends that such films "narrate the passing of the old Hollywood through this figure of the aging actress." She goes on: "The central characters in these films are all thus marked by time twice over: as aging women they are marked as outside desire, and as aging stars, as image, they are both frozen and transitory."[7] In Lupino's appearances in both *The Twilight Zone* and *Charlie's Angels* is the suggestion that time stops in film. In television, these examples seem to imply, time marches forward. Certainly, that notion makes sense in the context of the medium; as originally a broadcast form, TV is able to come to us "live" and is therefore not unlike a kind of living, transforming thing. Jane Feuer describes this ideological phenomenon as such: "Live television is *not* recorded; live television is *alive*; television is living, real, not dead."[8]

A series itself teeming with former Hollywood stars, two episodes of *Columbo* imagine Hollywood history—and its fear of aging via the female star—similarly to films such as *Sunset Boulevard* and appearances like those by Lupino in the 1960s and 1970s. "Forgotten Lady" (5:1; Sept. 14, 1975) opened the fifth season. Its title carries with it the same valence as the television episodes in which Lupino appeared as an aging star: the fear of loss brought by the ravages of time and the changes to media culture. Film, however, has the capacity to enshrine the star. The opening of "Forgotten Lady" demonstrates this belief. We begin at a nostalgic Hollywood event: the screening of an old film starring the episode's character Grace Wheeler Willis (Janet Leigh). This event gives rise to her brainstorm that she return to her former glory by producing a new version of one of her old musicals on stage. And when her rich husband refuses to bankroll the venture, she kills him when she is purportedly watching one of her former films on 16mm in her home theater. The film she views, *Walking My Baby Back Home*, was in fact a vehicle for the actress Leigh (and owned at the time by Universal, which made for easy use on the series, produced by NBC-Universal). Embedded in this scene and into the episode is thus not only the fictional character's former glory days but also the history of Janet Leigh's own stardom. Notably, the "over-the-hill" character is played by an actress who was only forty-eight at the time; paradoxically, her character is old enough to have been a star when Columbo was in high school—a highly unlikely scenario since both actors were born the same year.

When Willis's old dance partner and former paramour, Ned Diamond, asks if she wants to cancel her plans for the musical after her husband's death, she says she wants to go forward, as "Rosie" would have done. "But Rosie is a character in a film," Ned says. "There's no difference," Willis wistfully replies. Willis, it seems, is living not only in the past but—not unlike Barbara Jean Trenton—even in the world of fictional film. Diamond ultimately designs another fiction for the detective, as he confesses to the crime so that Willis—whose delusions of grandeur past are at least in part a result of a malignant brain tumor—is now safe from prosecution in her final days. His affection for the actress undisguised, the lieutenant agrees to this ruse, demonstrating another way in which the lieutenant is not only "relatable" as an "everyman," but also, again, relation-able. Another happy ending for a Hollywood film–inspired episode.

4.4. The forgotten actress and days gone by ("Forgotten Lady," 5:1; Sept. 14, 1975)

Broadcast three years earlier, "Requiem for a Falling Star" stars Anne Baxter, most famous for her eponymous role as Bette Davis's cunning assistant in *All about Eve*, as a now-aging movie star herself and double murderer named Nora Chandler. When Columbo questions the seeming would-be victim of the most recent crime, Hollywood scandalmonger Jerry Parks, about what information he's collected on Chandler over the years, the yellow journalist declares, "Who cares about an aging actress, sliding downhill?" Columbo quickly responds, "Hey, she's still important on TV, and on the late-late show I don't miss a picture she's in." Thus, we have the episode most explicitly about classical Hollywood film. Like "Forgotten Lady" and "How to Dial a Murder," this one is played for a kind of sentimental value. Perhaps that's because, as Nora herself exclaims, "Hollywood is fighting for survival"—whose survival, as Columbo himself implies, is threatened, of course, by television.

Yet part of old Hollywood studios' survival at this point is also *indebted* to television—to the late-late shows that play films of yore, as well as to television series like *Columbo* that showcase Hollywood icons such as Anne Baxter, Janet Leigh, Ray Milland, and Ida Lupino. Thus, while surely the film industry is on the cusp of change at this moment in history, all is not yet lost, and, despite the title of this particular episode, nostalgia is not quite in order. "Requiem," in fact, begins with a scene at Chandler's latest movie shoot: we see a woman walk toward the glass wall of a shower and shoot a gun several times through it, her victim dropping to the floor. After his on-screen death, the woman turns around and announces, "Darn, missed him!" as the crew all around breaks into laughter. The actual murder the actress commits comes a few minutes later in the episode, after she becomes afraid that her assistant, Jean Davis, will share her (as yet unknown) secrets with Parks.

Such complex diegetic sequences recur throughout the episode, so that we might briefly mistake Chandler's film shoots for "real" events taking place in the episode. In fact, the two are repeatedly commingled. For instance, following Columbo's interrogation of Parks after the seeming attempt on his life, the detective comes upon Parks and Chandler meeting furtively, and he attempts to gather evidence concerning who might want to see Parks dead (Jerry barely disguises his look in Nora's direction when he claims he can't think of anyone in particular). In the scene that immediately follows, Nora is interrogated by another detective, with a uniformed police officer watching over the scene. In the midst of her response, she pauses, admitting to forgetting her lines (a scene echoed by William Shatner's "Detective Lucerne" four seasons later). Later, immediately after Columbo reveals to Nora that he is certain Jean was the intended victim, rather than Jerry Parks, we cut to a shot of Nora driving, being followed by a police car, sirens blaring. Yet we quickly learn that this scene, too, is another shot for the film she's making. Through this associative, parallel editing, each of these cases simultaneously equates the world of the fictional film and that of *Columbo* and also differentiates between them. On the one hand, the film shoots imagine Nora's very real anxieties about getting caught by the "real" detective Lt. Columbo. The fictional world of the film thus offers a means of understanding the "real" world of *Columbo*'s diegetic universe. And, yet, in contrast to the world of *Columbo*, the movie world is one where there are no real consequences for her actions—except celebrity, of course.

In a final plot twist in which Chandler's films have a bearing on the present case, Columbo's brother-in-law phones to alert him to a broadcast of one of Chandler's movies while the lieutenant is in her bungalow; he turns on her television set to watch her appear dressed as a man, plotting with a lover on the phone. We witness here his own revelation that not only did Chandler kill Jean, but she also killed her own husband many years ago (and her fears that the first murder would be revealed are the motive for the second). In a strange sense, then, the televisual world that Columbo the character witnesses and that *Columbo* the series inhabits is precisely that which puts an end to Nora Chandler's film fantasies—which can now only live on in television reruns of her old movies.

Therefore, the relationship between television and the movies is a twisted one, as our television detective uses what he's learned about the staging of Hollywood productions to catch the killer. Throughout the episode, of course, Columbo follows Nora about on her set: "As long as I've been in Los Angeles," he tells her, "this is the first time I've ever been on a movie set." Not only watching shoots on set, he also tours the backlot with a prop man, and he even meets legendary costume designer Edith Head, who appears in a brief cameo as Nora's own designer—and as the purveyor of a new tie for the lieutenant. "Is she the one I see on the Academy Awards?" Columbo asks, and shortly thereafter the three of them stand before a desk laden with the trophies. This reference is a neat nod to the ways in which televised awards shows, like the Oscars, keep "old Hollywood" stars alive, therefore furthering the symbiotic relationship between the two industries.[9]

But then this scene is significant in other ways, too. Alongside his own television viewing, costumes and props become Columbo's final means of catching the murderer. Once he realizes Nora murdered her husband—and, though not yet explained to the viewers, buried him under an old movie prop, the lavish fountain in her backyard—the detective borrows a Shriner's ring, which he intimates belonged to her husband. Upon this revelation—which takes place in front of a rear projection screen on set—Nora becomes undone, racing home after Columbo has

4.5. Film and television provide the solution ("Requiem for a Falling Star," 2:5; Jan. 21, 1973)

4.6. Special appearance by Edith Head ("Requiem for a Falling Star," 2:5; Jan. 21, 1973)

left her in order to check that the fountain is still intact. Once there, the jig is up, as Columbo has been lying in wait for her. He reads his own jottings about the case aloud to her, as if reviewing the plot of a film— or a television series—and she summarizes the details of both murders in turn, as if giving the lieutenant "notes" on his scene construction.

Though alluding to the struggle between the two media industries, this episode hardly demonstrates the triumph of television over film. In fact, "Requiem" is explicitly and implicitly built on the foundations of the Hollywood classical era, perhaps a little like the fountain built over the dead husband's body. Not only is the plot about a film star, but it also stars one herself. And Baxter's appearance, furthermore, is yet a springboard for other neat links both to her most famous film and to classical Hollywood more broadly. Thus, whereas Jean's relation to Nora could hardly be equated with Eve's to Margo Channing's, the situation does bear some similarities: the assistant is preparing to leave her mentor; Jean's exit is enabled by a figure not unlike Addison deWitt in Jerry Parks; and, ultimately, if perhaps in an overstatement when it concerns the Bette Davis vehicle, the mentor would rather see her protégée dead. The names of both characters offer a little reference or rhyming to those in *All about Eve* as well: Jean's last name is Davis, after all, and "Chandler" is not so far removed from "Channing" (nor is "Jean" so removed from "Eve"). In other homonymous connections, Nora, too, seems an indirect reference to Norma Desmond of *Sunset Boulevard*, the all-time definitive fictional aging star (barely removed from reality, of course, since Gloria Swanson's legendary director Erich von Stroheim appears as Norma Desmond's butler and driver). Playing such name games might seem only that—a fun game for the avid viewer—but its roots are there in "Columbo" itself: a name Link and Levinson may have borrowed as an homage, via a minor character, to another Billy Wilder film, *Some Like It Hot*.[10]

The Televisual Double Agent

Television in the 1960s saw an emergence of spy TV—from *Danger Man* (1960–62) and *Secret Agent* (1964–66) (which together developed into *The Prisoner* [1967–68]), to *The Avengers* (1961–69), *I Spy* (1965–68), *The Man from U.N.C.L.E* (1964–68), and *Get Smart* (1965–70). These spy series ranged between the cerebral, the global, and the comedic— sometimes merging all forms together. Of course, each series—and thus its respective take on the genre—was largely based on the persona of the spy himself. Some spies, like John Drake of *Danger Man* and *Secret Agent* (whose name really was taken and replaced with a number, as the song goes, in *The Prisoner*), worked largely with their wits and charisma; others, like Maxwell Smart of *Get Smart*, depended on ingenious gadgets, luck, and a charming partner to catch their nemeses; global tennis star–cum–agent Kelly Robinson of *I Spy* worked with a little of each. Three of the actors who played these iconic spies—"secret agent" Patrick McGoohan, *I Spy*'s Robert Culp, and *U.N.C.L.E.*'s Robert Vaughn—were three of the four performers, who also included Jack Cassidy, who turned up as repeat offenders in *Columbo* episodes of the 1970s (McGoohan also played a murderer in two episodes of the later version of the series). McGoohan, Culp, and Cassidy, moreover, consistently followed the very star persona developed through their television work in the 1960s.[11]

Given that McGoohan was largely known as a "secret agent" on television, he fittingly plays characters on *Columbo* who are involved with the government and national defense, directly or indirectly: as a headmaster at a military school in "By Dawn's Early Light" (4:3; Oct. 27, 1974) and as a spy in the following season's "Identity Crisis." The winner of an Emmy Award for a guest performance in the first of these outings, McGoohan was the most lauded of guest stars on the series. He also directed two episodes in the first run of the series: "Identity Crisis" and "Last Salute to the Commodore"; and he appeared in two episodes and directed three of the reboot of the series. His signature on the series was perhaps emboldened by his friendship with the star. In his memoir, Peter Falk writes, "The Columbo franchise, myself, Universal Studios, and the NBC network—we all are indebted to Patrick McGoohan for his huge contributions to the show. He did everything. He wrote, directed, acted and he did them all brilliantly. He single-handedly lifted the show to new heights."[12] Certainly his directed episodes reflect some license with the formula, if not exactly scaling "new heights."

Interestingly, given that his role as Nelson Brenner in "Identity Crisis" is marked by a range of disguises, his choices as a director also, to some effect, disguise the conventions of the series. "Identity Crisis" has the lieutenant uncharacteristically leering at a belly dancer (one of the only blatant sexist moments in the original series as a whole), and throughout, it includes extraordinarily extended pauses in conversation, almost unbearable in their duration, even for a die-hard fan. The seeming banality of the detective's conversational tangents is equally met by Brenner; staring at one another during a discussion of cigars, they appear to be in a standoff over who can break character first. "Last Salute to the Commodore" was hardly an audience favorite (though Mark Dawidziak's *The Columbo Phile* calls it "enchanting," with the claim that Levinson himself was "delighted" by it).[13] Moreover, it reverses the normal structure of the series: we do not witness the murder in full at the beginning, but rather see a lengthy reveal at the end of the episode that looks a lot more like Agatha Christie's Poirot at work. Falk also plays the role in a much hammier manner than usual, seemingly parodying the character more than embodying him (this will become more of the norm in the reboot, which, unsurprisingly, Falk had hoped McGoohan would executive produce).

McGoohan's two directed episodes, moreover, appear in a season that is rife with departures. Four of the six episodes in season 5 include some form of international intrigue, and one takes place outside of the United States. Leaving the more localized context of Los Angeles, class, in these cases, is also less central to the plots and to the characterizations of both the murderers and the detective. Rumored by some insiders as the possible last season of the series (in fact, it was followed by two more years' worth), it seemed that its fifth official year was undergoing something of an identity crisis of its own, weary of its formula and other limits imposed on its typing of murderers.

Robert Culp's roles, on the other hand, were almost shockingly uniform, a kind of analogy for the stability of the series. Each character he played seemed to have an anger-management problem (in that he either overly managed or undermanaged it), and in all three episodes his character worked, in some form or another, with recording and/or broadcast technologies. His first appearance, in the episode "Death Lends a Hand," which earned Levinson and Link an Emmy for writing, gives us a key to understand both his appearances and the series as a whole. As Brimmer (the character is given no first name), he is a security expert, a private investigator of sorts, who looks into corporate and personal affairs. Like so many characters on the show, he is also a blackmailer. In his case, he tracks down cheating wives, gives their husbands a "clean bill of health" on their marriages, and then blackmails the wives for either money or information, as he threatens he will otherwise spill the beans. The episode opens with him readying the scene: from the security monitor in

4.7. Double vision ("Death Lends a Hand," 1:2; Oct. 6, 1971)

his office, he watches his appointment enter the building, so he situates a mysterious guest in one room, for whom he sets up a sound system so that she can overhear his meeting. He then informs the husband, Arthur Kennicut (Ray Milland), that his wife is faithful; upon Kennicut's exit, he enters the other room to inform the wife, Lenore, that she now owes him, or he will send compromising photographs to her husband. As Brimmer returns home that evening, he finds that Lenore Kennicut (Pat Crowley) has made her way in ahead of him, where she informs him that she refuses to go along with his plan. In a fit of rage, he slaps her—we see the act in slow motion, which intensifies the violence (a rare moment on the series)—and she cracks her head against a table. An accidental murderer but a very intentional blackmailer, Brimmer at once goes about cleaning up the scene. What follows is simply remarkable.

Brimmer's own glasses begin to function as split screens, like tiny rounded television sets, each showing different actions from different moments in time. In one lens, we see the events conceivably happening during the moment at which they are taking place; in the other, we see the immediate future. This device might seem surprisingly experimental for a show that became known in many ways for its narrative formula and its primary character's predictable habits and favorite lines. Of course, the series included other conventions—such as the very training of the detective in cultural forms—but it is hardly a conventional show. Or, at least, it was more replete with visual and technical experimentation than a casual viewer would imagine (or possibly remember). "Publish or Perish," which I will discuss shortly, features another split-screen effect, seemingly presaging the 2001–10 series *24*, though actually a replica of earlier work, such as the opening of the 1960s series *Mannix*, itself also created (if not ultimately written) by Levinson and Link. Other episodes offer brief fantasy sequences. "The Most Dangerous Match" begins with a dream sequence that is not entirely unlike Salvador Dali's design for Alfred Hitchcock's *Spellbound*. "A Matter of Honor" similarly features an opening dream sequence; presented in extreme wide angle and no diegetic sound, it displays the near-fatal bullfight of the dreamer. In "Lady in Waiting," we see the killer imagine her brother's murder, which ultimately does not work out quite as smoothly as she had planned. The pilot, "Ransom for a Dead Man," features repeated flashbacks, increasingly menacing and distorted, as the detective closes in on the killer. And in the final season, "Make Me a Perfect Murder" returns to the split-screen effects of earlier episodes like "Publish or Perish" and Culp's "Death Lends a Hand."

In all these cases, *Columbo* the series plays with visual possibilities for television production perhaps analogously to the detective's psychological play with his suspects. In each of these ways, the series offers us alternative ways of seeing television and detection. To punctuate this idea: the proof of the murder in "Death Lends a Hand" is also predicated on the supposed loss and reappearance of the victim's contact lens in Brimmer's car. This coincident plot device neatly demonstrates the series' literal and figurative concerns with optical devices—those things that help us see more clearly. And given that the two lenses of Brimmer's glasses also look a lot like tiny television sets, this early episode declares, however implicitly for the obsessive viewer, its fascination with television itself. In watching this series, after all, we are using a kind of optical device for understanding television detection.

Culp's other two episodes further highlight the work (and myths) of time-based media forms. Whereas "Death Lends a Hand" showcases video surveillance, "The Most Crucial Game" gives us broadcast radio, and "Double Exposure" (3:4; Dec. 16, 1974), which I will focus on in a later chapter, combines a look at audio recording and film editing. In both cases, the killer is fluent in various forms of mass-consumer technology, and audio technologies in particular help to establish the killer's alibi. In essence, Bart Kepple, the killer in "Double Exposure" (who is also a blackmailer like Brimmer), draws on now-outdated (and illegal) psychological tactics in order to produce subliminal advertising in film. In order to manipulate his audience, he also manipulates multiple technological forms: photography, film, and audio recording. Culp's Paul Hanlon of "The Most Crucial Game" is more of a businessman than a technological expert, but he depends on the liveness of radio, as well as the timing of a professional football game, to falsify his whereabouts to his imminent victim. The live game, furthermore, first helps initially establish his alibi for the murder and then ultimately allows Columbo to break it. The consistency of Culp's roles marks a relation less to his former television appearances (though they do draw on his manner quite well) than they mark a particular obsession of the series through him as a "repeat offender." That is, his roles together reveal the series' oft-displayed interest in time-based recording technologies, and Culp himself becomes a stand-in for this element of the show.

Hovering between the consistency of Culp's outings and the costume and disguises of McGoohan's roles, a third actor, Jack Cassidy, also played three different murderers on the series. In his case, his appearances, too, were neatly linked to his other work in television, though perhaps in a broader sense than were either McGoohan or Culp. That is, he appears always as an "actor" of sorts—the definitive guest star and the definitive duplicitous criminal. Though best known as a terrific Broadway actor (the winner of a Tony for acting in a musical, he was nominated three other times), Jack Cassidy was primarily a professional guest star on television in the 1960s and 1970s, likely taking TV gigs to supplement his income and to work around his Broadway career. This part as "guest star" was true even in his one recurring role, as Oscar North in the 1960s sitcom *He & She*, created by Leonard Stern, who also made *Get Smart*, *McMillan & Wife*, and *The Snoop Sisters*. The "he" and "she" of this series were Dick and Paula Hollister. Dick is a cartoonist, responsible for the comic *Jet Man*, which has been adapted into a television series. Oscar North plays the live-action Jet Man, which means, of course, that Jack Cassidy plays the role of an actor—which is a neat, if implicit, acknowledgment of his ongoing "role" as "guest star" on the series itself. After all, his regular appearance is announced in the credits similar to the ways in which guest stars are tagged. At the end of the actors' credits, the title reads "and Jack Cassidy as Oscar North." As North, he is basically *always* acting—and, moreover, "playing" suave while appearing rather silly.

As the narcissistic "talent," Oscar North seems to be a precursor to Ted Baxter of *The Mary Tyler Moore Show* (a role Cassidy was said to have turned down, though he did make one guest appearance as Baxter's brother Hal in "Cover Boy" [Oct. 23, 1971]). The comic relief in a sitcom, Oscar simply drops into scenes from time to time to allow for an integration between or distraction from plotlines. For instance, in the episode "The Background Man" (Oct. 25, 1967), North flirts with Dick's new assistant, Rosemary, whose utter cuteness has made Paula— and Dick—a little uneasy. Oscar asks her, "What are you doing tonight?" When she responds with "nothing," he suggests, "Good. *Jet Man* is on at 7:30. Watch it." He later quotes fictional character Jet Man himself, declaring, "Greatness is lonely work—the greater you are, the lonelier you are" with a seriousness that is, of course, rather difficult to take seriously.[14]

Cassidy continues in the vein of the professional guest star in his appearances on *Columbo*. His roles are more varied than either those of McGoohan or Culp, though, interestingly, in each he works as an entertainer of sorts and in each case he is involved in a masquerade. Two episodes cast him in the publishing arena (three episodes total concerned this field in the first round of the series): in "Murder by the Book," he kills his mystery-writing partner, and in "Publish or Perish" (written by Peter S. Fischer, who was the cocreator, with Levinson and Link, of *Murder, She Wrote*), he is a publisher who kills off one of his best-selling authors when he tries to move to a different genre and new publisher.

In his third showing, "Now You See Him" (5:5; Feb. 29, 1976), he plays a magician known as "The Great Santini." In each of these cases, he plays a character who is not as he appears—either to the outside world or to the criminal investigation.

For instance, in "Murder by the Book," he plays Ken Franklin who kills his cowriter, Jim Ferris, because he is about to leave their partnership. As we learn, Franklin was hardly a creative force in the team, taking credit for work that he simply did not produce; having to set out on his own would expose this masquerade. A ladies' man, Franklin lives high on the hog; he drives luxury cars, owns extravagant art, and keeps a second house along a lake near San Diego. His motive, as with so many of *Columbo*'s killers, is money. Without the partnership, he won't have a steady income. But with Jim dead, Franklin can draw money from an insurance policy and therefore continue to live off the masquerade of being Ferris's writing partner. The irony is that the plot for the murder—which Columbo finds etched in Ferris's own hand on a scrap of paper—was the only one Franklin ever came up with himself for one of their mysteries.

In "Publish or Perish," Cassidy's second outing on *Columbo*, he's again not a literary talent himself, but he still works in the publishing business, this time as the executive Ryan Greenleaf. Greenleaf hires a bomb enthusiast named Eddie Kane (one of the few real nuts who appears on the series) to kill writer Alan Mallory (played by legendary Mickey Spillane); he frames himself for the murder, while also establishing a clear alibi. Planting evidence that would seem to indict him but securing an alibi that would demonstrate his innocence seems an ingenious plan—suggesting, in an utterly meta way, that he only *looks* like a murderer. But, in fact, it inextricably binds him to the crime, a connection that is itself established both narratively and visually. So, in another split-screen sequence, the screens reveal simultaneous events; at once we see Greenleaf's alibi verified as he fakes drunkenness and plows into a vw bus and, elsewhere in LA, the murder of Mallory by Kane. Here Greenleaf is placed in the same space of the television screen with the act of murder, if not in the exact space of the scene of the crime, revealing what we already realize is true: a direct connection between him and the shooting. (In an echo of "Murder by the Book," Greenleaf also creates a sham suggesting that Kane was the actual author of Mallory's new book on the Vietnam War.)[15]

And then, of course, there is the Great Santini in the fifth season's "Now You See Him"—essentially a charlatan by profession, but, even more significantly, also a former Nazi officer who has changed his identity since the war. In fact, the threat of the exposure of his criminal and political past drives him to murder his blackmailing boss via an act of "magic"; he sneaks away during the part of his act when he is supposedly trapped in a steel box that is in turn submerged in a tank of water. This is the perfect trick: after all, now-you-see-him-now-you-don't is practically the very essence of an alibi. Moreover, the magician's code does not allow him to reveal his trick to Columbo, thus seeming to ensure the secret of the murder as well.

Because this episode is itself a direct link to that which is implicit between murder, magic, and detective fiction, it's useful here to know that Levinson and Link were themselves practicing magicians. In fact, they devised "Now You See Him" in order to learn how a particular magic trick, the zig-zag, was done. The zig-zag is an act in which the magician's assistant is held in a box while the magician stabs the box with a variety of knives and swords; to learn how it was done, Levinson and Link ordered the box for the production of the episode. By coincidence, the magician's code was inadvertently kept, as the wrong machine arrived. (They later learned there was no "trick" involved—or so says magician Link—that in fact the space is merely small enough for the assistant to dodge the swords while kept inside.) But this makes for a wonderful story, and most certainly it points to the shared element between mysteries and magic, which, as Mr. Link himself has said, is "deception."[16] The difference, of course, is that normally magic doesn't also contain a story. Narrative emerges with murder, and thus the mystery is plotted. "Now You See Him" is based on a complex plot of deception that goes well beyond the confines of the magician's act. Such expanding borders are represented sartorially as well. Part of the murderer's scheme entails him taking on an additional identity, or at least disguise: Santini dresses as a waiter to make his way through the lounge's kitchen and up to his boss's chambers. Cassidy's series of roles in *Columbo* therefore culminates in this episode, as the character he plays here engages in a triple masquerade: he is a former Nazi playing an American magician playing an ordinary waiter.

In a sense, Cassidy's character and performance neatly remark on that of Columbo himself. In this episode, in fact, the lieutenant appears on the scene in slight masquerade. Instead of his signature raincoat, he is wearing a new jacket, a gift from his wife that he then repeatedly attempts to lose throughout the show. As he initially begins to enter the restaurant where the crime took place, an officer on duty tries to stop him, but Columbo quickly identifies himself. Says the officer, "I didn't recognize you, Lieutenant. You look different somehow." Columbo responds, in a funny voice, "I've had a haircut." Suggesting he doesn't know what the officer is referring to, his veiled facetious comment is typical of the character, if uttered in an atypical voice. For, like the Great Santini, Columbo always pretends that he is something other than he is; that is, if he appears less wise than he actually is, it's all the better to catch the criminals off guard—and, in fact, to garner their help in trapping themselves. At the same time, Columbo's constant reappearance in the murderer's lair is akin to, if also the reverse of, the magician's ultimate trick. The game Columbo plays, after all, is now-you-see-him, now-you-see-him-again. These likenesses and disparities come to a head when Columbo attends the Great Santini's magic act. He offers a challenge to the magician, betting that he can't get out of a pair of handcuffs he has with him. Santini manages to work his way out of them, but this only means Columbo has secretly won the game, for he was testing to see whether he could pick any such lock.[17] He therefore masquerades as the "loser" of this round only ultimately to win the game between them.

While I don't mean to cast aspersions on the vocation, actors are also charlatans by profession—especially when they are very good. That is, it's an actor's work to masquerade, believably, as someone they are not. But while this "act" is descriptive of every player on the series, in the case of Cassidy it is also descriptive of his ongoing work on television—never quite a stable persona, he is rather one whose persona is set only by its incessant variations. By reading across his appearances on *Columbo* alongside his other television performances, we can recognize him as

4.8. Now he's a waiter ("Now You See Him," 5:5; Feb. 29, 1976)

4.9. Now he's in a new coat ("Now You See Him," 5:5; Feb. 29, 1976)

the ultimate guest star or "character actor." Moreover, in each role on the mystery series he acts as something other than what even his fictional character is: a drunk driver and a wrongly accused man, a good writer, and even a non-Nazi. The detective himself is never so nefarious, but he is a character who is forever acting for his suspects. Though not exactly a charlatan, Lt. Columbo repeats his masquerade with every episode.

5 Between Columbo and Cassavetes

Sloppy Kisses

In one of my favorite scenes of the entire series, which appears in the episode "Playback," Columbo has let his dog run on the suspect's (and victim's) property while he speaks with the killer, Harold Van Wick. As Columbo and Van Wick take leave of one another, the camera cuts to the killer's wheelchair-bound wife, Elizabeth, played by Gena Rowlands. She and Columbo's dog have found one another, and he is climbing up on her lap, giving her kisses as she pets him. When Columbo comes upon them, he apologizes for the dog, eventually shooing him away so that the two of them can talk. He follows Elizabeth Van Wick to a flowerbed, where she cuts a few chrysanthemums and offers them to the detective to bring home to his wife. "Oh, she loves flowers," he says to her. As they continue to speak, he holds the little bouquet in his hand, crossing his arms so that the flowers offer a smattering of purple against his signature raincoat.

Why do I love this scene? My initial answer is obvious: it's the dog and the character Elizabeth's affection toward him. That dog rarely gets such loving attention; vets attend to him and a dog trainer tells Columbo he's a hopeless student, but, with the notable exception of young Steve Spelberg in "Mind over Mayhem," characters almost never give him any love. The detective himself repeatedly admits that he doesn't even have a name for him (matching the lieutenant's own lack of a first name).

5.1. A pack of two ("Playback," 4:5; March 2, 1975)

But here this perfectly beautiful woman—coiffed blonde hair, casual green gown—gently nuzzles the dog as the camera and, eventually, the detective, too, look on. And thus my own affection turns from the dog to the two characters—and to their relationship to one another as the two actors Falk and Rowlands.

First airing on March 2, 1975, "Playback" comes on the heels of John Cassavetes's film *A Woman under the Influence*, which was released November 18, 1974, and which starred Falk and Rowlands as a volatile married couple. The film's camera is nearly as volatile as its characters, as when it moves with Nick and Mabel Longhetti as they chase each other around the living room, closing in on Mabel's pained face or Nicky's mad gestures. It relentlessly holds on Mabel as she unravels or on Nick as he sits on the sofa, exhausted. It runs up the stairs as Mabel flees into the children's room, and it lays bare Mabel's breakdown in their kitchen. The story of a tumultuous marriage that involves in-laws and children alongside the husband and wife, *A Woman under the Influence* was a family affair in its casting as well as its narrative: Rowlands and Cassavetes had been married for twenty years by 1974, Rowlands's mother plays Mabel's mom, Cassavetes's mother plays Nick's, and the fictional couple's three children are played both by Cassavetes and Rowlands's own kids and the son of Seymour Cassel (a regular in Cassavetes productions since his first film, *Shadows*, in 1959). Such casting was typical in Cassavetes's work, with these familial relations extending to the actors, like Falk and Ben Gazzara, who grew to refer to Cassavetes as a brother.

Watching Columbo's eyes gently soften as he stares at Elizabeth when she cuts the flowers or plays with his dog, I see not just the characters of a fictional scene but also the layers of collaboration between these two actors. And in those layers, I see, too, the polar opposite of their performances between these two works made at roughly the same time. There in the detective's solicitousness toward the victim's daughter and in Elizabeth's kindness toward the lieutenant's absent wife are the vestiges of the emotion between them in Cassavetes's film and, I believe, Falk's respect toward Rowlands (Falk himself describes his awe of Rowlands's performance in an interview they produced for Criterion's release of the 1974 film). Am I "reading too much into" the glances between them or in the detective's hands and gait as he pushes Elizabeth's wheelchair through the house? Perhaps. But what I *am* "reading" is the historical, professional, and personal context of their work together, caught in a moment of this series I love.

Love—and a range of other emotional states of being—circumscribes Cassavetes's work. As he declared, "I have a one-track mind. That's all I'm interested in. Love and the lack of it."[1] His stated role as a director, after all, was to draw out raw emotion from his actors. Arguably, most of Falk's richest work as a performer is in the films he made with Cassavetes as either his costar or director. In *A Woman under the Influence*, Falk plays a man who is by turns difficult, bullying, ambivalent, and loving: he is a figure who is simply uncertain as to how to manage his feelings and those of his wife. In *Mikey and Nicky*, Elaine May's film in which Falk and Cassavetes star as old friends, the ambivalence of Falk's character is upped a notch. The film tracks them as Nicky (Cassavetes) calls Mikey (Falk) to help him out of a jam with the local mobsters for whom they work. Fearing a hit has been taken out on him, he persuades Mikey to crisscross Philadelphia in the middle of the night, from a bar

5.2. Falk's range in *A Woman under the Influence* (John Cassavetes, 1974)

5.3. Falk and Cassavetes in *Mikey and Nicky* (Elaine May, 1976)

to a girlfriend's house to a cemetery to the movies until Nicky temporarily disappears. While Cassavetes plays his character in an erratic, almost neurotic style, Falk plays it attentive, focused, and ultimately angry as he chastises his friend for only calling when he needs him and for otherwise making fun of him behind his back. This anger, we soon learn, appears to be at the root of his double-cross, for he's put a tail on his pal at the bidding of the local mafia boss. In *Columbo*, the intensity of those emotions is in check, whether with Cassavetes or Rowlands or most other actors and characters with whom he interacts, but such emotion forever hovers on the outskirts of his performances. Thus, I turn to this oeuvre not to suggest a disparity between *Columbo* and the work Falk did with this icon of New American Cinema, but because I'm interested in the intersections between the two and the ways in which the latter shapes, however lightly, the former.

Dogpile

Selectively reading, I could easily trace a trajectory of parts that primed Falk for his eventual signature role. Just as easily, I could trace another trajectory that set him on a seemingly opposite, if parallel, course. For instance, his part as a killer in *Murder, Inc.* and his performance as Ramos Clemente in *The Twilight Zone* ("The Mirror"; Oct. 20, 1961) presaged his collaborations more with John Cassavetes than his role as the detective. In the *Twilight Zone* episode, as I noted previously, he is a peasant-turned-militant-leader, whose volatility is much more akin to his turn as Nick Longhetti in *A Woman under the Influence* or as Mikey in May's film. At the same time, the logistics of his television career in the period leading up to *The Trials of O'Brien* did largely follow ongoing stints in anthology-based series, and *Trials* itself sets him up—even as he resisted it in some ways (as in his reluctance to star in a full-season series)—toward the part of *Columbo*. But these parallel trajectories remain intertwined from the early 1960s over the next fifteen years; not only are they impossible to disentangle, but their intertwining itself points to a commonality across the roles, as two sides of the same coin.

Throughout the 1960s, when Falk was nominated twice for Oscars and Emmys simultaneously, he continued to establish his reputation as a serious actor on film and television. In fact, just following his first stint as Lt. Columbo in *Prescription: Murder*, he also made his first appearance in a Cassavetes film, *Husbands*, the story of three friends (played by Cassavetes, Falk, and Gazzara) who travel to London together after the death of their friend. An extraordinarily significant director in the

New American Cinema, Cassavetes was known through three signature elements in particular: a realist aesthetic, rehearsed improvisation, and raw emotional performances that emerge out of each.

The preparation and shooting process for *Husbands* point to the blurriness between "fiction" and "real life" in Cassavetes's work. The three men not only rehearsed together, but Cassavetes as director invited the other two actors to contribute to the development of their characters.[2] When shooting in London, the three of them also spent afternoons and evenings together away from the cameras, building a relationship among themselves. Cassavetes would remark, "The time devoted to making a film is just an extension of the life of everyone involved."[3] Or, as he claimed about a scene in *Husbands* between Archie and his love interest, "This is not love or a relationship that men and women have in a movie. . . . It is like in real life."[4] Though Cassavetes would claim that these characters in the film were the men themselves—"It *is* us. It's *us*. Yeah, these people are me"—his point here is not that the actors were, say, in love with their female costars, but rather that the expression within the film is continuous with real-life expression of emotion.[5] And such expression was most manifest in the relations between the three men within and outside of the film. In his memoir, Gazzara describes the end of work on *Husbands* as creating "a kind of postpartum depression." As he says, "It was an experience that led to deep, personal friendships that would last a lifetime."[6] What "eventually had to happen," in other words, was the friendship between them.

Given that Cassavetes's work straddled independent film and mainstream cinema, it must have been a surprise to no one that as part of a promotional appearance for *Husbands*, the three stars—Falk, Gazzara, and Cassavetes—would join Dick Cavett on his talk show, which bridged the same independent and mainstream lines as Cassavetes's work. Cavett begins his September 21, 1970, show with some trepidation over the fact that it will be his first forty-five-minute time slot to accommodate ABC Monday Night Football. Then, after referring to their recent *Life* magazine cover that promotes *Husbands*, he half-jokingly announces his guests as follows: "They're all in the wings now, taking the theater apart. Before they do, would you welcome John Cassavetes, Peter Falk, and Ben Gazzara!"

5.4. Dogpile on *The Dick Cavett Show* (September 21, 1970)

In this notorious appearance, the three actors upend Cavett's show. From the get-go, together they take over by asking the questions themselves and directing the action over the host. Falk begins by petulantly asking Cavett if he just referred to the three of them as "animals," and Cassavetes says, drawing the camera to him, "Can I say hello to my mother? And to Sonny and the construction crew at Universal, I say hello." Gazzara stands up and shouts, "Hello, Sonny!" Cavett first asks if "the bar is open backstage" and then moves to a question about the film. The three refuse to speak; in fact, they quickly reveal they had planned not to speak at all for forty-five minutes. From here on, the episode is literally full of pratfalls: Cassavetes is the first to stand up, turn around, and fall to the floor as if he's been shot, Gazzara follows his lead shortly thereafter, and not long after that the three throw themselves onto the floor on top of one another in a dogpile. Falk bares his leg; Gazzara takes off his left shoe and sock and demands that everyone look at the "white stuff" on his feet (later explaining his wife put powder in his shoes); Cassavetes rests one of his legs on Falk's lap. The three indeed seem visibly "smashed," as Cavett himself suggests. Eventually they even briefly drive the host off his own set in feigned (or perhaps very real) exasperation.

Looking back on this episode over forty years later, Cavett recalled: "I think I watched it a year or so ago and it seemed even worse than I remembered it. When the circus was going on, with shoes coming off and smelling each other's feet—which may be an image I have conjured [indeed it was], but something close to it—and falling down, as if *that* were funny, just a bunch of louts out encouraging each other in their stupidity."[7] Such loutish behavior is surely what makes Cavett announce, "This is the reason I didn't join a fraternity." But for all the "horror" and "embarrassment" that Cavett documents (and which frankly seems an overstatement, given his own relatively good humor throughout), this display is also very much a demonstration of the men's refusal to contain their emotional lives. Moreover, the three do get serious as they discuss the film, with Cassavetes himself leading them into a more considered conversation, even apologizing to Cavett and emphasizing the respect they have for him. Gazzara praises Cassavetes as "the most humble, open, tenacious, and remorseless" filmmaker "in trying to . . . make the picture work" (along with claiming he wanted to physically come to blows with him), and Falk also manages to make an impassioned speech about working with Cassavetes, describing the differences he understands between "sentiment" and "sentimentality" (an earlier somewhat phony speech he makes about friendship and truth, on the other hand, sends Cassavetes into a silent giggling fit as he sits next to him). He lists those emotions that he thinks don't normally get expressed on film: "delight, hope, irritation, anger, friendship, love, bewilderment, confusion." And he goes on to say, addressing the audience (and refusing to address Cavett directly), "I found out I was more alive than I thought I was." Cassavetes puts a stop to this direction in the conversation, repeatedly opting instead to speak in platitudes, suggesting simply that the film is good and people should see it. But he also repeatedly attempts to acknowledge their wives throughout the appearance, ultimately, as the show begins to wind down, announcing, "I really would like to preserve my marriage."

Half-joking, half-exasperated, Cavett asks the trio to do the same to "Carson and Griffin." And indeed they did take this show on the road; Dick Cavett's show was one of three major appearances on talk shows, including also *David Frost* (July 10, 1969) and Johnny Carson's *Tonight Show* (Feb. 7, 1971).[8] Aside from Cassavetes tumbling out of his chair—first spontaneously and then on command—and jokes about Falk's hair, the three were least rowdy with Frost. In an appearance lasting nearly thirty-five minutes (inclusive of commercials) and less focused on antics, the threesome had the time to attempt to define some of the central tenets of the film. In his opening introduction of the evening's guests, Frost had promised that talking about *Husbands* "is going to lead them to talk about women, which is going to lead them to talk about who knows what they are going to talk about." And so begins the interview: after Cassavetes initially answers Frost's question about what the film is about, he says, "They fall in love with life and they try to make everyone else fall in love with it." For much of the rest of their appearance, together, along with host Frost, they attempt to unravel what this means. In so doing, they describe and disagree over what constitutes a marriage between a man and a woman, what constitutes male friendship, and what it means to be "turned on by life." Throughout the conversation, the three men interrupt each other and try to better articulate one another's thoughts. When Falk claims that a husband can't be friends with his wife, for instance, first Cassavetes briefly interrupts him, and then Gazzara chimes in: "Peter has a profound point but he didn't make it. I'll make it." Or, when Frost asks Cassavetes what he wants "people to have at the end of the picture," Cassavetes insists that he hopes "young people will understand that there are no bad people—not that there are no boring people . . . but that you can have a hell of a good time out of nothing. . . . Taking a chance on life is a start." Frost pushes him on this notion, and Falk intervenes.

What's particularly interesting about appearances like this one is that it allows them to delve deep into their conversations. Though what they announce may be at times vague, maddening, idealistic, or even, as Cassavetes calls himself, "silly," they reveal an actual desire to understand or unravel ideas, to get at the core of what it is that they're trying to express or that the film is trying to express. And through their conversation and performances—whether falling off chairs or interrupting each other—they also reveal how they relate to one another. What I see in the appearance on both Cavett's and Frost's shows in particular is that

Peter Falk is more interested in being like John Cassavetes—describing and practicing his "philosophy" of life and certainly his philosophy of acting—whereas Ben Gazzara remains somewhat removed from the two of them. Perhaps Gazzara's posture is part of his own performance style or maybe because he longs, too, to direct, or, perhaps, in the case of their promotion for *Husbands*, simply because his character is also more independent from the other two in the film.

These talk shows provide more than just a commentary on the relations between the three men; they also stand for the very format of broadcast television itself. That is, the talk show or variety show is emblematic of television as a whole in the ways such shows can include multiple formats and segments (including the commercials, but also moving between songs and conversations, performances and sketches).[9] It may appear to lack a coherent "narrative" as we find in, say, a mystery series, but it gives way to other narratives about the production of the stories we see and those who make them. This narrative is augmented by the commentary that develops out of the serendipitous relationships between the segments, too. For instance, preceding the appearance of the *Husbands* threesome on *Frost* is a performer who sings while alarmingly smacking himself in the head and on the thigh with a tin tray; such physical comedy prefigures Cassavetes's falls from his chair. Their appearance is immediately followed by songstress Julie London, who sings "Makin' Whoopee," which seems eerily related (possibly quite consciously designed by the Frost team) to the conversation they've just been having. And, finally, the next guests are Yoko Ono and John Lennon, who continue a philosophical conversation with Frost about the meaning of artistic practices.

Such appearances are illustrative of some of those cultural and countercultural ideals and beliefs that circulated through the late 1960s and early 1970s. Of course, countercultural and dominant cultural objects and beliefs regularly intermingle on the television screen. This is certainly apparent in the range of talk shows that Falk and his pals visited; in 1974 when he and Cassavetes appear on *The Tonight Show* to promote *A Woman under the Influence* (and give a nod to *Mikey and Nicky*), they share jokes with Carson, but the format doesn't allow for a real chance to develop an understanding of the film. Cassavetes baldly admits they are there because he's afraid they won't otherwise be able to fill the 2,600-seat theater they've engaged for the opening in Los Angeles. And Carson seems neither as sympathetic nor as willing to push the guests in their ideas; in spite of the fact that Cassavetes had appeared four times in the past on Carson's show, Falk is the primary guest of the two of them: he's the bankable, recognizable star who has brought his incomprehensible, arty filmmaker friend along.[10] Moreover, Carson mispronounces both Cassavetes's and Gena Rowlands's names, and at the end of their stint he refers to the film as "Lady under the Influence," markedly revealing, in whatever minor or major ways, that these figures are not part of his primary cultural environment.

Such is American television from the wane of its first Golden Era into the 1960s and 1970s; it could sustain the intellectual and the mundane, the thrilling and the "boring." As these various appearances show, it could even sustain one of the central creative forces representing New American Cinema. After all, like Falk, both Cassavetes and Gazzara alternated between film and television work during this period (though increasingly Cassavetes avowedly did so in order to keep afloat financially). Each of them revealed elements of performance and character that would return in Cassavetes's direction of them. Their respective work in the 1960s demonstrated an emotional intensity, and each actor played some version of thugs or cops, or at least men struggling with the lines drawn by the law. In guest roles they were often on the wrong side of the law, but on their series they were detectives and lawyers: Cassavetes appeared as the eponymous "jazz detective" in *Johnny Staccato* from 1959 to 1960, five episodes of which the actor directed; Gazzara played a cop on *Arrest and Trial* (1963–64) and a lawyer in *Run for Your Life*, in which he plays a man with a fatal diagnosis, leading him to live his life as if he would die the next day (1965–68); and Falk was a defense attorney who often solved the crimes of which his clients were accused in order to prove their innocence in *The Trials of O'Brien* (1965–66). They also were each forever brawny, not-quite-leading men, even when they were in the starring role. Gazzara's performance style is suave and assured, even distant, as if he doesn't quite belong on this medium. In the first episode of *Run for Your Life*, a somewhat marginal character (played by film actress Celeste Holm) calls Gazzara's character, the lawyer Paul Bryan, "quite a cool client." He stands removed from the rest of the crowd but is ever vigilant. A sly dog. In his Emmy-winning performance for "The Price of Tomatoes," the 1962 episode of *The Dick Powell Theater*, Falk is a hapless but ultimately dogged working-class truck driver, a lovable but restless mutt. In "You Got to Have Luck," a 1956 episode of *Alfred Hitchcock Presents*, yard-dog Cassavetes plays murderer Sam Cobbett, just escaped from prison. At once controlled and unpredictable, he moves frenetically—he shifts and smolders—like the jazz detective he plays in *Johnny Staccato*. When the heat is on in his headlining series, his own temperature rises. Getting too close to the killer of "Luck" can be fatal; and in *Staccato* the detective must keep his own distance, or he will be swallowed up by those around him and the camera that hovers near.

Admittedly, to follow the Falk/Cassavetes connection is to fall down a rabbit hole (and here I play a hound myself, rather than dear Alice)—a wonderland of late 1950s and 1960s television and 1960s and 1970s film. Leading in multiple directions, deeper and deeper, wider and wider, this investigative path, by turns, mesmerizes, disorients, and coheres. I wander through this maze of connections, uncertain sometimes where to maintain my look. In one direction I find their late 1950s and early 1960s television appearances on *Alfred Hitchcock Presents* or anthology series like *The Goodyear Playhouse* or *The Chrysler Theater*. Another path leads to the individual television series mentioned earlier. Inevitably, these intertextual connections give way to interpersonal ones when the three star together in *Husbands*. And then I am back on the path on which I started in the first place: the three of them together, a family of forty-year-old men who take their act on the road, diverge, and then meet again—however, always separately—in the 1970s television series *Columbo* and in their autobiographical productions decades later.

Those styles that preceded their work in *Husbands* together were likely one of the primary reasons for Cassavetes's desire to work with these two actors—they nicely complemented him in looks and manner, yet each had a particular personality of his own, personalities punctuated in interviews of the period and their own later writings. Granted, on the small screen, Falk would never be the detective Cassavetes himself played in *Johnny Staccato*. Perhaps this is in great part because in those early years Falk is always in the process of learning—as an actor when he's working with

Cassavetes, or as the detective when he's in his signature role. His role is to observe, to learn, to comment—traits that will reappear when he plays himself-as-Columbo in Wim Wenders's *Wings of Desire* (1987). Thus, when the three take their antics (far less rowdy, to be sure) to *The Tonight Show* with Johnny Carson, Falk himself largely plays the observer; leaning back in his chair, he tilts his head toward his director and friend, smiling through his antics. Or, as on Cavett's and Frost's shows, he attempts to parrot or echo the philosophy of his director. As he says to Cavett's audience, he never would have learned that he was so "alive" without having worked on *Husbands*, and he never would have known how unchallenged he'd been as an actor outside of Cassavetes's film.

All in the Family

In the conversation between Falk and Rowlands that serves as part of the "extras" in the Criterion release of *A Woman under the Influence*, Falk recalls the challenges of working with Cassavetes in *Husbands*, and Falk's declaration that he would never work with him again as a director. But, as he goes on to proclaim, when the film was completed, he realized he had more to learn from Cassavetes, a sense that Cassavetes must have held in his back pocket when he needed a male lead for *Woman* when Ben Gazzara wasn't available. Several months after Cassavetes's own turn in *Columbo*, at a gathering with Elaine May when the actors were preparing to work on *Mikey and Nicky* with her, Falk announced that he wanted the part of Nick Longhetti. Cassavetes recalls that he initially "had no idea that he could play the part" but then cajoled him to take it based on a little reverse psychology, not unlike a ploy the lieutenant might devise: "I said, 'Peter, I don't know if you could play that. What kind of a part is that for you to play, a heavy? You're the most loved character in the world.' *Lying!* I *wanted* him to play it!"[11] In working with an actor he knew well, Cassavetes then revised the character of Nick in order for them together to resist "*fictitious* emotion."[12] But he also asked Falk to share in the financing of the film, so that together they put up $250,000. Cassavetes mortgaged his home, while Falk used earnings from *Columbo*. At the time, Falk was not only the "most loved character" but also the highest paid actor on television. As *Broadcasting* reported in October 1973, he earned $100,000 for each ninety-minute episode.[13] For an actor playing a notoriously underpaid cop—and one who details his $11,000 salary to the murderer whom Cassavetes plays one year earlier—this figure might seem ironic; but it was also certainly handy in allowing both Cassavetes and Falk to pursue independent work outside of mainstream film or television.

And, of course, these fields of work—performance for Falk, acting and directing for Cassavetes—intermingled in ways that went beyond the actors' own bodies moving between the arenas. For instance, if *Woman under the Influence* was a family affair, so, too, was *Columbo*. At least, seeming to model after Cassavetes's practice, Falk used his influence to bring in the Cassavetes "family" over a period of three seasons. Rowlands appears in the fourth season, Cassavetes guests as a murderer in the second, and Gazzara directs two episodes between the third and fourth seasons. Moreover, four different character actors who were regulars in Cassavetes films also had multiple bit parts on *Columbo* over the years: Val Avery, Timothy Carey, Fred Draper, and John Finnegan. In the Cassavetes films, which had relatively small casts (and which almost always included various family members), these frequent appearances were hardly coincidental. Val Avery, in fact, even appeared in episodes of both *Johnny Staccato* and *Run for Your Life* before his work in *Faces*, his first Cassavetes film; he appeared on four episodes of *Columbo* over its first five seasons. Appearing on six episodes of the original and seven in the reboot, Finnegan was the most prolific *Columbo* extra of these four actors; he also had brief appearances in the late 1970s Falk film *The In-Laws* and several years later in *Big Trouble*, which reunited *In-Laws* stars Falk and Alan Arkin and which Cassavetes himself ended up directing.

This intersection of major and minor players in *Columbo* can therefore be neatly situated through the work these collaborators did in film, organized largely through the charismatic leadership of Cassavetes. In fact, "Étude in Black," in which Cassavetes plays the murderous, philandering orchestral conductor Alex "the Maestro" Benedict, visually demonstrates the very movement between screens that Falk performed through their ventures together. This star-studded episode crosses several industries and eras: first, of course, is New American Cinema filmmaker Cassavetes as the Maestro; his wife is played by theatrical

5.5. John Finnegan, member of the Cassavetes pack ("A Friend in Deed," 3:8; May 5, 1974)

5.6. Timothy Carey, member of the Cassavetes pack ("Fade in to Murder," 6:1; Oct. 10, 1976)

and film actress Blythe Danner, just off her 1970 Tony Award for *Butterflies Are Free*; classical Hollywood star Myrna Loy plays the Maestro's mother-in-law (who holds the purse strings, much like Rowlands's fictional mother in "Playback"); NBC and Universal television player James McEachin appears as the Maestro's assistant, Billy; and indie filmmaker James Olson plays Paul Rifkin, musician and ex-lover of the victim. Add to this lineup Steven Bochco as the writer for the episode (based on a story by creators Levinson and Link) and longtime television director

5.7. Columbo plays "Chopsticks" ("Étude in Black," 2:1; Sept. 17, 1972)

Nicholas Colasanto (best known for his role as "Coach" a decade later in *Cheers*, he was also a longtime friend of Gazzara's, having directed several episodes of *Run for Your Life*).[14] Such a cast of characters was certainly not unusual for the series, but the intersections this cast represents are part of what crystallizes the episode's allegorical commentary on Falk's and Cassavetes's own crossovers between entertainment and artistic arenas.

Even more suggestive than the cast are those scenes that extend this commentary. The Maestro has attempted to perfectly orchestrate the murder of his blackmailing lover and star pianist, Jenifer Welles (Anjanette Comer), when he kills her by knocking her out and leaving her to die from leaked gas fumes (all the while dressed in his tux, accessorized with sunglasses as he completes the scene of the crime). But, while Columbo is dispatched originally for what appears to be a suicide, he knows, of course, "from the beginning" who the murderer is, as the Maestro himself observes at the end. In the opening to the final third of the episode, he makes this case known to the conductor.

The scene begins with a long shot of Columbo playing "Chopsticks" on a grand piano on the stage of the Hollywood Bowl. He is joyfully working at perfecting the little tune, playing it again and again, even sounding out the melody with his mouth; the Maestro hears the song as he steps out of his sports car and approaches the stage. After watching the detective for a moment, he bursts into ironic applause, and the detective bashfully continues playing. What follows is a scene between them that appears as a kind of rehearsed improvisation, much as for Cassavetes's own films: the lieutenant pulls out Jenifer Welles's typewriter to show him a clue. He stumbles at first as he attempts to show Benedict how the note in the typewriter had to have been inserted into the machine after it was already typed. Becoming increasingly confident in the scenario he sketches, Columbo begins to rehearse his theory of the crime, suggesting that a lover had staged the suicide. As Benedict walks away from the lieutenant, the detective calls out, "Suppose it was you." This stops him in his tracks. Columbo insists that he's not saying it *was* him, but just suppose, for the sake of his theory. Here his performance has shifted from what might seem a rehearsed improvisation between a bungling police detective and a self-assured conductor to a carefully staged presentation—but one that is itself another kind of rehearsal, such as for a future arrest. The detective's method here is not unlike that which Cassavetes employed as a director, and the commonalities between them are striking as the two of them appear onstage and on-screen together. And, of course, as the detective exits the Bowl, stage right, he turns to add "just one more thing," revealing that his superiors have approved his theory and officially assigned him to the case. "That's my specialty, you know," he says. "Homicide."

On the heels of this interaction between them, the next scene also smacks as an homage to Cassavetes—though this time as a television actor, rather than an infamous film director. Following a commercial break, Columbo appears on a balcony of a club as jazz music wafts toward him. This scene—consciously or not—echoes a common image of Cassavetes as *Johnny Staccato*, "jazz detective." A throwaway detail, perhaps, but one that nevertheless resonates when we watch it with Cassavetes in mind. And, indeed, throughout the episode, Benedict appears on a multitude of literal screens, heralding his roles across texts

5.8. James McEachin on screen as "Maestro" departs ("Étude in Black," 2:1; Sept. 17, 1972)

and media formats. In fact, the episode begins with Benedict directing the look of the cameras to the television director who is preparing for the evening's live presentation of a Hollywood Bowl concert. Alongside his right-hand man, Billy (McEachin), and looking directly into a camera aimed at the stage, Benedict tells the director ("Frank") that he has some ideas for the night's recording. Seated at a console board, staring at the four screens in front of him with a technician on either side (one white, one Black), Frank asks Benedict what he had in mind. "I would like one on me as usual," the Maestro begins, and then he goes on to suggest, "I want to get away from these usual dull looks that we get around here." While this scene paints the Maestro as narcissistic and annoying, the character's demands—to "get away" from "dull looks"—are also analogous to Cassavetes's own approach as a director. This implicit link between Cassavetes and big and small screens becomes increasingly apparent as the episode continues. As Welles's death is discovered, for instance, a montage begins, which moves from a broad image of Benedict conducting the orchestra, to an image of his performance as seen through a series of television monitors, to the police bursting through Welles's door as the music soars. As the camera moves in for a close-up, we even see Benedict's own recollection, as revealed through a flashback to his loss of his signature carnation at Welles's apartment. The picture freezes, and it cuts again—now to an image of the conductor on a small television set, its monitor framed perfectly within the set that the audience watches at home. Shortly thereafter the shot moves from the television set to reveal the detective and a doctor, apparently standing over a patient on a table. As we soon see, the patient is the detective's basset hound (in his first appearance on the series), whom Columbo must bundle up after some shots in order to head over to the scene of the crime.

The lieutenant and these attendant screens continue to dog the conductor. In what will be the penultimate scene of the episode, Columbo has returned to the vet's office, where he sees the same orchestral performance on the doctor's television. And in a scene that will be echoed in season 4's "Playback," television itself guides the detective toward a solution of his case. Whereas in "Playback" Columbo watches a repeat of a play in a football game in order to recognize that, of course, not everything we see on television (or via surveillance cameras) is "live," in the case of "Étude in Black," he realizes that live performances are recorded for subsequent play, thus offering evidence of their original moment of production, including the absence of Benedict's carnation in his lapel. Hence, in the final scene the detective organizes a special screening for Benedict and his wife, Janice.[15] Whereas "Camera 1" and "Camera 2" led to television monitors as the episode began, now we see a film projector and screen and a bank of monitors set side by side.

Here the detective offers a mini close reading of the two images: the video-recorded orchestra appears on one of the four television monitors and a recording of the nightly news is set on the film screen. (This ending also resembles that of "Playback," which, of course, costars Rowlands.) In the orchestral performance, Benedict is without his carnation; in the aftermath of the victim's death, he wears it. Throughout this scene Columbo has directed various characters to assist in the presentation of these moving images, cueing the television director Frank to turn off (and turn on) the lights and asking another police officer to run the film projector and then pause it. In considering the images, he utilizes his cigar as a pointer—not unlike the conductor's wand that is still in Benedict's own hands. Upon the revelation first of the visual proof and then of Janice Benedict's confirmation that she did not witness her husband put the carnation back on after the orchestral performance,

5.9. Television (and dog) solves the case ("Étude in Black," 2:1; Sept. 17, 1972)

the Maestro bows to the detective's performance.[16] "Goodbye, genius," he says to Columbo. He then taps his wand toward his wife in adieu and says goodbye to Frank as he's escorted out by a police officer. After ensuring that Janice will be escorted home, Columbo sits back down in front of the screens and asks Frank to play the concert again. The last image appears as a freeze-frame: the detective sits before a bright television monitor, with the darkened film screen to his left.

In the final image from "Étude in Black," when the film projector is turned off and its screen goes black, television quite literally gets the last look. But not only does it share the space with vestiges of film (technically, visually, and historically), it is also revealed time and again to be more than one thing. Hence "Étude in Black" points outward in multiple directions: to Falk's collaborations with Cassavetes in film, to the appearance of Rowlands in "Playback," to the directed episodes by Gazzara, to the appearances of the three men on contemporaneous talk shows, even outer still to Gazzara's, Cassavetes's, and Falk's television performances in the late 1950s and early 1960s. Thus, looking

5.10. Televisual evidence ("Étude in Black," 2:1; Sept. 17, 1972)

at Cassavetes's appearance in the second season—not unlike looking at the final image of the episode—reveals the confluence of circumstances that suggest the multifaceted layers that shaped Falk's work in and out of *Columbo* in the 1970s. Gazzara's directed episodes, "A Friend in Deed" and "Troubled Waters," also reveal such layers, as each contains scenes and elements that, in their intimacy and intensity, appear to belong more in a Cassavetes film than in an episode of *Columbo*. Together, these examples point to the ways in which the series demonstrates movement between mainstream television production and independent cinema, enabled, of course, by the star Falk and his personal relationships with other professionals in the field. Surely, then, Falk's work between *Mikey and Nicky*, *Woman under the Influence*, and *Columbo* reveals his versatility as an actor. That versatility is constitutive of an emotional range as well: the alternately loving and volatile Nick Longhetti, a detective by turns stumbling and self-possessed, a character and an actor who looks lovingly at Gena Rowlands and knowingly at John Cassavetes. Recognizing this flexibility is not just a means of describing Falk as a

5.11. Gazzara shoots it Cassavetes-style ("A Friend in Deed," 3:8; May 5, 1974)

5.12. Gazzara directs Columbo ("Troubled Waters," 4:4; Feb. 9, 1975)

performer and Columbo as a character; it's also a method for an investigation of television. After all, to understand television is always a matter of knowing "just one more thing." Often that one more thing is a state of feeling—a fondness apparent between characters or performers or, perhaps, my own affection for not just Columbo or *Columbo* but also for Cassavetes and Rowlands and Falk themselves, which breathes life into my experience of episodes made five decades ago.

Living Remembrances

The notion of being or becoming "alive" is a thread across Falk's and Gazzara's memoirs, as well as one appearing throughout Cassavetes's interviews about his work in film, and it's often tied to a depth of emotion. Gazzara was drawn to work with Cassavetes after he saw *Faces* in a packed theater. He writes, "I'd never seen the camera go so close and remain so long on an actor's face. And I'd hardly ever seen an actor's face project as many thoughts and feelings on-screen."[17] As he goes on, "*Faces* had structure and yet, as in life, things were never resolved neatly. Nothing seemed acted or directed or even written. It just *was*."[18] Such insistent claims about parallel states of being between film and life or the performer and character recur again and again with all the men. In response to a series of questions about his role in the film—repeatedly trying to get at the difficulties the film posed for him—Falk finally simply states, "There was no character . . . there was me."[19]

Of course, actors are ever "living" beings; they are professionals whose very job is to move between those roles that they embody. This is not to say an actor like Falk simply plays himself on-screen, but his body is identified with the character: quite simply, he shares a body with the character he plays. Cassavetes's approach to making film was to extend that bodily fact by engaging the actors' emotional experiences. He continuously picked up on the emotion that a body feels and expresses, and he utilized that emotion as a connective tissue across real life and fiction. Such is the work, perhaps, of any good director or good film, but for Cassavetes and those actors who were sympathetic to his work, emotional expression was at the core of film. Rather than work through a well-crafted story, he sought to explore "incidents": events in life that may be mundane or shattering. In the case of *Husbands*, he described the premise as such: "Basically what we started with was ourselves in kind of a simple idea of a guy dying—what it would mean to us if one of us—one of our close friends would die and how we would handle it, and just took it from there."[20]

When Cassavetes laughs in a documentary for the French series *Cinéastes de notre temps* made during *Faces*, he is irrefutably alive, brimming over with feeling that can't be contained by the very spaces he occupies. The French team follows Cassavetes moving incessantly around his house as he describes his work on *Faces*, and the camera can hardly hold him as he laughs, gesticulates, and talks nonstop. Even in *Columbo*, the Maestro runs up a set of stairs rather than taking them one at a time like an average person. Much of his claims about the "authenticity" of emotions or that a film like *Husbands* was simply "him" are admittedly elusive, bordering on platitudes. But his relentlessness attached to the capture of a feeling is contagious. His costars Gazzara and Falk believe in this mode of acting and being, as evident in their range of biographical works, whether interviews, talk-show appearances, or their respective memoirs. And those memoirs, too, are resolutely consistent—not only with other performances or sources, but with one another, as if they composed them together. Given that the form of the memoir is less linear than the autobiography—telling the story of an aspect of one's life, such as one's work as an actor, rather than attempting to capture the telling of a life as a whole—this overlapping history across Falk's and Gazzara's works makes a kind of structural sense.

Gazzara and Falk write in harmony about their friend Cassavetes, even while they reveal their wildly different modes of expression. Both actors joined Cassavetes during his final months to read through a play he'd penned called *Begin the Beguine* (a seeming "sequel" to *Husbands*, given Gazzara's description). Shortly thereafter, Cassavetes died. Gazzara describes how he flew from Rome for Cassavetes's funeral, where he "had to step away. I couldn't stand still. I paced and cried." He notes, "Peter Falk was wearing the same navy-blue coat he'd worn in the opening scene of *Husbands*, so many years before. That picture opened with John, Peter, and me going to the funeral of our best friend—and here it was, the real thing."[21] In other words, Gazzara points out that Falk returned to the beginning of their work together, effectively coming full circle. Falk's own final chapter on Cassavetes in his memoir *Just One More Thing: Stories from My Life* is "a tribute," in which the actor focuses less on his own loss and more on a description of his friend as "teeming with feeling, emotional, yet extremely intelligent."[22] He goes on: "A complex man—he had antennae like Proust, but he was a competitor like Vince Lombardi. He was a wild animal. But at the same time the family was central to his universe. These are times when it's easy to be pessimistic. But if the tribe can produce somebody like John, there is still hope."[23]

Perhaps, however, the penultimate chapter of Falk's book is even more telling. Here he retells a story that Cassavetes told him in his last days. Suffering from cirrhosis of the liver, Cassavetes had struggled climbing down the driveway from his house to get his newspaper. Every day his dog Cosmo walked along with him, leading the way, but Cassavetes described to his friend how one morning Cosmo held back and followed him. Falk prints Cassavetes's account as if it's part of a screenplay:

JOHN

He showed me a lot of consideration. He's an unusual dog. And when we got to the top of the driveway, you know what he did? He went all the way back to the very end of our property and when he finally got there, he threw up and died. Peter, do you think he was trying to tell me something?[24]

Falk introduces this anecdote by noting that he's "sometimes in a daze," thus again echoing those stories Cassavetes and Gazzara have both told about him; "maybe—just maybe—that's why John chose to tell me this story about his dog."[25] So while the story is about how his dog set an example for his human companion, it's also about how Cassavetes continued "to set the standard" for his friend, even in dying. Twenty-two years later, Falk followed his friend to the grave; both are buried at the intimate Westwood Memorial Park in Los Angeles.

6 An "Obsessive Preoccupation with Gadgetry"

> *He stands there, looking dreamily at the TV set.*
> —Steven Bochco, "Étude in Black"

Knowing Television

It is a terrible thing for a media studies scholar to admit, but I have never been a big gadget person or even very technologically minded. Growing up, I was never much for electronics; as a mark of my own time, I didn't even have a Walkman as a kid, though I listened to my brother's on occasion. As I got older, I continued to eschew new technological thingamajigs. I didn't have a CD player until well into the 1990s, and, until recently, every gadget I did have (my first iPod, even TiVo) were gifts from friends. Of course, the exception to this rule was the television, but even that has been, first and foremost, largely a delivery system for narrative and then, as I made my way in the academic world, the object and tool for much of my work. Aside from fooling around with my mom's reel-to-reel recorder, what I did learn about technology as a kid—and, in fact, about film history as well—largely appeared to me through television, specifically through *Columbo*. Most distinctively, for instance, I remember learning how movie projectors work (not exactly a new technology, I admit, but one that fascinated me). Thus, from the

6.1. The cue blip that started it all ("Make Me a Perfect Murder," 7:3; Feb. 25, 1978)

episode that haunted me for decades, "Make Me a Perfect Murder," I was a student not only of how television works but of film technology as well. I learned what a "cue blip" is when Kay Freestone kills her boss— or so I inaccurately remembered—between reel changes. From then on, whenever I saw the flash in the corner of the screen at the movies, I imagined murder.

Columbo taught me more than I might even have realized at the time, and I've realized since that it tells us much about culture, particularly technological cultures, in the period during which it ran. Through its investigative structure—not just of murder but also of American culture in the 1970s more broadly—it embodies multiple histories: developments in television format, intersections with other media industries (and histories), and perspectives on emerging technologies. Taking a cue from that flash in the corner of the screen, I want here to draw some links between those emerging technologies, television, murder, and, of course, its investigation.[1] After all, the technological objects on display in the series are embedded with history: they narrate a history of technological change of the era, and they discretely link technology with time. Allowing for the detective's investigation of such emerging devices, the series also implicitly invites an investigation into the work and the myths of television itself.

If chapter 4 looked at how, at least in part, *Columbo* knew film history, this chapter is an attempt to show how the series demonstrated a case of knowing television.[2] At once, it was a series that revealed a range of cultural knowledge to its viewers and that understood and taught us about the medium itself. In "Negative Reaction," Lt. Columbo states this claim directly himself. On the trail of a professional photographer, who has staged the kidnapping and murder of his wife, the detective goes to a camera store to follow up on the model used in the faked kidnapping. Milling around the store, he comes upon reverse images of a photograph on a magazine cover, and the clerk gives him a brief lesson on printing from the negative. "I'll be a monkey's uncle," Columbo responds. "You learn something every day."

Along with the infamous oft-repeated line "just one more thing," this phrase could be the perfect motto for the series, for every episode offers the detective an opportunity to learn something new. And with this new knowledge comes a reiteration of what he already knows about class difference; time after time, as I've discussed elsewhere, our working-class detective is pitted against a wealthy murderer whose own cultural knowledge is largely class-based. Hence, every murder, whether because of the context where it's taken place or because of the profession or "obsession" of the murderers themselves, sets the scene for the detective's accumulation of knowledge. Indeed, the first three iterations of the series neatly present a broader arena for the context in which we as viewers also learn. In the original made-for-television movie *Prescription: Murder*, we learn about psychology; in the pilot, "Ransom for a Dead Man," the general setting is the law, as the killer and her victim were lawyers; and in the first official episode, "Murder by the Book," the framework is mystery writing itself. *Columbo* is, after all, a series about the psychology of the murderer and the detective, the implicit legal ramifications of crime, and the very plotting of the event (and, by association, the plotting of the series itself). Moreover, "Ransom

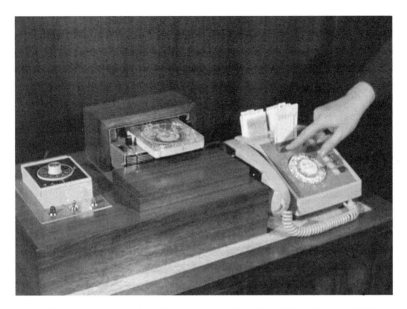

6.2. A phone recording system ("Ransom for a Dead Man," 0:1; March 1, 1971)

for a Dead Man" sets up the series' fascination with technology and its relation to time, for the murderer utilizes a reel-to-reel recording system on her phone to authenticate her husband's existence after she has, in fact, already murdered him.

Such technological objects produce a bridge between television and other electronic forms (as well as one between technologies and class structures). In effect, this trope incites questions about the relation between technologies and crime, or even between murder and television. For there is indeed a relationship. In the episode "Playback," for instance, the killer's mother-in-law and future victim announces that he has an "obsessive preoccupation with gadgetry." Though perhaps less malevolently so, the same could be said for the series as a whole. After all, the statement of the soon-to-be-victim of "Playback" is an echo of the detective himself in "Ransom for a Dead Man," when Columbo tells the murderer, "I remembered how you liked gadgets." Across the series, several other murderers' crimes or alibis are enabled by or hinge around a particular technogadget: the answering machine, tape recorders, surveillance systems, the VCR, even a robot. The display of and instruction concerning these various gadgets throughout the run of the series provide a kind of material history, one that allows the series to produce not only fictional narratives but also documents of its particular time and place. As we might do in relation to cocreators Levinson and Link, we read technological change, too, as Columbo does.

Our instruction also comes with another kind of relational history: the new gadgets are often situated, at least through the context of the series as a whole, within a broader history of recording technologies, including photography and film. To illuminate the context the series produces, I will move from a consideration of photography and film apparatuses to emerging technologies of the period to television itself. In almost all of these cases, image-based technologies function as a means quite literally to mark time. In other words, they are almost always bound to the killer's attempt to set an alibi and/or function to set the time of death. In "Negative Reaction," the alibi for the murder is even both set and undercut by a photograph. A professional photographer, the murderer, Paul Galesko (in an amazingly devious turn by Dick Van Dyke), stages a photograph of his wife as a kidnap victim; placing a clock on the mantel, he sets it to 2 p.m., a time for which he can account for himself. In the final scene when the detective confronts the killer about his crime, Columbo unveils a huge blow-up of the same photograph, but, based on what he has learned about photographic printing, he has reversed the image so that the clock reads 10 a.m., the inverse of 2 p.m. In his desperation to prove that the detective has printed a negative image of the photograph—and therefore to save his own alibi—the killer ultimately exposes himself when he unwittingly identifies the camera used in the commission of the crime.

If photography exposes time, moving-image—or "time-based"—media set time even more frequently in the series. Usually, it's less the medium itself than the apparatus for screening it that demonstrates time. In two episodes, for instance, a film projector is shown to us as a tool of exhibition, but it also functions as a tool for murder when it is used to set part of the killer's alibi. In fact, in "Make Me a Perfect Murder," the episode that was such a crucial part of my own media education, first

6.3. The photographer's alibi ("Negative Reaction," 4:2; Oct. 6, 1974)

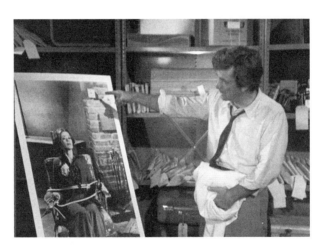

6.4. The photographer's misstep ("Negative Reaction," 4:2; Oct. 6, 1974)

the audience and then the detective get a lesson in how the changeover of reels works. Our soon-to-be murderer, Kay Freestone, has already rehearsed the event with the help of a small cassette recorder and the sound of her own voice counting down from four minutes in real time (itself a tour de force that could hardly be imagined on television screens or any other devices in the twenty-first century, the era of split attention). For the main event, she enters the projection booth in order to prepare a screening for studio and network executives of the made-for-television movie she has produced. The scene is played out through a dual context of instruction and bloodshed. The projectionist, Walter (played by James McEachin, who, recall, appeared on *Columbo* three seasons prior, in which he stared into a television monitor at the television director), greets her with "VIP time, huh?"[3] "Oh, it's murder," Kay responds. "You got all nine reels here?" He answers, "Ninety minutes, nine reels." As the audience quickly calculates—ten minutes per reel—the instruction on reel changes begins, with Kay's threat to Walter: "If you so much as make one mistake in a changeover, I'll kill you."

And thus begins Walter's showman's performance of what might seem an otherwise quotidian, behind-the-scenes task. Like a circus ringmaster, magician, or African American vaudevillian, Walter demonstrates the magic and pragmatics of movie technology or, rather, explains the science of what seems like magic. As he does so, he gestures toward the instruments: the projector, the counter, the screen. He begins with a twirl of his hat:

> Yowza, Miss Freestone. Your film is gonna go through this gate at the incredible rate of ninety feet per minute, you just watch this little ol' counter here. And no sooner will this first reel finish up, when I will see two little flashes of light out there in the upper right-hand corner of your lovely picture. Then I will, with lightning speed, switch over to this projector here [he moves across to demonstrate "lightning speed" by a slow-motion run; we cut to a shot of Kay watching, arms crossed, smiling at his performance]. Not only will your big shots not know that I have switched a reel, they will not suspect one lil ol' thing.

Kay applauds: "Bravo, Walter."

Throughout this sequence, Walter is shot in the center of the frame, with a reaction shot of Kay in the middle of his performance, as a means of enunciating the instructional bent of his monologue. But, of course, his explanation is more for the audience's benefit than for Kay (who is partly a stand-in for us), as she already knows how to run the projector. Still, the scene does set the stage for the commission of a crime. When Walter exclaims that the VIPs "will not suspect one lil ol' thing," we easily catch the double entendre. He suggests that the executives (also a little like us, the television audience) won't know there is a method to the magic of the projection. But read slightly differently, in the context of

6.5. A lesson on projecting ("Make Me a Perfect Murder," 7:3; Feb. 25, 1978)

Kay's threats, this statement suggests that Walter and Kay are committing a crime by projecting a film. And indeed, as it quickly turns out, the changeover is the cover-up for her crime, but it's hardly Walter whom she wants to kill. In fact, Kay sends Walter on an errand and promises to manage the next reel change, both to keep him out of the way and to ensure her own alibi. Moreover, to complete her alibi, she resets the clock on the projector itself, as if to represent time-shifting mechanisms only just introduced for home use.

In this case, as with other such scenes and alibis throughout the run of the series, we therefore see how the scene behind the scene is important not just to the killer's alibi but also to film and television production and exhibition. Thus, from the scene of instruction, we cut to the "VIPs": the boss says to Kay, "Roll when you're ready." We then shift to the projection booth and see an actual demonstration of the process, with a close-up on the projector's counter when Walter winds the clock to 09:00. He flips the switch, checks the focus, and wishes Kay luck. The image shifts now to the title screen of Kay's film: "The Professional"—a designation that seems to remark on Walter's work as well as Kay's (and which also anticipates Columbo's).

In "Forgotten Lady," an episode that kicked off season 5, we also witness the work of a film projector, but in this case it's when the projector essentially breaks down, splitting the film in the midst of its projection. Thus, from the murderer herself, we learn how to repair, or splice, film. Film is also the context and the drive for the murder she commits. Here our killer is an aging Hollywood star, Grace Wheeler Willis (played by Janet Leigh); she wants to return to her glory in show business, but her husband won't bankroll a film. So she murders him, claiming that at the time of his demise she was watching one of her old films in the screening room downstairs. Columbo, however, realizes that fifteen minutes remain unaccounted for during the event, as the movie lasts 105 minutes, whereas Willis's screening took two hours. He knows that Willis had to repair the film in the middle of the screening, but he suspects she was able to do this in much less than fifteen minutes. Thus, to test the veracity of his estimate—less for his own proof and more for the benefit of the murderer's former costar, Ned Diamond (John Payne), who has become her current advocate—Columbo orchestrates a scene when he's invited over to her place for a night at the movies.

Columbo and Grace's old friend Ned arrive in tuxedos for the evening; the former star appears in evening dress with such a graceful elegance that it seems incomprehensible that she can't find work in Hollywood or on Broadway. The problem, it seems, as with many similar roles for women on television during this era, is that she continues to live in the past, or at least wants to relive her former, lost glory. This evening is illustrative of that drive, for she's screening an old film for her guests. Therefore, this sequence cuts between two primary spaces—the screening room and the projection room—with Grace moving between them. As she first exits to check on the projector, Columbo and her former costar remain in the screening room and discuss her alibi.

"The film broke," says Columbo, referring to the night of the murder. "The film broke," responds Ned. Columbo continues: "You can see the actual splice. You can see where the film is mended together. Thirty frames are missing." His companion responds, "That's innocent enough. It accounts for the missing time. The film broke and had to be repaired."

But Columbo answers, "That would depend on how long it takes to repair it, wouldn't you say?" At this point, the men are interrupted by the actress, who shares with them a photograph album, inviting Lt. Columbo to have a laugh: "Look at those shoes." And here is where it becomes difficult to precisely describe this scene, for Columbo responds with such warmth and such affection to this woman who he knows is a murderer that the complexity of his own role in this case becomes palpable. He glances at the photograph and says, "They are funny, aren't they?" He then looks her in the eye and says, "You were pretty. They didn't affect your eyes." Thus, at the moment that he is orchestrating exactly the event that will trap her, or at least expose her, he also seems to adore her, holding his gaze on her for several seconds. This scene is yet another in which murder is not really the focus of the series but rather an opportunity to investigate something else entirely—in this case, another era of the movies, lost time, and the very material nature of film itself, whether in the body of the actress or the strip of celluloid.

The group finally sits down in Grace's screening room, which, like the actress herself, has a casual, graceful elegance. Most likely more luxurious, but not *entirely* unlike the rooms where we might be watching *Columbo*, it is unmistakably part of a larger domestic space: with one side of the room open to the rest of the home, the perpendicular walls house the window through which the film is projected on one side and the wall that holds the screen on the other. The film on-screen is thus situated in this domestic space, with a lamp to its right and armchairs in front (with the three viewers sitting near the back of the wall). As the film begins, the camera moves so that we see the three figures in the darkness, their cigarette and cigar smoke rising to meet the light of the projector. The scene patiently cuts between the audience and the image of the film on-screen. Rendered thus patiently, the scene erupts again when the film breaks: we see a jagged edge of the film, and then the screen turns completely white. After Grace rushes back to fix the film, Columbo admits that he "tampered with the film to make sure it would break." As much a test as it is a point of instruction, Columbo whispers, "Let's see how long it takes her to repair the film." He watches her through the window between the projection "booth" and the screening room. Through his point of view, we see her at the splicer reel, and Columbo narrates the

6.6. The projector's glare ("Forgotten Lady," 5:1; Sept. 14, 1975)

6.7. The lieutenant's gaze ("Forgotten Lady," 5:1; Sept. 14, 1975)

course of events to his companion and to us: "Seems to know what she's doing. Knows how to work the splicer. You see, actually this is a very simple procedure. Even a child could do it." It takes her only a matter of seconds to cut the film and then tape and repair it on the machine, which means, of course, that she can't exactly account for the fifteen minutes of "lost time" the night her husband was murdered.

In both cases the projector sets the killer's alibi, as in each she claims that she had to be present in order, respectively, to change the reel or to view the film at a particular moment. Thus, the projector, like other forms of technology on the show, is associated with time. Of course, that is the work of any alibi—an explanation that situates a person in one place at one particular time, for, obviously, a killer can't be in two different places at once. Interestingly, though, this exception to the space-time continuum is always the suggestion of film, in an ontological sense. That is, on the one hand, there is the time of the original recorded event, and, on the other, there is the time at which that event is re-placed in the new time and place of the theater. These two hands are of the same body—of film as a form, or maybe, again, ontologically speaking, of the film viewers, who are at once in the physical theater (or other viewing space) and in the time/space of the film before their eyes.

Surveying Technology

Perhaps because film conceptually enables a viewer to imagine being in two places at once—the site of viewing and the site of the world of the film—in these instances film itself does not function as the alibi or that which undoes the alibi; instead, that comes from the machine that runs the film, an electronic device. In several other episodes, electronic recording technologies are used to design alibis, to seemingly allow the *killer* to be in two places at once: the place where he or she commits the crime and the place where she or he is situated in time by the device that documents their presence in some form. For instance, in the case of the episode "Playback," our killer, Harold Van Wick, is the president of his mother-in-law's multimedia company, but what she disapprovingly calls his "obsessive preoccupation with gadgetry" is producing a deficit both in his attention to work and in the company's finances. His mother-in-law therefore wants to oust him from his position and replace him with her seemingly less efficient son; given the nearly inexplicable wifely devotion of her wheelchair-bound daughter (played by Gena Rowlands—Falk's costar in another medium altogether, as I noted in chapter 5), the mother invites her son-in-law for a private conversation in order to sack him. She demands his resignation and threatens him with blackmail—proof of his extramarital affairs she will show her daughter—if he refuses to go along with her plan. Through a complicated technological setup in which he plays multiple roles in its visual production, the son-in-law proceeds immediately to orchestrate her murder.

Van Wick has installed in the house a security system whose control room is situated next to the library. This sequence begins in the control room; Harold stands amid the machines: a video deck, monitors, reel-to-reel recorders. From this establishing shot, the image cuts to offer us a point of view behind him, with the reel-to-reel tape in front of him. He presses the buttons to create "playback" (marked as such above the button), and the camera pans up so that our view now shifts to the screen of the monitor, with the first image slightly staggered, alerting us that this is a recording rather than the space of the library "live." Reminiscent of the opening sequence of "Murder by the Book," no dialogue appears; we hear only the sounds of the machines buzzing along, with Chopin emanating from the living-room stereo in the background. As Harold leaves the room, we cut to the house's private security cottage, where three screens are set on a desk before their private guard, Baxter (played by Herbert Jefferson Jr., known for his role as Lieutenant Boomer in the 1970s *Battlestar Galactica* film and television series). He holds the posture of a working television viewer—slightly slumped in his chair, but attentive to the screens before him. From Baxter, we return to Harold, who begins to set the scene in the library, using his remote-control clicker to move the doors to the library slightly. As we return to the image of the guard and his monitors, we become aware—that is, if we are as attentive to our screen as he is—that he is seeing something different than what is actually taking place at the time. Now Harold returns to the control room, where he resets the machines to begin recording again.

From here, the scene cuts to Harold's mother-in-law sitting on the sofa. She finishes her glass of brandy with a little flourish, unwinds her feet, and stands up, turning off the Chopin and opening the door with a clap of her hands. She is in a good mood; she's fired her son-in-law, put things right. But after she walks out the door from the living room to the hall, she hears a crash from the library and turns to investigate. Here she finds Harold, who immediately shoots her as she turns to go back out the door. At the moment that he fires at her, the scene shifts to the control room, where we see her fall in black and white on the monitor's

6.8. A staged alibi for the viewer ("Playback," 4:5; March 2, 1975)

screen. The camera then pans down to the machine, following the reel-to-reel recording of the videotape. From the tape we then cut to Harold live in the library and his mother-in-law dead before him. And again we cut to the guard, Baxter, who continues to attentively watch the monitor, seeming to be vaguely unsettled by something, even though the images on the screens in front of him remain the same.

Now the killer continues to go to work: he turns off the recording, and as he picks up a timer, the phone rings. Harold enters the library to answer it. For the first time in a nearly three-minute stretch, dialogue ensues. It's his wife, Elizabeth, who has awakened because she thinks she's heard something downstairs. He reassures her as he grabs an envelope from the table and puts it in his jacket pocket. Upon his return to the control room, he rewinds the tape, plugs the cord from the video machine into a timer, sets the timer by his watch, and inserts a second cord (connected to the monitor) into the plug labeled "recorder." He leaves the room, clicks the door closed with his remote control, steps around his mother-in-law, claps the front door open, and exits the house.

As I said, the killer plays a variety of roles in this production. He acts as both set designer and director as he establishes the scene, manipulating lighting, framing, and objects in the mise-en-scène. Adjusting the video board, he plays editor (and, in the context of live television, director). One of the primary actors in this recorded theater, he walks along designated cues in preparation for his invisible performance. And, like a projectionist, he organizes the running of the videotape for his initial audience member, the security guard. Throughout, we follow the minute mechanical details of this setup through the close-ups of the machines. The cords and buttons guide us, as do the screens in the control room and the security guard's cottage. Such detail allows us to recognize both what is recorded and what is "live" and surely indicates the difference between them. By pointing to all of these technical elements of its construction, this scene allows us to witness the very process of a television production and ultimately the illusions we come to accept of the form. That is, because television has the capacity to be broadcast live, it carries with it what Jane Feuer has called its ideological "liveness."[4] Yet, time and again, *Columbo* reveals the myth of televisual liveness, demonstrating instead the ways by which recording technologies intercede to merely produce the *sense* of a live broadcast—a lie or illusion that murder is dependent upon. In this unveiling of television's illusion, episodes like "Playback" suggest that our own view is the most "live," if also the most highly produced. What makes it so "live" is that we are offered multiple views; we witness simultaneous times. Thus, our view—that is, of *Columbo* itself—is also the most foolproof. Over and again, in fact, television as an on-screen object even exposes the time of death.[5]

This concomitant veiling and unveiling of the work of recording technologies is part of a number of episodes of the series, each managed in a slightly different context. In fact, we get a somewhat similar orchestration of events as in "Playback"—and therefore a similar construction of an alibi—in an episode from season 3 entitled "Double Exposure" (written by Stephen J. Cannell and starring Robert Culp in a similar role to one he played two seasons prior). In this case, the episode opens with the killer's preparations. The second shot we see is a glass case displaying a set of guns. From this image we cut to a close-up of a hand

6.9–6.12. An obsessive preoccupation with gadgetry ("Playback," 4:5; March 2, 1975)

hitting the play button on a small cassette recorder: a voice announces from the machine, "Nothing can happen in this country until someone sells something. We are . . ." The hand hits "stop" and rewinds. Another cut reveals a medium shot of the man to whom this hand belongs. He then exits from behind a curtain on a stage, and the credits begin with the information already revealed to us by the presence of the actor: "Guest Stars ROBERT CULP." From here he exits the stage and then the larger auditorium. He unlocks a closet door and increases the dial on a thermostat. We cut again to see him standing before a light table, expertly splicing one frame of a filmstrip: a glass of soda with ice. He then splices a larger strip of film and sutures the single frame into it. As he plays the reel of film on a Steenbeck, our point of view shifts between what's on the screen before him and an image of him watching it. As he winds the strip of film very slowly, we see the frame with the soda appear between other frames of a desert scene. After he sets the film to rewind, he checks and then unscrews something on the back of the security monitor with images of the hallway outside. He is interrupted by the need to check the film, which is just rewinding. A veritable media multitasker, he then returns to complete the first job, eliminating the image from the security monitor—almost caught by the projectionist who enters the room just as he is finishing up. This entire sequence, like that in "Playback," is without dialogue; aside from the recorded device on tape, we hear only the whir of machines as the killer readies himself. But after the projectionist enters the scene and thereafter, we begin to understand the context for the criminal act through their discussion.

A psychologist of consumerism whose stock-in-trade includes subliminal advertising and blackmail, Dr. Bart Kepple (Culp) is on the brink of being exposed by his client Vic Norris, who refuses to give in when Kepple shows him compromising photographs of Norris and a young woman. So Dr. Kepple designs a murder to take place during a screening of a film about advertising and consumer desire, which he narrates live behind the stage curtain. A master of manipulation, his goal is to create such overwhelming thirst in his intended victim that he will leave the auditorium, at which point Kepple will exchange the audio recording for his own voice, exit the room from behind the stage, and shoot his victim in the hallway. As he readies himself for this event, we see the intermingling of multiple formats in one fell swoop: analog audio, video, and film. The liveness of broadcast television, represented by the video feed that we will see Kepple disconnect, is a potential threat but also a potential lie—and here one of many, each enabled by recording technologies. A cassette recorder will fake the killer's presence in an auditorium; the still images he inserts into a film strip (itself revealed as a series of still images as he cuts and splices them), aided by the increase in temperature in the room, will produce a "false" sense of thirst through a subliminal messaging technique; and, of course, the video feed itself is turned off so as not to produce any electronic and/or human witnesses of the murder he is about to commit.

In what is a rather remarkable sequence, we see a series of machines and a series of screens—in both "sequential" and "adjacent" formats, terms that the media theorist Anne Friedberg offers by way of distinction in her description of the common structure of moving-image windows (with the sequential dominant, of course, as the sequence represents a continuous flow of images). But as Friedberg also notes, "The . . . television viewer is a *montagist*, composing a sequenced view from a database of channels and delivery formats, a random set of synchronic alternatives to the single-screen view."[6] In both "Playback" and "Double Exposure," *Columbo* offers such an image of the television screen and viewer as replete with multiple views, multiple formats. Juggling them appears in each case as a nefarious act, the work of a killer. But witnessing them— is that another kind of work? I would suggest that in the same way that we see these various machines and screens coexist on the television set, the murder and its solution are also simultaneously rendered for us. In other words, by witnessing the arrangement of murder, in this case enabled by television form to become "montagists," we learn how to detect its solution. In fact, Columbo ultimately solves the case in "Playback" by reading carefully the image that the killer provides as his alibi—noting, in particular, the appearance of an object on the scene that belies the "liveness" of the murder caught on tape. And in "Double Exposure," he traps Kepple through copying his own methods, having spliced still photographs of himself investigating his office into a film that Kepple runs for clients.

While I find these various scenes in "Playback" and "Double Exposure" to be remarkable in and of themselves—especially in their magnification of machines and technological processes—what might be equally remarkable is the similarity between the two of them. Yet I don't think the repetition of this trope of the technologically inclined murderer is a simple formulaic element of the series. Rather, it indicates the series' fascination with emerging technological forms. In this way, decades after its making, the television-media text *Columbo* reveals media objects to be what Lisa Gitelman calls "denizens of the past."[7] Part of what those objects contain, moreover, is the history of surveillance culture in the early to mid-1970s. After all, the FBI had become known for wiretapping many prominent figures, such as Martin Luther King Jr., and for infiltrating organizations such as the Black Panther Party and the American Communist Party. US presidents had been audiotaping their phone conversations for years, but, of course, in 1972 the story of President Richard Nixon's wiretapping of the National Democratic Party headquarters broke. At this point, too, the nation witnessed displays of work with recording technologies through Nixon's assistant, Rose Mary Woods, who both took partial responsibility for the erasure of key tapes surrounding the Watergate break-in and demonstrated how she managed to misuse the machines. In a March 1974 feature article, "Rose Mary Woods—the Lady or the Tiger?," Nora Ephron even documents the machines that Woods used, from the "cumbersome" Sony tape recorder she originally worked with to transcribe (and potentially erase) the notorious recording of June 2, 1972, at Camp David, to the new Uher 5000 she used back at the White House.[8]

Surveillance technology, particularly via Nixon's audiotapes, was therefore in the air, and *Columbo* certainly reflected this cultural moment, even referring to a commentary on this phenomenon in an episode about a murderous police commissioner. In the midst of the investigation of a second murder during "A Friend in Deed," Columbo asks another detective how he understands the behavior of the burglar, who apparently changed his modus operandi and became a killer. "Haven't you heard of *Future Shock*?" he responds. "Times have changed." To look at a 1970s television series like *Columbo*, which moves at what seems like an unusually slow pace in the context of twenty-first-century media production, it might seem hard to imagine its era as one that was also characterized by rapid technological change, which Alvin Toffler's book *Future Shock* (1970) defined in terms of information overload. The acceleration of change—whether industrial, architectural, medial, fashion, or other—was so rapid that it produced in consumers and citizens a sense of "future shock." Moreover, Toffler wrote, "Without time, change has no meaning."[9] Over and again, *Columbo* documents these changes via the variety of media forms that it represents, inevitably linking them to time itself. And linked to change, to technology, and to time, both

Toffler and *Columbo* show, is knowledge. According to Toffler, "If technology . . . is to be regarded as a great engine, a mighty accelerator, then knowledge must be regarded as its fuel."[10] He is largely describing the imagination needed to develop changing technologies, but, of course, these relations are circular. With change comes the impulse to understand. And this is Columbo's modus operandi.

Besides these longer meditations on emerging media forms, the series does indeed show a preoccupation with gadgets, even if they play only a brief or supporting role in the plot. Indeed, this fascination was there from the beginning, in the pilot, "Ransom for a Dead Man." In yet another episode starring Robert Culp, "The Most Crucial Game," the killer's alibi is at first preserved and then broken through a combination of surveillance recording of his phone and a transistor radio. In "An Exercise in Fatality," the killer regularly records his phone conversations, so he is also able to splice parts of one to create the pretense of a conversation with the man he has already murdered; in a neatly layered representation of old and new media, his efforts are showcased as he projects a 16mm film for his party guests. And both "An Exercise in Fatality" and "Short Fuse" briefly showcase answering machines. Add to this the fascination with moving-image media, and we might see television itself as a kind of information-gathering system, a knowledge accelerator.

Television's Realignments

In the case of *Columbo*, I see inscribed within it a history of media objects, but media transformation was certainly a fascination of its time of production. This particular fascination with technology in turn reveals an element of the most infamous line of Marshall McLuhan (who, like Toffler, was also in the air during this period): that the medium is the message. In a chapter entitled "The Gadget Lover" in his *Understanding Media* (1964), McLuhan explores the work of medical researchers and theorists in order to draw a link between media forms and human bodies in an attempt to define this fascination and its effects. As he writes, "The principle of self-amputation [is] an immediate relief of strain on the central nervous system. . . . Whatever threatens its function must be contained, localized, or cut off, even to the total removal

6.13. "Boy genius" Steve Spelberg ("Mind over Mayhem," 3:6, Feb. 10, 1974)

of the offending organ."[11] He then argues that electronic technologies function as an extension of that nervous system, one set outside of ourselves. But these extensions are also forms of self-amputation (especially of our "organs" and of our senses); as such, they also *fragment* us. This warning about our social and psychic fragmentation through electronic technology is central to McLuhan's argument.[12]

Nowhere is this notion clearer in *Columbo* than in the episode entitled "Mind over Mayhem," also part of season 3, two episodes after "Double Exposure," and penned by Steven Bochco, Dean Hargrove, and Roland Kibbee. Set at the "Cybernetic Research Institute," in this episode the soon-to-be murderer and head of the institute, Dr. Marshall Cahill, learns that one of his colleagues is going to blow the whistle on his son for plagiarizing research that has just won him a major award. Cahill encodes a robot—called "Double-M 7"—to stand in for him as the behind-the-scenes programmer of a war game for institute guests. This robot itself is the ultimate gadget, especially in McLuhan's terms. A recurring fantasy of this era, the robot is designed to carry out all those tasks we humans find annoying. In a remarkable scene, Columbo meets the designer of this robot, twelve-year-old "Steve Spelberg." Columbo quite reasonably assumes that the kid is the child of one of the researchers, but as Steve says, "I might as well tell you now. I am a boy genius." He then goes on to explain how Double-M 7 functions. This scene holds two marvelous references at once. The robot, after all, is "Robby the Robot" from *The Forbidden Planet* and *Lost in Space*, among other guest appearances. And the kid is a neat reference to "boy genius" Steven Spielberg, who hung around Universal Studios as a teen and, in his early twenties, had directed the first episode of the first full season of *Columbo*.[13]

Still, McLuhan's critique regarding the "strain" on our "nervous system" is also implicit throughout *Columbo*. For one thing, as I have said, these devices allow people to commit murder, a definitively inhumane act. As Columbo exposes the nefarious *uses* of these tools—which might be somewhat nefarious in and of themselves to our low-tech, underpaid detective—the series also suggests a privileging of *television* as an electronic medium, at least when it is used appropriately. Several episodes even suggest that the medium of television itself can help catch the criminals. This is true in episodes when Columbo finds clues via the television, such as in "Étude in Black," as I discussed in chapter 5, or in episodes such as "Double Shock" (2:8; March 25, 1973), in which a television's malfunction marks the time of death. Other examples are "Requiem for a Falling Star," when a television airing of an old film starring the killer sparks a clue for the detective; "Dead Weight," when Columbo watches television in a bar and sees a news story on the killer's illustrious military career; "Any Old Port in a Storm," in which Columbo is reminded via television of the weather on the day the victim died; and "Make Me a Perfect Murder," when he catches a key segment of the diegetic made-for-television movie as his own television is being repaired. The notion that television might help enact and then land a murderer also surfaces in "Fade in to Murder," when we are introduced to an emerging ancillary technology for television itself, the VCR.

Appearing in the penultimate season of the series, "Fade in to Murder" features Ward Fowler (William Shatner), an actor who plays a

6.14. Technological and temporal alibis ("Fade in to Murder," 6:1; Oct. 10, 1976)

television detective called "Detective Lucerne" and who kills his black-mailing, rich producer. To do so, he drugs a friend during a live base-ball game on television, sets his VCR to record the rest while he runs out to commit the crime, and then returns home to rewind the game and awaken his friend so that it seems only a few moments have passed while he was out. The VCR provides the killer's alibi, but it also es-sentially "records" a clue to his crime. Toward the end of the episode, Columbo arrives to have a further discussion with the killer. The scene opens with Ward Fowler, performing as Lucerne, recording Columbo. As Fowler follows him around the room, the camera is plugged into the television, so we simultaneously see the live action take place and the recorded performance on the television screen in the middle of the frame. After Columbo repeatedly interrupts his own pretend interroga-tion with laughter, Fowler ends the taping, rewinds the tape in the VCR, and puts the camera away. The two men sit side-by-side at the edge of a table like old chums (a chess set and an Emmy statuette behind them) and watch the TV together. The image cuts between a medium shot of the

6.15. Ward Fowler shoots Columbo ("Fade in to Murder," 6:1; Oct. 10, 1976)

television, our two viewers, and then a close-up of the screen, so that eventually their on-screen television virtually engulfs our own. At the end of the viewing, Fowler turns off the set, and Columbo begins another (very friendly) interrogation, starting with a question about the cost of the VCR. When Fowler tells him, "Three thousand, not counting the camera," Columbo responds incredulously, "Three thousand? Dollars? I could get a new car with that—not that I need one."

The layers of self-reflexivity throughout this episode are therefore both performative and technological, dependent, as they are, on three primary conceits: Columbo's ability to "act" as a "bad" detective, the notoriously "bad" actor William Shatner's ability to act as one who thinks he is a better one, and Columbo's investigation of this new recording machine. Originally airing in October 1976, "Fade in to Murder" appears in the midst of the development of the new domestic apparatus; Betamax comes on the scene in 1975, while VHS appears in 1976.[14] As with other gadgets similarly presented and investigated in the series, here we get a brief material history of this emerging technology: a visible evidence of emerging technological tools, an instructional guide for their use, and an acknowledgment of their monetary cost. As this particular machine records a live sporting event, the series records a historical and cultural moment in which this machine emerges. The VCR in particular, moreover, allows for a self-reflexive admission of the series' own modus operandi: its dual investigation of cultural objects and the instruction of the detective himself in their operations. Part of this self-reflexivity is connected to the act of detection itself. Unlike other procedurals in which technological forms are the tools of the investigators, in the case of *Columbo* these gadgets are *objects* of his investigation. As Columbo himself learns to understand these objects, rather than acting as a tool for its acquisition, technology provides the confirmation of the knowledge he already holds regarding the identity of the murderers themselves.

The Death of Television: Long Live Television

To conclude, I want to return to the episode with which I began: "Make Me a Perfect Murder." Like "Fade in to Murder," also set within the context of the television industry itself, this episode features a woman who has just hit the glass ceiling. Her lover and boss is invited to take over the network's base in NYC; when he first tells her the news, she thinks he's inviting her along, and when he disabuses her of that idea, she thinks he's leaving her in LA to run the show there. But that's not the case either. After spurning her so, the lover says, "You wanna sue me? Shoot me?" He tosses a gun on the bed and says, "Make me a perfect murder, babe." As the title of the episode, this line is an enticement: for the character, the audience, and the show itself. After all, no murder on the show is ever exactly perfect, since Columbo always solves them. However, as narratives of murder—especially because they are replete with the solution—the series' episodes come pretty darn close.

And Kay Freestone does stage if not a perfect murder, at least an impressive technologically syncopated one. The success of her alibi is, of course, predicated on time. As a woman in the television industry, she's able to work across media objects and formats in order to time the events perfectly. Hence, as I noted in the beginning, she first resets the clock on a projector to suggest that the reel will need to be changed sooner rather than later. After assuring Walter, the projectionist, that she can do it herself, she uses an audiotape of her own voice to help her keep time. During a four-minute segment, the primary dialogue we hear, beyond the startled response of the victim, is the recording of her counting down four minutes on a small tape player as she travels through the building in order to commit the deed.

During the course of his eventual investigation, another lengthy and technologically centered sequence takes place, which I described in the introduction. Trained by the technical director in the workings of the director's console, complete with the seven screens before him, the lieutenant is pleasantly fascinated, showing the television audience he's a quick study when he plays with the board after the director leaves. However pleasurable in this moment, the detective's mechanical training serves him well later in the episode when he traps Miss Freestone. Through a fairly complicated ruse, he organizes a meeting at an amusement park, where the made-for-TV movie she's producing is being shot. Freestone attempts to hide from him in a production trailer, but Columbo uses the television machinery to track her down. Speaking into the ether to her, she responds, and he realizes that she can see him through a camera on the set. When we return to Freestone's point of view, we see Columbo himself from different angles, on multiple screens, insisting that he talk with her. Attempting to refuse, Freestone also tries to rid her screens of the detective, frantically pushing buttons to alter the cameras' input. But the lieutenant's doggedness here appears to extend to technology. The more buttons she pushes, the more insistent is his image on the screens, even while it becomes increasingly distorted. Columbo appears through glitches, from different angles, and, in one monitor, surfacing in black and white. And in another monitor, he even shares his own image with that of a geometrical shape from the earlier scene at the studio. Glitches and all, our detective here controls the television apparatus itself.

I started out by suggesting that *Columbo* is about the investigation of its contemporaneous technologies alongside murder. In fact, I would say, murder becomes a delivery platform for our understanding of technological and cultural forms, revealing a particular manifestation and subsequent history of an evolving intermedial culture. In other

6.16. Columbo is live ("Make Me a Perfect Murder," 7:3; Feb. 25, 1978)

6.17. Televisual contortions ("Make Me a Perfect Murder," 7:3; Feb. 25, 1978)

words, television inscribes a history of itself in its fictional narratives like *Columbo*. Ironically, then, with murder as a delivery platform, the series also guards against the death of television.

I want here to conclude by suggesting both something even grander as well as something grounded in our everyday experience with the medium. This duality—of the grand and the mundane, a dream and a material thing—is spelled out early on in the series, through the script for "Étude in Black," when Columbo appears in his vet's office and "stands there looking dreamily at the TV set."[15] To begin with the grand: by exposing the fallacies enabled by electronic and recording technologies—that someone could be somewhere *else* at some *time* (indeed, *any*where at *any* time)—Columbo is also realigning the time-space continuum. After all, technology might help save time or seemingly mask it, but it cannot control time. In "Make Me a Perfect Murder," then, this temporal realignment (or the acknowledgment that technology does not control time) is enabled by television itself. Appearing in 1978, in the final season of the original series and toward the end of the broadcast era, this episode anticipates the destabilization on the part of its own medium in the era to come; no longer simply marking time, television will become part of a media culture that insists on shifting time. Yet, as the series ultimately privileges television above other electronic media, it effectively attempts to establish its own alibi in the age of acceleration. Like the eponymous detective, television doggedly tracks time and makes history in the 1970s. In particular, *Columbo* works through television's role in the process of the sorts of fragmentation and auto-amputation that McLuhan cautioned against some twelve years prior.

At the same time, in reimagining the "golden age" of television and trying to grasp on to the broadcast era before it loses its place, "Make Me a Perfect Murder" at once critiques and situates television as a singular, stabilizing force—one that is embodied by Columbo himself, our low-tech genius, and by the singular set in our living rooms during the age of its broadcast. After all, even while "television" is ethereal—in its broadcast (or cable or digital) signals and its amorphous textual forms—*Columbo* shows again and again that media forms are also material things. Though time slips through our fingers, the television set itself is the thing that we touch, even as it's replaced by other technological gadgets on which to watch. In effect, we now hold television in our hands every day—which may be part of the dream, or the shock, of the future itself.

7 Columbo's Reign

OF LIFE AND DEATH AND DETECTION

I was in disguise in disguise in disguise.
—"Sam Diamond" (Peter Falk), *Murder by Death*

In my own obsessive preoccupation with *Columbo*, the film and television texts I've gathered together here have a cumulative thrust. Over time they spin less like a spoked wheel and more like the spiral of DNA; in this double helix, their fictional and material narratives twist around one another. I look at one text, and I see it imbricated in another. Those overlaps become compounded as I watch and read and write, both clarifying and complicating the essence of *Columbo* itself, as the ancestry and the inheritances of the series spiral together. And then, by the time of the original series' end, Columbo as a character and *Columbo* as a series begin to turn on themselves.

Thinking through the "DNA" of the series is to recognize not only its ancestry and structure, but also its progeny and its mutations.[1] Thus, in spinning this analogy, I want to consider how, like the basic structural unit of DNA, *Columbo*'s texts and intertexts are also bound together.[2] They are structurally joined through the industries of film and television and through those figures—Falk, Levinson and Link, Cassavetes, and many, many others—that move between the series' constituent parts. Traces of this character are left on Falk, whether it was Falk's personality that intrinsically shaped Columbo or his role as Columbo that shaped him as an actor. In turn, knowledge of Peter Falk as Columbo clings to the viewer even when the actor appears outside of the original show and/or outside of the original role, whether in films of the same era or in those films that are part of the series' and the character's own "progeny."

Given how the series and its eponymous character shift over time, this metaphor could be pushed further to include the gene-editing tool CRISPR. Standing for "clustered regularly interspaced short palindromic repeats," CRISPR and its mutagenic ability possess an uncanny parallel to a description of television itself. After all, able to alter DNA sequences and modify gene function, CRISPR could also describe those "mutations" of the original series and of the eponymous character himself: if the continuous strand of original DNA is *Columbo*, other television series and films act as its gene-editing tool. Like a pair of molecular scissors, other texts insert themselves into the series, changing the meaning of the whole itself and thus creating a mutation. Furthermore, as the parts integrate into one another, the function and the expression of the whole have the potential to shift, to twist, to tangle together. In fact, it's precisely because the double helix itself is not perfectly symmetrical that it makes sense as an analogy for a means of understanding *Columbo*'s textual and intertextual formation, for it displays a sort of distorted mirror image of itself even before the more formal manipulation of an "editing tool."

Such asymmetrical, even distorted, turns expose themselves in moments within the original series, such as in "Murder under Glass." In this second episode of the final season, with a plot that concerns the murder of a chef by a blackmailing restaurant critic, our detective seems to have magically accumulated knowledge, or at least he reveals knowledge we might have only sensed he had. If in the first official episode, "Murder by the Book," he claimed that the one thing he knew how to cook was an omelet, in "Murder under Glass" he is suddenly an expert at Italian cuisine (and, moreover, speaks Italian as well). It's not just his cooking powers that have transformed; the detective's performance (or that by the actor Falk) has also shifted to become a little less sincere, a little more smarmy. He exaggerates the traits with which we're already familiar, whether in his pauses, his gestures, or even the drawl of his voice. And in that performance, this episode gestures toward the reboot that will emerge a little more than a decade later.

Perhaps Falk's performance in "Murder under Glass," directed by future filmmaker Jonathan Demme, was itself informed, or "edited," by two movies Falk had recently made—both spoofs of the detective genre, in which he plays a version of the titular detective. As I've noted, he made two films with writer Neil Simon (both directed by Robert Moore): *Murder by Death* in 1976 and *The Cheap Detective* in 1978.[3] Capitalizing on the emerging popularity of the parody film in this era, each cast Falk as a hardboiled detective of sorts. In *Murder by Death*, he is Sam Diamond, cloaked in a trench coat, speaking out of one side of his mouth like a poor man's Humphrey Bogart in a Raymond Chandler adaptation. He joins four other famous detectives—all spoofs on various characters, including Dashiell Hammett's Nick and Nora Charles, Agatha Christie's Hercule Poirot and Miss Marple, and Earl Derr Biggers's Charlie Chan. In contrast to the others, Sam Diamond is not just hardboiled; he's also hardscrabble. In a debate over whether murder is a "business," he lectures the other detectives about their own hidden riches. Apologizing to Mrs. "Charleston" for being so blunt, he says, "Sorry if I'm shocking you, ma'am, but I never had time to go to finishing school. My school is the streets, and looking down the barrel of a revolver is my teacher. I get fifty dollars a day and expenses when I can get 'em, gentlemen." He claims to owe his secretary (and mistress), Tess Skeffington (Eileen Brennan), three years and two months' back pay, as he announces that he doesn't solve murders for the money. But as the mystery unravels, so does Diamond's persona. In the act of attempting to unveil the murderer, he and Tess first spin a homophobic tale of Diamond's motive for killing the host (played by Truman Capote). But he soon after admits he isn't responsible at all: he is merely an actor playing Diamond.[4] Breaking character, he also breaks the film's fictional era: "[I'm] JJ Loomis. I'm an actor. I do impressions. I did the Carson show six times last year." And here, too, he sounds like someone else, for the staccato rhythm of his sentences sounds a lot more like Lieutenant Columbo, and the Carson reference is, of course, a lot more like Falk.

But even this unveiling is a ruse; as the film comes to an end, the characters realize the entire plot was a fabrication, with no one and nothing as it claimed or appeared. Driving away, Sam declares to Tess, "I was in disguise in disguise in disguise." Such a description could certainly be applied to William Shatner's character, known alternately and over time as Ward Fowler / Detective Lucerne / Charles Kipling / John Schnelling, in "Fade in to Murder," which screened on NBC four months after *Murder by Death* played in theaters. And it can also be increasingly applied to Falk's roles that emerge over the next several years, including when he plays the lieutenant again for ABC's reboot of the series. (Such disguises and mutations take a step further in the series *Mrs. Columbo*, which Levinson and Link refer to as "such a flagrant ripoff, and . . . so ill-conceived," that they "declined to participate" in its production.)[5] In fact, these parodies, spoofs, and metanarratives function in some ways like the formula of the series itself, as they are themselves dependent on the knowledge we already have before the detective enters the scene. But then this parallel begs the question: If the original *Columbo* trains its viewers in knowing television, what do these subsequent narratives reveal? How might they shape an understanding of the detective in the original and in its progeny of sorts when the detective returns to television over a decade after his initial departure?

If one thing in particular kept me working endlessly (perhaps doggedly) on this long labor of love, it was not merely the sense of the loss of that love that such completion often brings. Rather, it was also the looming duty to write about the reboot, which aired on ABC from 1989 to 2003 as a series of twenty-four movies. If I wear my heart on my sleeve sometimes when it comes to the original series (and when it comes to Falk, to Levinson and Link, to Cassavetes and Rowlands, and so on), I will here lay my cards on the table. I do not like the reboot. The skeleton of the original remains present in the structure of the mystery and in Falk himself, of course. But it's not the same series. It's not even a series in the sense that the original was, even if the original was also itself a series of "movies." For one thing, it lost the continuity of the original, and then it also lost much of the original's sensibility. Yet while I acknowledge my own (and my research assistants') dislike of the reboot, I do not mean to disrespect Falk—whom I greatly admire—or others involved in its production, particularly the original cocreators Levinson and Link, as well as others who worked closely with Falk in his later years. Rather, I want to recognize the ways in which it was and also was not *Columbo*. Therefore, I will indeed discuss it here, as it's an intrinsic part of the overall text and intertext that comprise *Columbo*, but rather than focusing on it either as a singular entity or as a continuation of the original, I will set it in relation to other works of the 1970s and 1980s as part of Falk's post-*Columbo* oeuvre—and hence its "edited" DNA. But first let me begin again with another ending.

First and Last

It's commonly recognized that we remember exactly where we were when we have heard news of extraordinary cultural events: the political assassinations of President John F. Kennedy and Martin Luther King Jr.; the attack on the Twin Towers; the announcement of victory or loss in significant elections. And, of course, we remember where and when we hear of personal news, such as the loss of someone we love or an announcement of a friend's pregnancy or birth of a child. Those moments of devastation and expectation stay with us, awash with details. Such moments stay with us because of their extraordinariness amid our ordinary lives—the shock of terrible or wonderful news. But we remember our ordinary habits, too: for me, this would include late Sunday afternoons in the early 1990s in Brooklyn, when my friend Aline and I would turn on the television set to watch *Columbo* in syndication on a local New York station, or weekday summer mornings in Milwaukee where I would sit on my green sofa and watch the series with breakfast when it aired regularly on A&E. I remember, too, bringing DVDs of the series into my dad's "senior living" apartment to watch together quietly over lunch—an attempt to revive an old memory for him as he was losing others. And I remember watching the series with my mom in the late afternoons a few years before then, when she took care of me following surgery. The first episode we watched during that time, in fact, was "A Stitch in Crime," about a surgeon who attempts to kill another surgeon, and it wracked her as she sat in the rocking chair to the left of my bed.

On June 24, 2011, I was taking a local bus home from work in western Massachusetts, when I checked the email on my phone. I had a message from a colleague I didn't know well, but one with whom I had recently shared a panel at our college about our current research, and I, of course, had been talking about *Columbo*. His email had the subject line "sad news about Peter Falk," with a message simply containing the link to the obituary in the *New York Times*. It was the first I heard of it, and I spontaneously began to weep, surprising myself with this depth of feeling. *I didn't know him*, I kept telling myself, and then I would silently respond, *but I loved him*. It's not remotely an overstatement to say that, though I felt alone on that public bus in Massachusetts, I wasn't remotely singular in my grief, as he was beloved throughout the world. In fact, during this same period, close friends of mine were traveling in Paris, and they brought home magazines for me with Falk on the covers, celebrating his life and announcing his death.

I had seen a public version of this global and local phenomenon in Paris myself, two years earlier when I watched *The Princess Bride* (Rob Reiner, 1987) at a repertory cinema in the Latin Quarter. The film begins with a mother tending to her son at home from school because he's sick. She announces that his grandfather has stopped by to look in on him, and he groans. The door opens, and there is Peter Falk as the grandfather, entering with aplomb: he spreads his arms outward, as if to say "Ta-da!" The Parisian audience (mostly young, it seemed to me) screamed with delight. Their response matched that within Wim Wenders's film *Wings of Desire*, produced the same year as *The Princess Bride*, in which Falk plays a version of himself, having traveled to Germany to make a film about World War II. When the actor walks through the streets, young people chant from windows above: "CO-LUM-BO! CO-LUM-BO!" Falk would refer to this real-life phenomenon in various interviews: "I've been to little villages in Africa with maybe one TV set, and little kids will run up to me shouting, 'Columbo! Columbo!'"[6] Granted, he also once claimed, "No one was put on this earth to be so well known by two billion strangers."[7]

But then Falk was and wasn't known by two billion strangers. That is, Falk was known as the fictional character he played, and this sentiment—the belief in "knowing" him and the affection for him—was borne out in much of his work during and after the completion of the original run of the series. In fact, even "knowing" Columbo the character is a funny thing. After all, we almost only ever see him at work. We know

7.1. The grandfather's entrance (*The Princess Bride*, Rob Reiner, 1987)

his habits of detection; we know that he is always up to the job. Outside of work, we largely see him at the vet's office with his dog or perhaps grabbing a bowl of chili at a little dive. We're not entirely sure he truly has a wife, and he (or the writers) is inconsistent on whether or not they have children. His impact on both the murderers he haunts and the audience who adores him is based on this sort of partial knowledge, stemming from misdirection. Falk would describe being drawn to the character precisely for this quality: "the basic thrust of a guy appearing less than he actually is."[8]

In this last chapter on Falk's work, as I consider an amalgam of texts produced near the end of the original series and after its initial run, I will continue with a method born through circles and spirals. To quote from an infamous line he shouts during *The In-Laws* (Arthur Hiller, 1979), I am tracing this work through a "serpentine" pattern of references—from television to film, from comedy to drama, from international and independent to US industrial productions.[9] And as in the scene from *The In-Laws* when Falk's character, Vince Ricardo, drags dentist Sheldon Kornpett (Alan Arkin) as they dodge bullets from a low-flying plane, my own approach (back and forth, stop and start) is directed by Falk. Of course, he is himself often directed by the most well-known character he played. Hence, I want here to remark on a series of patterns in Falk's work from the late 1970s through the early twenty-first century, forging an understanding of the "Columbo" presence across them, even in absentia.

Return to Character

Not unlike with "Sam Diamond," in the first half of *The In-Laws* it's unclear if Falk's character is as he appears, or even as he says he is. The film's premise begins quite simply: Sheldon and Carol Kornpett, the parents of a bride, Barbara, are preparing to host her wedding. The groom, Tommy Ricardo, and his parents, Vince and Jean, come for supper with the Kornpett family so they can finally all become acquainted. But Vince Ricardo is a little off. He tells an unbelievable story of tsetse flies that he encountered in the "bush" of Central America: "They have tsetse flies the size of eagles," he recounts. "In the evening I would stand in front of my hut and watch in horror as these flies would pick children off the ground and carry them away." As he speaks, Sheldon appears unfazed, while Jean clutches her chest and Carol gasps "My god." Vince continues, describing the villagers chasing the flies: "You can imagine the pathetic quality, waving these crudely fashioned brooms as these enormous flies carried off their children to an almost certain death." At this, Sheldon becomes more overtly skeptical: "Are you sure these are flies you're talking about?" Sheldon's suspicions go unnoticed by Vince, who continues with more preposterous details, describing the children grasped in the "beaks" of the flies. Now Sheldon appears bemused, interjecting: "Beaks? Flies with beaks?" Vince goes on to describe the "red tape" of the jungle, claiming that the flies were "protected . . . under the Guacamole Act of 1917." And with this utterance, a flash of mirth briefly crosses Vince's/Falk's face as well. Finally, Barbara interrupts her father to ask for some more wine before he continues his own interrogation of Vince. From this moment forward, the film inevitably invites us to wonder about Vince: Is he or isn't he the person he says he is? This is the question Lt. Columbo himself implicitly poses. After all, Levinson and Link designed the detective as "a character who's very bright but doesn't seem to be." As Link stated for a 1973 *Time* article on Falk, Columbo was "somebody who's not got much of an education and no social graces but takes advantage of his shortcomings."[10] In other words, one might say, he's a fellow who never had time for "finishing school."

It is impossible to do justice to such scenes from *The In-Laws*—especially to the weird and wonderful performance by Falk. Arkin himself performs perfect comic disbelief, whereas Falk's Ricardo (mostly) seems to believe the outrageous tale he tells. And as the film progresses, the improbable becomes inextricably linked to paranoia—governmental plots of collusion, surveillance, and conspiracy. Paranoia was hardly an explicit feature of *Columbo*—quite the opposite, really, in part because even in those episodes about governmental intrigue, the political is personalized between victim and killer. But, of course, paranoia was omnipresent in many films of the era. Coming at the end of this decade, which trafficked in political and cultural fears of conspiracy, as well as hybrid genres, *The In-Laws* integrates paranoia with comedy. And its comedy is richer because of Falk's performance, particularly as it is built on what we know from his role as the lieutenant. How can we possibly believe this man who appears to be something other than what he says or seems? But then again, how do we refuse him, too? Like the dogged lieutenant, Ricardo is persistent—and, like the detective, he is insistently charming.

Whereas Falk portrays a figure who is at least largely on the side of the "law" in *The In-Laws*, he plays a hood in films of the same era, as in *The Brink's Job* (William Friedkin, 1978) and *Cookie* (Susan Seidelman, 1989). These latter gigs recall both *Mikey and Nicky* and his early television work.[11] Playing both with and against type, such roles all dance around the law, reviving and resisting patterns developed in his first twenty years as an actor. Moreover, the fact that he costarred with John Cassavetes in May's film, while Gena Rowlands appears as his wife in *The Brink's Job*, is evocative of the other pattern of work he developed over the decade. In cast and character, then, this series of films reveals at once Falk's range during the period largely encompassing the original run of *Columbo* and those ways in which he could not escape that eponymous role.

Falk's late 1970s films preceded his partial, and early, retirement from acting. During that latter period he took up drawing and painting in earnest, and he made only two appearances in films in the first half of

7.2. Falk plays the dubious charmer (*The In-Laws*, Arthur Hiller, 1979)

the 1980s.[12] But in the mid-1980s he was drawn back into regular work, first for a revival of his work in 1986 with Alan Arkin in *Big Trouble*. Like *The In-Laws*, this film was also penned by Andrew Bergman, and Bergman started as director, though Cassavetes took over the helm (and retained the full credit for that role) in great part as a favor to Falk. A messy caper inspired by *Double Indemnity*, the film was nearly pulled from theaters and ultimately met with a mixed critical response. Forgiving its "haphazard" qualities, for instance, *New York Times* reviewer Vincent Canby notes that the film largely appears to be a "collaboration among friends."[13] The last film directed by his friend before his death in 1989, *Big Trouble* bore some personal significance, but more notable was Falk's work in 1987 and the years that followed.

In Wim Wenders's 1987 gorgeous masterpiece *Wings of Desire*, Peter Falk is listed as a "special appearance"—special, in part, because he plays a version of himself, the actor Peter Falk. As the film begins, we follow an angel's observations throughout the city of Berlin and beyond; this angel, Damiel (Bruno Ganz), is unseen by all humans except for small children, and he has the ability to listen in on the thoughts of the people he witnesses. Thus, he even appears in the aisles of a plane on its way to Berlin, where Peter Falk seems to be studying his lines for his part in a film. After he arrives at the set, Falk talks to a teenager who describes to him the narrative of a book, and the actor comments that "it's not too plausible." The kid says, "It's more realistic than the film we're making," to which Falk responds, "People like detective stories. So any excuse to make a detective story. It's dopey, but this is dopey, too." The two are interrupted by a woman who takes the actor's picture, and Falk intercedes in turn: "Erika, come on, give me a break. No more pictures." The film is structured by the various intersections that these interactions suggest: scenes shift through the meeting of characters as if they are passing the baton in a relay. Hence, while the photographer moves away, Falk stops a costumer to complain about his hat. Carrying on a conversation while the camera pulls away to focus on other elements of the set, Falk says, "I want to look like a German. I want to look anonymous." And now the camera finds him again, in front of a mirror, with the angel Cassiel (Otto Sander) at his side. Falk and the costumer each dismiss various options, such as one that makes him look like "Humphrey Bogart" or another that makes him look like a "gangster." Upon finding the right one, she tells him, "You look like somebody's grandfather." He nods at his reflection in the mirror as the angel Cassiel passes him.

As Falk wanders away in his new hat, the camera hovering above him like an angel lightly over ground, we are privy to his thoughts. He muses about his old detective's coat, interrupting himself to ask, "What is it, Peter? Why does your mind stray?" As he moves away, other performers appear, their thoughts available to us via Damiel. Momentarily Falk comes upon a woman and asks to sketch her, the two of them wondering about one another. Falk's mind continues to wander a bit as he sketches: "These people are extras. Extra people . . . extras. These humans are extras. Extra-humans. . . . Yellow star means death. Why did they pick yellow?" And so it goes. Later Falk strays again, wandering through the ruins of the city. He thinks, "Walking, looking and seeing. I wish you were here, Grandma." In his lovingly erudite study of Wenders's film, Christian Rogowski remarks on the poignancy of this moment. However inconsistent the character "Falk" plays in the film, Rogowski writes, "Falk's self-deprecating American-Jewish mannerisms attain greater depth by way of giving him a German-Jewish grandmother (with her admonitions of '*Go spazieren!*'), a gesture that ties Falk's character

7.3. "You look like somebody's grandfather" (*Wings of Desire*, Wim Wenders, 1987)

more closely to Berlin's traumatic history and issues of remembrance."[14] As Falk continues his walk through the streets of Berlin, his thoughts again run between the quotidian and the profound: "This must be the station they told me about, with the funny name. Not the station where the train stopped, but the station where the station stopped." At this point a group of young men pass him, and one of them asks, "Isn't that Columbo?" His friend responds, "Don't think so, not with that shabby coat." Within this film, Falk is at once Columbo and not-Columbo, an American who wants to look German, and a man who now resembles a grandfather, the very role he played in *The Princess Bride* the same year.

Being Lieutenant Columbo

Together Falk's own affection for the eponymous character along with these cinematic appearances as versions both of himself and of a detective set the foundation for his portrayal of the lieutenant the second time around. Thus, in 1989, eleven years after the final season of the original and two years after *The Princess Bride* and *Wings of Desire*, Falk returned to television as Columbo, in the ABC made-for-television movies that ran intermittently for the next fourteen years. The ABC iteration of *Columbo*, like the original, began as part of a wheel series: the ABC *Monday Mystery Movie*, which also included *Gideon Oliver* (starring Louis Gossett Jr.) and *B. L. Stryker* (which brought Burt Reynolds back to television). The following year, *Columbo* was part of the ABC *Saturday Mystery Movie* wheel series, of which *Christine Cromwell* (starring Jaclyn Smith) and a reboot of *Kojak* (with Telly Savalas) were also a part (the latter was particularly notable, given that *Columbo* and *Kojak* were programming rivals in the 1970s). Overall, the twenty-four films that aired on ABC mostly appeared from mid-season into spring. After its only consistent run during its initial two years, the new *Columbo* was no longer part of a wheel series. Four episodes appeared in the winter and spring of 1989 on Monday nights, and six episodes ran from November 1989 through May 1990 on Saturday nights for the first five and Monday for the final one. After these first two years, *Columbo* became even more of a "movie" than a series. Three films apiece appeared over the following three years (on inconsistent nights), and five final films ran over the next several years from May 1995 until the final one was broadcast on January 30, 2003.

Though starting barely more than a decade after the original series ended, the iterations of the show and the character himself are radically different. Granted, the scaffolding is largely the same: the murders still take place at the beginning of most narratives, the movies are filled with relatively well-known guest stars (though more are known from television than from film), the killers are rich denizens of Los Angeles, and Columbo still appears to the killers as absent-minded, seemingly not up to the task of solving their crimes. However, the tone—and with it some of the significant details that made *Columbo* so distinct— inexorably changed in the ABC movies. Some of those changes may be difficult to trace, subject to a viewer's loyalty to the original. But some of the changes are objective facts, pure and simple. Two marked losses took place before this reboot: the death of John Cassavetes on February 3, 1989, and the death of *Columbo* cocreator Richard Levinson on March 12, 1987. Whereas the surviving member of the team, William Link, helped to convince Falk to do another run, Link himself was downgraded from executive producer in the first year of the films to a "created by" credit with Levinson in the second year.

The inconsistency of scheduling matched the inconsistency of the production team. While about half of the twenty-four films were either penned or directed by someone who had been involved in the original, the involvement of these team members was somewhat scattershot, and usually these veterans of the original did not work alongside one another, with the exception of their collaboration with Falk. Ultimately, very few of the original writers and directors were on board with the new films, though the first season of the films did feature directors Leo Penn, Sam Wanamaker, and James Frawley; for instance, Wanamaker, who had directed the "Bye-Bye Sky High I.Q. Murder Case" episode in season 6, directed the fourth production in the reboot, and Frawley, who had directed three of the episodes of the final season of the original, reappeared to direct two of the new films in the first season. Even more significant was the lack of continuity of original writers. Only six of the twenty-four movies were written by veterans of the original series: Steven Bochco penned "Uneasy Lies the Crown" (April 28, 1990), Jackson Gillis wrote "Murder in Malibu" (May 14, 1990) and "Bird in the Hand" (Nov. 22, 1992), Robert Van Scoyk wrote "No Time to Die" (March 15, 1992), and Peter Fischer wrote both "Rest in Peace, Mrs. Columbo" (May 31, 1990) and "Butterfly in Shades of Grey" (Jan. 10, 1994). Actor-director-writer and friend of Falk Patrick McGoohan was involved with three different films late in the run. Very few of these veterans of the original series worked together in the reboot. Moreover, without a consistent group of writers, particularly in its latter years, each *Columbo* movie was pitched individually through the collaboration of Falk, his development director, and a packaging agent. Each movie, too, had a longer shooting schedule (at roughly nineteen days) than a conventional series episode, and each movie's budget ran from about $2.5–3 million.[15] Ultimately, as executive producer and, of course, as the star, Falk was the only real consistent player across the fourteen years of the production of the reboot.[16]

Let me return briefly to the DNA metaphor with which I began this chapter. Without many members of the original team—writers and directors who helped to form the character in tandem with one another, or who took over from veterans of the show with some overlap—the reboot morphed in terms of genre, the context for the murders (and therefore Columbo's own cultural investigations), and its overall sensibility.

And in the face of this mutation, compounded by the loss of consistent writers, more mutation occurred. In order to salvage the lineage of Columbo, perhaps particular traits of Columbo began to be snipped and inserted into the reboot's Columbo. An overreliance on a repetitive sequence, much like DNA, irrevocably altered their own expression as their frequency and order became nearly unnatural. Often when a break in DNA occurs, the cell uses a short strand of DNA as a template.[17] This is precisely what the writers attempted to do, using the template of the character quirks of Columbo. Yet, in the end, placing a mutated gene back into its environment has unknown implications on genetic diversity as a whole, which in this analogy is the writer's creativity.

Along with these changes in the writing teams, nearly every other aesthetic element also shifts in the reboot. Lighting, costume, music, and camera work are all updated to match the era. Gone are the duller hues of the 1970s, replaced with bright whites. With some key exceptions, performers and performances are altered as well; no longer awash with classical-era Hollywood stars like Janet Leigh and Ida Lupino or theatrical stylists like Jack Cassidy and Lee Grant, instead the series is largely populated by contemporary television stars (and guest stars). Falk himself logs less screen time than in the original as well. Certainly all of these changes are part and parcel of historical change, whether to television technology, fashion, the aging out of former film stars, or even the needs of the primary star as an aging actor himself. But the new look and sound of this iteration are matched in both tone and narrative details. For instance, some narrative elements of the series appear to be updated so that they are more consistent with other contemporary cop shows. Columbo frequently works with other officers, as if part of a workplace crime series (such as *Hill Street Blues*, which ran from 1981 to 1987) or a procedural team series (such as *Law & Order*, which premiered in 1990). Akin to *Murder, She Wrote* (cocreated by Levinson and Link with Peter S. Fischer), an actual family member even appears in the episode "No Time to Die" (Feb. 15, 1992) when Columbo's nephew's bride is kidnapped on her wedding day. In fact, this episode itself represents several changes to the original: not only has a relative taken actual human form, but the nephew is himself a police officer, so that Columbo works as part of a team of family members and cops. Significant, too, is the sexual threat posed to the bride; in fact, the subject of sex itself—and the relative sexualization of the lieutenant—is an early part of the reboot, which is another departure from the original.

The erotics of the reboot are often tied to the professional and cultural context of the murderers' lives. In particular, whereas in the original the occupations of the murderers had a pretty broad range—inclusive of writers and actors surely, but also scientists, psychiatrists, military personnel, an architect, a magician, a car dealer, a senatorial candidate, even a police chief—in the reboot the majority of the murderers are linked to entertainment. It's true that several of the original killers also worked directly or indirectly in various entertainment industries—such could even be said of the Maestro in "Étude in Black," advertising executive Bart Kepple in "Double Exposure," or even the infamous chess champion of "The Most Dangerous Match"—but these were peppered in with other fields, and even those strictly connected to film or television lent the lieutenant the opportunity to learn about various technological forms. In the latter iteration of the series and of the lieutenant, entertainment industries dominate the murderers' milieus. And for those who do not work in entertainment, their wealth is frequently tied with celebrity, to the extent that even the killer dentist of "Uneasy Lies the Crown" cleans the teeth of the stars (including one whom he murders) and plays poker with a group of largely B-list actors who have cameos in the episode. In some of these cases, the capital on which the killers depend is in turn dependent on sex: the romance novel ("Murder in Malibu"), soft-core pornography ("Columbo Cries Wolf" [Jan. 20, 1990]), even sex therapy ("Sex and the Married Detective" [April 3, 1989]). And it also seems that sex sells in terms of the *Columbo* movies themselves.

Though the lieutenant was ever bashful in the original series, the series was hardly prudish; murders took place over money *and* love, and we are often privy to sexual relationships, if not actual sex scenes. After all, in the very first outing of Columbo in "Enough Rope" and then *Prescription: Murder*, the murderer kills his wife, using his mistress as his accomplice. And in the final season, the plot of "How to Dial a Murder" hinges on a husband seeking revenge on his late wife's lover. Certainly more than one episode features sexualized women, whether the young yogi fiancée, Lisa Chambers (played by "Catwoman" Julie Newmar), in "Double Shock," the swimsuit-clad fiancée of the victim in "Any Old Port in a Storm," or the denizens of the "fat farm" that the murderer, Viveca Scott (Vera Miles), runs in "Lovely but Lethal." That said, a sense of modesty was written into these scenes within the scripts and through Falk's performance. For instance, when the detective comes upon Newmar's "Lisa" as she stretches on the balcony, legs in the air, he turns away, embarrassed.

Alternately, either the original scripts or their ultimate productions over the initial run bear out this modesty. For "Lovely but Lethal," Jackson Gillis penned Columbo's entrance into killer Viveca Scott's grounds as follows:

> EXT SUNBATHING AREA
> And there checks himself abruptly. For it's a sunbathing area. And there are a couple of squeals and some scrambling for bikini tops. But Columbo is already whirling to face the gale.

In the previous season, scenes in the original scripts by Gillis for "Requiem for a Falling Star" feature acts of dressing and undressing, as well as already-undressed women, which were either ultimately cut from the actual episode or toned down. For instance, exploring the studio sets searching for the killer, Nora Chandler, "He rounds a corner and almost bumps into some girls in dancing costume. Sidesteps safely, moves on. He is like a kid in a candy store as he stares about." But when he happens upon the women's wardrobe, Gillis writes:

> The angle widens as Columbo comes puffing into a view to stop beside him—and now we see the sign "Women's Wardrobe"—also, through the open doorway, a couple of very scantily attired girls.
>
> Inside, other girls are disrobing entirely. Columbo winces, tries to make his away around without looking at them—and so he doesn't see Nora appear in doorway to one side, his glazed eyes are focused on infinity and he almost knocks down a dressmaker's dummy.[18]

Here, Columbo appears both bashful and respectful, a trait that Gillis toys with in the scenes that follow with Chandler. As Chandler rips off Columbo's tie for a new one from the costume department, offered by

Edith Head herself, "Columbo becomes putty." But a following scene was excised from the final version, likely for the ways it took the detective's bashfulness to a more literal level, losing the series' signature nuance.[19] As Nora asks the lieutenant to help unzip her dress, Gillis describes the following:

COLUMBO

(fumbling obediently, eyes turned)
Uh—yeah! Certainly!
And he bolts as her dress starts to fall to her feet.

If these earlier iterations recognized Columbo's sense of modesty, by the reboot, the lieutenant's modesty is a running gag, with the plots and circumstances of the plots tearing away the seams of the original. Subtlety and ambiguity are traded for more blatant forms of eroticism, even at times a kind of unsettling lecherousness.

Several plots of the films in the 1980s and 1990s center explicitly around sex, even when outside of the killer's professional milieu. In his second turn as a killer in "Butterfly in Shades of Grey," for instance, William Shatner hardly plays a role in which the killer is "sympathetic" (a claim he insists upon in "Fade in to Murder"). Now he is right-wing "shock jock" Fielding Chase with an apparent sexual attraction to his adopted daughter, Victoria (Molly Hagan). He kills his associate and friend of his daughter, Gerry Winters (Jack Laufer), because Gerry has tried to help Molly get out of Chase's clutches. Falk himself penned the episode that precedes Shatner's; entitled "It's All in the Game" (Oct. 31, 1993), this one is a take-off of *Chinatown*, complete with Faye Dunaway in the role of mother and murderer, though Falk tones down elements of the 1970s film on which his work is based. In this case the man she kills is not her (and her daughter's) father, though he was a philanderer who was having affairs with both mother and daughter. Furthermore, over the course of the episode, Dunaway's character, Lauren Staton, attempts to seduce the detective; he plays along when she takes him to a romantic supper, and he accepts her extravagant (and frankly thoughtful, if vicariously flirtatious) gift of a dog bed as well as a new tie (which Chase appears to be wearing in the episode that follows).

The turn to the overt subject of sex in these episodes is less a significant issue in and of itself—after all, it matches the fare of ABC programming in this general era—than it is symptomatic of a broader shift to a heavier hand that characterizes the plotting and performance throughout the reboot. Part of the complexity of the original run of the series was its inclusion of the detective's learning process, particularly about emerging technologies. Granted, his ongoing education occasionally continues in the reboot; for instance, the solution to the murder of "Butterfly in Shades of Grey" is predicated on an understanding of mobile-phone technology and cellular networks, which enabled the killer to seemingly be in two places at once. But, on a new television network, with increasingly relaxed regulations in the 1980s, a great part of what the lieutenant seems to learn has to do with sex, whether "personal" or "professional": an adopted father's attraction to his daughter, a woman who unwittingly shares a lover with her daughter, soft-core publishing, sex therapy, and so on. This attendance to sex, then, is attached to a frequent dependence on familiar traits of the series and the detective. And rather than being a holistic part of the character and plot, these traits themselves drive both the action and performance.

This superficial approach to the character is quite literally written into the scripts, even that by veteran writer Steven Bochco. In his script for "Uneasy Lies the Crown," Bochco describes the detective at one point as follows: "He toys with the gearshift lever, puffs his cigar and thinks Columbo thoughts." In his 2002 interview with the Television Academy, Bochco describes the mentorship he received from Richard Levinson and William Link regarding writing for a character and an actor. In particular, they taught him how to "underwrite" the character in order to "let . . . the actor fill the role." As Bochco paraphrased them, "Peter Falk is Columbo, so you don't have to write all of that stuff."[20] However, his indications in "Uneasy Lies the Crown" seem to be taking that advice to the extreme. Indeed, the shorthand he offers in the script is a far cry from Bochco's writing for the original series. In "Murder by the Book," the writer consistently describes Columbo and other characters with a subtlety that becomes integrated into the performance of actors, surely, but that is also characteristic of the series' overall sensibility. For instance, in his depiction of the scene when the victim's wife meets with

7.4. Falk rewrites *Chinatown* with Dunaway ("It's All in the Game," Oct. 31, 1993)

her husband's coauthor (and killer), Ken Franklin, for the first time after the murder, Bochco shows Columbo's patient watchfulness in action:

INT. HOUSE. DAY.

They are still standing in the doorway as Columbo comes from the kitchen. Neither of them notices him and he remains silent, trying not to intrude on what is obviously a very personal moment.

Later in the same script, a description of Columbo perusing the crime scene simply reads, "Columbo prowls."[21] Even briefer than his later reference to "think[ing] Columbo thoughts," this early phrase is far more precise. Bochco here captures a condensed image of how Falk/Columbo moves through the spaces he occupies. Of course, visually and performatively, he may appear to be "bumbling," but in many ways, we as viewers know he is deceptively on the prowl, looking for the next clue. This sense is captured again in an interaction between Franklin and Columbo. After Columbo mentions a detail about phone records, "Franklin's annoyance vanishes. Once again he sees Columbo as an adversary to be dealt with." Through this description we understand the cat-and-mouse relationship between the detective and the killer as creating a culprit's constant swing between confidence and insecurity.

In the closing scene, Bochco writes, "Franklin is completely undone by now and he knows it. He doesn't say a word." The episode ends as Franklin says to Columbo, "I had you going for a while," to which Columbo responds, "Sure did." The description that follows reads, "This seems to please him in a way."[22]

Bochco's depictions of characters in "Étude in Black" are similarly evocative, almost novelistic. For instance, he describes the silent response of the killer (played by John Cassavetes, of course) to an utterance by Columbo: "It's a simple statement, with a sincerity Alex has probably never felt in his life, but he recognizes it. All insincere people recognize sincerity—it's how they learn to simulate it so well. At least he's sensitive enough not to say it glibly in return." Such nuance in Bochco's writing in these first seasons is demonstrative of the approach of the series overall. In these years, *Columbo* allowed for complexity in both the detective and the killers. Roland Barthes might refer to this sort of writing as "ambiguous." For the author, Barthes contends, "The feat is to sustain the mimesis of language . . . [such] that the text never succumbs to the good conscience (and bad faith) of parody."[23] Julia Kristeva draws on similar notions when she describes how Mikhail Bakhtin emphasized the importance of dramatic features in the "carnivalesque": "the laughter of the carnival is not simply parodic; it is no more comic than tragic; it is both at once, one might say that it is *serious*."[24] Whereas Bakhtin was drawing in part on Dostoyevsky's *Crime and Punishment*, Kristeva goes a step further via Antonin Artaud: "*laughter* is silenced because it is not parody but *murder* and *revolution*."[25]

As a performer in a series about murder if not revolution, Falk clearly thrived on more "ambiguous" characteristics in the original series, maintaining a level of sincerity, whether he was acting kindly or a little bit silly. Whether in his prowl through a room in "Murder by the Book," the self-conscious hamminess for Ward Fowler's video camera in "Fade in to Murder," or the gentle way he guides the wheelchair-bound Elizabeth Van Wick in "Playback," his bodily gestures themselves represent at once a sense of intelligence and of sincerity. By the time of the reboot, the intelligence is still there, of course, but the sincerity is often lost across the levels of production. His dimensionality has been condensed into just one thing: "Columbo."

7.5. Columbo plays TV detective ("Fade in to Murder," 6:1; Oct. 10, 1976)

"Different Kinds of Charm"

Such a reduction of the character is arguably at the heart of the various novels produced as unofficial tie-ins for the series. With one series published in the years of the original and another during the years of its revival, these novels follow two different patterns: some involve plots that are consistent with the original run in their focus on the murders of and by wealthy residents of Los Angeles, while some of the later iterations task the detective with solving mysteries linked to historical, notorious crimes—whether Jimmy Hoffa, Herbert Hoover, John F. Kennedy, or Charles Manson.[26] *Columbo: The Helter Skelter Murders* even begins with a prologue that places Columbo at the scene of the August 1969 massacre at Cielo Drive. Often exaggerating Columbo's character traits, the novels overall bear elements of parody without entirely succumbing to it; "no more comic than tragic," they are "both at once," though I'm not sure I'd exactly deem them "serious." For instance, the internal monologues within them function both similarly and incalculably differently from the internal monologue in *Wings of Desire*. That is, they draw on clichés of the series without the subtlety we see in some of Bochco's descriptions or in Falk's early performances. Take, for instance, *The Dean's Death*, in which the lieutenant is invited to lecture at a local college on his work. As he stands at the podium, "He felt himself get hot all over. He knew he should have better control of himself. He was just addressing a bunch of kids. Bright kids, though, awfully bright. Boy, he should have listened to his wife when she asked him why he should give his secrets away to a bunch of students who would only use them against him if they ever had to defend a murderer in court."[27] Here his internal monologue, while technically consistent with the detective's asides and associations, doesn't bear the same tone as it does in Wenders's film, perhaps in part because in *Wings of Desire*, the voice comes directly from Falk himself. But it also loses the nuance of the original series and of the types of descriptions that writers like Bochco posed in his early scripts. Indeed, as the scene goes on, Columbo begins to do "Columbo things": in looking for the notes for his lecture, he "began pawing mechanically, then a little desperately, through his pockets. . . . He pulled two envelopes and a parking ticket from the inside pocket of his jacket. Notes for his speech were penciled on the back."[28] Here "Columbo" is an easy target, reduced to predictable characteristics.[29]

In his 1995 interview on *Fresh Air* with Terry Gross, Falk complains about some of the early scenes in the original series: "I think that when we started to make the series, they would often write scenes that were supposed to be humorous, and those were the ones that made me very nervous." When Gross asks him why, he responds, "Because I didn't think they were funny, and they were kind of cute. And so I would tamper with those all the time to make sure that they were—that they were funny, that they were humorous, not [just] funny, and that they were more subtle and more believable." Oddly enough, in the later iteration of the character (in fact, at the time he was being interviewed by Gross), Falk himself often played up the "cuteness" of Lt. Columbo. It's precisely this performance that gives the reboot "episodes," like the unofficial tie-ins, a quality of parody. During the early run of the reboot, Falk claimed, "People can't get enough of that guy. I suppose that's true of me, too. How can you kick a character who's made you so much dough?"[30] He shows that he still has affection for the character he plays, surely, but he reveals a cynicism about the role as well: Columbo was bankable.

On *Fresh Air*, that cynicism is similarly tempered by pragmatism. Remarking on the impact the long-running role had on his work as a performer, Falk says, "I think arguably I probably would be a better actor if I hadn't spent so much time playing that one role. I think that kind of diversity and that kind of challenge—I might be a better actor. I don't know. I'm not sure. I think probably I would be. But so what?" His final question seems, at least in part, to gesture toward his refusal either to complain or have regrets about his choices as an actor, particularly since, as he admits to Gross as well, the role of Columbo made him so much "dough."[31] Shortly thereafter he also mulls over his work with Cassavetes. When Gross asks what was different about Cassavetes's approach to directing, Falk initially just says, "Everything." He then goes on to say, "Everything John did was original, everything. Every bone in his body was original. He was the most fertile man I've ever met. I'll never meet anyone as fertile as he was." And as the conversation continues, he muses on Cassavetes's aversion toward clichés, declaring that most human behavior has ambiguity. "There are different kinds of anger," Falk says. "There are different kinds of charm. They—they're not all the same, and there's mixtures involved at any given moment in time."

I admit it's speculation on my part, but I believe the loss of his friend affected Falk's work in the reboot of *Columbo*. The challenges that Cassavetes posed to him as a director (and as a costar, such as in *Mikey and Nicky* and "Étude in Black") inspired his performances, even when Falk was not working with Cassavetes directly. Certainly the first decades of his career proved his excellence as an actor, from his very early dual nominations for Oscars and Emmys through his work on *Columbo* in the 1970s and his concomitant spells with Cassavetes. It may be that he lost himself a little with the reboot, "playing" Columbo and therefore falling into a form of parody of his own character. In a sense, he was the character without the actor behind him. Or perhaps in the reboot's attempt to appear more "contemporary," it simply lost its timelessness.

In its focus at once on the Holocaust and angels living on earth, *Wings of Desire* is a film that is about both history and a sense of timelessness. And here Falk particularly displays his complexity as an actor by playing his own role as a form of duality: he is at once the actor Peter Falk and the character Lieutenant Columbo (in Kristeva's words, he is "ambivalent"). As his performance shows, Falk the actor is historically and perhaps forever bound to his most famous role. His oscillation or integration between these dual parts comes across in little details. Like the fictional detective, Falk also searches for things in his pocket that he either can't find or can't remember. As the man himself, the actor sketches in a notebook. As the actor who played the famous detective, Falk is greeted by strangers who recognize him as "Columbo" and even misrecognize him as not-Columbo. He is Columbo-as-Falk, Falk-as-Falk, and Falk-as-Columbo. And as the film begins to end, "Falk" appears to see the angel who is otherwise invisible, revealing to him that he had been an angel himself, having now lived on the earth for thirty years. Given Falk's well-known biography—he grew up in Ossining, New York; he had his right eye removed because of a malignant tumor when he was three; he joined the Merchant Marine in his twenties; and so on—I think we can be pretty sure he wasn't an angel who fell to earth circa 1957. But surely this characterization—that he's an angel on earth—reflects both the worldwide affection for the actor and the actor's sense of ease that's worthy of an angel.[32]

Interviewed about their work together in 1973, the actress Lee Grant noted, "Nothing really touches his equanimity. You could explode a bomb next to him, and he would just look at it with extreme interest."[33] This reference to his characteristic temperament, its own kind of charm, recalls to mind a "stars tour" I took around 2007, when the bus driver passed by Falk's house and announced that he was the nicest star whom tour groups came across, always waving at the fans on the ride. I nearly leapt out of my seat in the hope I might see him, opening his arms with the "ta-da!" of a grandfather, but I was never destined to meet him in the flesh. Four years later, sitting on a different bus three thousand miles away, staring at my phone and stunned by the news of his death, this moment might have crossed my mind. But more so I felt the loss of a greater presence on earth.

Epilogue

The original series *Columbo* came to an end on May 13, 1978. Like its multiple beginnings, from "Enough Rope" to *Prescription: Murder* to its pilot and its first official episode, it arguably also had multiple returns and multiple endings. But, to steal a line the detective himself utters on a bank of television screens at the end of "Make Me a Perfect Murder," I'm afraid I'll have to insist. As the seventh season's final episode, "The Conspirators," concludes, after all, the detective won't allow the ship to sail off to sea (and with it the means and motive for the murder). That would be too wishy-washy. For a man who didn't relish being in the water or the sky, it's fitting that this last episode would require a ship to come back to port. With the series thus grounded, everything that has come after this episode—whether the reboot, paperback novels and short stories, or self-reflexive references—is a mere echo, reiteration, transmutation.

However, I recognize that this book itself is a little more difficult to end than such a decisive statement as the above would suggest. Perhaps I am forever bound to the detective's stock line—"just one more thing." There's always been another text to which I can turn, another set of coincidences or relations I might discover or design. I've found myself wondering, do I need to devote a chapter to board games and cookbooks, to podcasts and fan fiction, to the novelizations in print and the reiterations online, or to Columbo's various memorials, including statues of the detective and his dog in Budapest and even a movement (part fanciful, part real) to change "Columbus Day" to "Columbo Day"?

These explicit, if ancillary, tie-ins ricochet and extend the original series and have made it hard for me to feel closure in any one ending. After all, a dish like "Janet Leigh's Cheese Soufflé" or "Johnny Cash's Chili," lodged in the pages of *Cooking with Columbo*, is at once material and ephemeral.[1] And those are two of the abiding qualities of television itself as a moving-image medium—making endings tricky, if not downright impossible. Indeed, the refusal of an ending seems part and parcel of the approach of some of the later tie-ins to the series, whether the 2018 cookbook or those novels that position the detective in relation to historical events, such as William Harrington's *Columbo: The Grassy Knoll* (1993), in which the detective finds connections between a contemporary murder and the assassination of President Kennedy three decades prior.

Perhaps the detective himself was never keen on goodbyes, almost always managing to find some redeeming quality in a killer, even as he shuffled the Hollywood elite to their fates in the denouement of each episode. Hence the episode's endings are often not merely resolutions but also moments of quiet reflection: Columbo sitting alongside the killer, the lieutenant alone with his thoughts (and possibly his cigar), or the detective as he witnesses the killer being led away. "Any Old Port in a Storm" concludes with the lieutenant discovering the killer, Adrian Carsini (Donald Pleasance), tossing priceless bottles of wine into the ocean. Reviewing the varieties and years, he tells him, "It must be killing you to throw all this stuff away." He goes on to confess his own plot that he used to catch Carsini—who gave himself away when he recognized a spoiled bottle of port at dinner with the detective—and the killer's eyes fill with tears. After Carsini in turn confesses to his crime, the two climb into Columbo's car. It's one of the only times when the detective takes a killer as a passenger, but in this case, as opposed to that in "Requiem for a Falling Star," he's not just taking Mr. Carsini for a ride, as he did with Nora Chandler. Before heading to the police station, they drive back to the vineyard together, where Columbo stops the car and pulls a bottle from behind his seat; he gives Carsini the cork to sniff as he pours a glass for each of them. Recognizing the dessert wine Columbo has chosen, the vintner says that it's "very suitable for the final course." He turns to our detective and declares, "You learn very well, Lieutenant." As the last line of the episode, Columbo looks at him warmly and responds, "That's the nicest thing anybody's ever said to me."

Those endings in which the killer confesses to Columbo surely confirm what the detective—a good student indeed, perhaps even a genius—already knows. They simply fill in an odd detail or two, sometimes commenting on their remorselessness or their regrets. In "Fade in to Murder," the murderer, Ward Fowler, even remarks on his own ending in the meta-language of television narratives: "I believe that in this killing, the murderer has the sympathetic part." Yet he realizes, in the convention of television detective stories, that he necessarily, if unconsciously, left a clue for the actual detective to discover. Snapping his fingers in lament, he declares, "Damn. I had to forget something. That's always how the third act ends. You see, I've had no rehearsal as a murderer: I'm, after all, a detective." Of course, Ward Fowler is and is not a detective. The same could be said about the fictional Columbo himself—a fantasy of a detective so immersive that he follows the actor into other roles. I like to think I've taken on part of Columbo's character myself, even if I'm a mere textual detective, an intertextual sleuth. After all, my own study is also a kind of investigative game, not entirely unlike the one the detective regularly performed. It's not the cat-and-mouse game that the series presents between the detective and the killers he tracks. But then, Lieutenant Columbo was neither a cat nor a mouse. He was forever a dog with a bone. As am I. Unwilling to give up or give in, I am the viewer and scholar who writes about a series I have loved so much over time that I don't want it, either the show or the book, to end. Yet, in regard to the writing, I'm afraid I'm going to have to insist.

But as for the viewing, that's the beauty of television as a narrative form and as an archival system: it forever promises the possibility of the return of the familiar, whether through the design of digital platforms, time-shifting technologies, or the serendipity of cable syndication. Like television, this book, too, is a kind of archival system. And like other archives—or like all books—it includes the stamp of my own DNA, which has become bound in my methods of reading, the texts to which I've turned, the "mutations" I've enabled or designed. In my serpentine methods of intertextual research and in the circularity of those returns that are embedded throughout my study (one might call them preoccupations),

I have become bound to this text, and it clings to me, too. Parts of the series and my own reading methods and writing practice have become integrated into one another. These twists and entanglements are essential components of analysis, and they are indications of the ways in which the very form of this study is informed by the series itself—not just in the detective's repeated returns or his varied tangents, but also in my own tangents, interconnections, and even collaborations.

In the end, I hope that my book might be recognized as a microcosm of the series and of television overall. After all, *Columbo* has forever taught me how to understand television—and how, in effect, to understand writing about it. And in this way, there's more permanence to television than we might imagine.

Notes

Prologue

1. A writers' strike occurred during the first six months of 1960, though conditionally writers could produce work for live television, which led Levinson and Link to develop the teleplay for "Enough Rope." A *Hollywood Reporter* review of the first production for *The Chevy Mystery Show* described it—and I quote verbatim—as "a live mystery show, or 'live' on tape or whatever" (Powers, "The Chevy Mystery Show," 9). With many thanks to Mark Quigley for this archival gem.

2. I use the same indicators for all episodes, noting season, episode number within season, and original airdate. For the reboot, which I will discuss in the final section, I shift just to dates, as the episodes were ultimately not part of a regular season but were effectively made-for-television movies, like the first two iterations ("Enough Rope" and *Prescription: Murder*).

3. In the play, Columbo asks Flemming to take him on as a patient: "I seem to bother people. I make them nervous. Maybe you can tell me why." And he goes on, "My wife says I ought to have it looked into. So I told her I know a psychiatrist. And I figure if I come to you, say once a week, we could get it ironed out." He worries, in fact, that he's "too suspicious." See Link and Levinson, *Prescription: Murder*, 53–54.

4. The year Levinson and Link won the Emmy for "Death Lends a Hand," all of the three writing nominations were for *Columbo*.

5. Interestingly, it was *McMillan and Wife* that *TV Guide* claimed was the "most anticipated" of the series, but it neither racked up the awards nor has had the long life and afterlife of Falk's show.

6. Dean Hargrove wrote and produced the pilot, but Universal asked Levinson and Link to return for the first season. After a year with *McCloud*, Hargrove,

who was under contract as a writer/producer with Universal, came on as executive producer in the second season.

7. The change in writing and directing staff might have been related to the fact that the fifth season was intended to be the last.

8. William Link discusses this phenomenon in an interview: "William Link Interview Part 5 of 9," Television Academy, https://interviews.televisionacademy.com/interviews/william-link?clip=116592#topic-clips.

9. For instance, the French television guide *TéléPouch* ran both a former interview with his wife, Shera Danese, as well as a tribute (Ragaine, "Adieu, Columbo"). The "TV magazine" of *Le Figaro* ran a similar homage, with a photo spread (Galiero, "Columbo").

10. See, for instance, Curran, "Why the World Still Loves 1970s Detective Show *Columbo*." Also note the UCLA Film and Television Archive's virtual screening of "Enough Rope" on April 1, 2021, curated by Mark Quigley, the John H. Mitchell Television Archivist: https://www.cinema.ucla.edu/events/2021/04/01/chevy-mystery-show-enough-rope.

Introduction

1. Eco, "Can Television Teach?," 15.

2. Interestingly, another academic volume about the series was published after I initially completed my own; it is entitled *Columbo: Paying Attention 24/7* (by David Martin-Jones).

3. To answer the question "Is Netflix television?," Sarah Arnold considers how the delivery platform is not like "linear television," yet she also notes that it is situated "within the same institutional landscape of television [which] makes it a competitor with television industries for television viewers" ("Netflix and the Myth of Choice/Participation/Autonomy," 50). Her analysis goes on to focus on the "datafication of audiences," as she considers the ways that Netflix (like other streaming platforms) utilizes algorithms to understand viewers' preferences and behaviors, in order to better target content to them. Doing so is a means, also, of eliminating viewers' agency or control—an argument that many fans of streaming platforms have made about "linear" television.

4. For these divergent but related approaches, see R. Williams, *Television*, originally published in 1974, as well as Ellis, *Visible Fictions*, originally published in 1982.

5. Browne, "The Political Economy of the Television Super(Text)," 176.

6. Browne, "The Political Economy of the Television Super(Text)," 177.

7. Houston, "Viewing Television," 184.

8. White, "Crossing Wavelengths," 51.

9. For another example, see Flitterman-Lewis, "The Real Soap Operas."

10. Kinder, *Playing with Power*, 2. Like Mimi White, in her 1985 essay "Television Genres: Intertextuality," Kinder traces the development of genre through intertextual methods and connections. As White puts it, "The study of genre involves systematized familiarity"; "rules" and recognition are therefore developed across a series of texts ("Television Genres," 41). Kinder's analysis considers in particular how children are cognitively trained through television's "familiarity" in order to "gain an entrance into a system of reading narrating" for both paradigms and the generation of new combinations (*Playing with Power*, 41). This comprehension of textual design, moreover, Kinder argues, goes hand in hand with a kind of ideological reasoning, especially as it involves an understanding of the subsequent "rules" guiding gendered roles and distinctions.

11. Naficy, "Television Intertextuality," 42.

12. Naficy, "Television Intertextuality," 46.

13. Gray, "Television, Black Americans, and the American Dream," 378. Moving between fiction and nonfiction programming, Gray emphasizes that those "assumptions that organize our understanding of black middle class success and under class failure are expressed and reinforced in the formal organization of television programming" (384).

14. White, "Crossing Wavelengths," 52.

15. White, "Crossing Wavelengths," 56.

16. Importantly, intertextuality is a much broader category than self-reflexivity. And, as I'll go on to note, parody is just one manifestation of self-reflexivity. With the exception of the analysis of the reboot of the series, its ancillary texts, and a couple of episodes, such as "Fade in to Murder," I'm taking an intertextual approach in a direction beyond parody.

17. Murphy, *How Television Invented New Media*, 80. She goes on, "Today, television's channels, networks, tubes, program guides, and more are all part of a media logic used both by those who make and distribute old and new media and those who use it" (81).

18. "Each word (text) is an intersection of word (texts) where at least one other word (text) can be read" (Kristeva, "Word, Dialogue and Novel," 36, 37).

19. Kristeva, "Word, Dialogue and Novel," 37.

20. Kristeva, "Word, Dialogue and Novel," 43.

21. Kristeva, "Word, Dialogue and Novel," 39, emphasis added.

22. Kristeva, "Word, Dialogue and Novel," 48.

23. Kristeva, "Word, Dialogue and Novel," 49, phrase drawn from David Hilbert.

24. Kristeva, "Word, Dialogue and Novel," 58.

25. Borges, "The Garden of Forking Paths," 54.

26. Borges, "The Garden of Forking Paths," 54.

27. Borges, "Blindness," 116.

28. Such a focus can be limiting, especially when it's confined to "new" television series in order to update anthologies or remain "current" in the offering of volumes. For a critique of this phenomenon, see Hastie, "The Epistemological Stakes of *Buffy the Vampire Slayer*."

29. See Feuer, "The Concept of Live Television," and Sobchack, "The Scene of the Screen."

30. The claim that watching a streaming platform like Netflix or Hulu is categorically different from "watching television" seems akin to HBO's past tagline: "It's not TV—it's HBO." Such claims follow a similar kind of value judgment to that which Michael Z. Newman and Elana Levine ascribe to varying forms of contemporary television criticism: "We argue that it is a mistake to accept naively that television has grown better over the years, even while such a discourse is intensifying within popular, industrial, and scholarly sites. In contrast, we argue that it is primarily cultural elites (including journalists, popular critics, TV creators and executives, and media scholars) who have intensified the legitimation of television by investing the medium with aesthetic and other prized values, nudging it closer to more established arts and cultural forms and preserving their own privileged status in return" (*Legitimating Television*, 7).

31. See Tryon, "'Make Any Room Your TV Room.'"

32. Levinson and Link also acknowledge the works of Austin Freeman and G. K. Chesterton as inspiration for the structure of the inverted detective story (Levinson and Link, *Stay Tuned*, 88, 93).

33. Moreover, the portrait of Mrs. Melville will later reappear as background artwork in "The Bye-Bye Sky High I.Q. Murder Case."

34. The alliteration of their names—Ferris and Franklin—are also neat parallels to Levinson and Link. Even more specifically, the F is nearly an inversion of an L.

35. Franklin also commits a second murder, when he is blackmailed by a shop owner by the lake regarding the first murder.

36. This is one of the only episodes of the original run in which the murderer doesn't directly kill for money ("Try and Catch Me" is another).

37. Of course, this isn't the only time he uses such a phrase. In "Negative Reaction," he responds to a pawnshop dealer, who teaches him about cameras, "You learn something new every day."

38. A consideration of conversational formats is part of the focus of Christyne Berzsenyi's 2021 volume *Columbo: A Rhetoric of Inquiry with*

Resistant Responders, which was published after the completion of my manuscript.

39. The victim was not a blood relation, as the killer repeatedly states. He was married to her beloved niece, and she killed him because she believed he was responsible for her niece's death.

40. As I'll discuss in a later chapter, this emphasis on time could also be neatly connected to another analytic work circulating in the cultural zeitgeist at the time: Alvin Toffler's *Future Shock*.

41. Ginzburg, "Clues," 101.

42. Ginzburg, "Clues," 115.

43. Ginzburg insists on "flexible rigor" for conjectural paradigms, reveling in the seeming contradiction-in-terms ("Clues," 114).

1. Mapping the Detective

Epigraph: William Link quotes Peter Falk in an interview: "William Link Interview Part 5 of 9," Television Academy, https://interviews.televisionacademy .com/interviews/william-link?clip=116592#topic-clips.

1. In a neat coincidence, at one point Fresco uses the phrase "any port in a storm," which will become an episode title on *Columbo* a few years later. Thanks to my research assistant Sam Hood for that insight!

2. Falk, *Just One More Thing*, 108.

3. See Falk, *Just One More Thing*, 51. Interestingly, in the original run of *Columbo* his glass eye is never mentioned, and, in fact, he was filmed in such a way as to minimize our recognition of it. In the reboot, however, the detective makes mention of it himself in "A Trace of Murder" when he quips to another character who has offered to help him out, "Three eyes are better than one!"

4. Falk would also continue to work in theater. In fact, he starred on Broadway with Lee Grant, the villain for the *Columbo* pilot "Ransom for a Dead Man," in Neil Simon's *The Prisoner of Second Ave.* in 1971.

5. Levinson and Link, *Stay Tuned*, 92.

6. A similar warmth and tenacity, moreover, could be ascribed to the two other detectives penned by Levinson and Link in the 1970s: Harry Tenafly and Ellery Queen.

2. Best-Selling Mystery Team

1. Levinson and Link discuss this move in a 1984 recorded conversation for a Writers Guild Foundation workshop on collaboration. Recording is archived at the Writers Guild Foundation (WGF).

2. Script held in the WGF collection, p. 1.

3. WGF collaboration workshop, cassette recording, 1984.

4. While the duo primarily focused on television writing after the 1950s, together they cowrote the novel *The Playhouse*, which was published in 1985. This work deviated from the detective genre; it functioned as more of a character study and a work of horror, focused on an older man, Mr. McGregor, who kidnaps two children and sets them up in his self-designed "playhouse" for his mentally ill daughter, who has lost her own children. Not unlike *Columbo*, the novel offers an examination of McGregor's criminal psychology, and it also enables its readers to understand and even at times to empathize with him. But unlike their iconic series and their made-for-television movies, it largely lacks the social consciousness of those other works. I am indebted to my research assistant Maeve McNamara for these insights.

5. After the death of Mr. Levinson, Mr. Link teamed up with David Black to create *The Cosby Mysteries*.

6. *Ellery Queen*, which ran for just one season, was also a precursor to the far more popular *Murder, She Wrote*, in which Angela Lansbury plays mystery novelist and amateur detective Jessica Fletcher.

7. Levinson and Link note in *Stay Tuned* that they left the helm of the series after the first season in order to pursue work on made-for-television movies (98).

8. I'm not sure if the character's name is an homage to Harry Caul of *The Conversation* (Francis Ford Coppola, 1974), but it's awfully hard to ignore.

9. Canby, "Suspense Melodrama."

10. *TV Guide* reported that the studio demanded this ending; it was not the spectacular scene the writers intended: "What begins as a crackling-good high adventure peters out at the end—the result of management's decision to hold back on a spectacular closing sequence, not the authors' idea" (*TV Guide*, "*Rollercoaster* Reviews").

11. When Mr. Link attended the premiere of Spielberg's blockbuster, his wife, Margery, turned to him and said, "Never say no to The Kid again" (conversation with Mr. Link, July 19, 2013).

12. Conversation with Mr. Link, July 19, 2013.

13. *The Gun* was directed by John Badham and was a Fairmont Foxcroft production, made in association with Universal.

14. See Hugo Munsterberg on "attention" in *The Photoplay: A Psychological Study*.

15. The chaplain is played by Ned Beatty, which is an odd twist, given two of his most well-known roles of the period: as Bobby in *Deliverance* two years prior and the evangelical studio head Arthur Jensen in *Network* two years later. He also appears as a hitman in *Mikey and Nicky* with Cassavetes and Falk in 1976.

16. Bazin, *What Is Cinema?*, 27.

17. Levinson and Link, *Stay Tuned*, 170–71, capitalization and inventive wording in the original.

18. Levinson and Link, *Stay Tuned*, 119.

19. Levinson and Link, *Stay Tuned*, 121.

20. Conversation with Mr. Link, March 2015.

21. Bear in mind, too, that their original screenplay was penned in the early 1970s and that their description of the compromise that resulted in the inclusion of "an ersatz liberal" was composed just a decade later. Perhaps the fact that this film was ahead of its time has something to do with the lack of attention paid to it in histories of LGBTQ representations on television, many of which primarily focus on contemporary representations.

22. His monologue also included statements that the network insisted Levinson and Link include as a means of appeasing homophobic viewers. As Doug begins his speech to Nick, he says, for instance, "Some people think this is a sickness." I've tried to characterize the writers' more progressive representation above.

23. Granted, the role of Doug was initially difficult to cast, as other actors did not want to be associated with gay identity. Martin Sheen declared in an interview decades later, however, "I'd robbed banks and kidnapped children and raped women and murdered people, you know, in any number of shows. Now I was going to play a gay guy and that was like considered a career ender. Oh, for Christ's sake! What kind of culture do we live in?" (quoted in Wright, "BTD Speaker Sheen Blasts Dems, GOP, Bush"; see also *Dallas Voice*, "Award-Winning Actor").

24. Conversation with Mr. Link, July 9, 2013.

25. Gray, "Television, Black Americans, and the American Dream," 379.

26. Wald, *It's Been Beautiful*, 38.

27. In the case of "Étude in Black," Steven Bochco's script described the Maestro's right-hand man, Billy (James McEachin) as "the assistant conductor, a black man" ("Étude in Black" script, held at the WGF [#35003], p. 5).

28. Levinson and Link, *Stay Tuned*, 28. Indeed, in *Stay Tuned*, they offer the wrongheaded assertion that the Black character Robert "is as racist as [the white character] Marlene" (29).

29. The movie was a critical success, earning an Emmy for Levinson and Link as the writing team.

30. The pilot of *Tenafly* preceded the premiere of the television adaptation of the *Shaft* films. The series also starred Richard Roundtree; it ran for seven episodes, starting October 9, 1973.

31. After *Tenafly*, Bradshaw wrote "Playback" for *Columbo*, as well as an episode for *Ellery Queen* ("The Adventure of the Eccentric Engineer"; Jan. 18, 1976). While *Tenafly* was his first writing gig, he continued to write for television on the heels of his work produced by Levinson and Link for over a decade, including an episode for *McMillan & Wife*, as well as for sitcoms and other cop/detective shows.

32. This is a smart, if fleeting, critique of racist paranoia on the part of cabbies, exactly twenty years before African American actor Yaphet Kotto's segment for Michael Moore's 1994–95 television show *TV Nation*, in which he repeatedly failed to hail a cab in New York City.

33. See Banks, *The Writers*.

34. Kristeva, "Word, Dialogue and Novel," 58.

35. The structure for writers was quite different in the reboot. With Falk as executive producer, first of all, the process had to commence with him.

36. He can laugh because he has quickly assessed the situation. "You're not intimidated," the gunman suggests, barely a question. The writer responds: "You don't have gloves on, your finger's not on the trigger, and there are no bullets in the cylinder." Here he shows he knows the rules of guns and the rules of murder, if not that of narrative economy. Moments later in the episode, after joining his coauthor at his getaway in San Diego, he is indeed murdered by gunshot.

37. Such sequences are not rare on the series. As another example, "By Dawn's Early Light" begins with a six-minute sequence in which the murderer prepares the scene, without any dialogue and with only sparse ambient noise, punctuated in the fifth minute by the nondiegetic sound of a snare drum (accompanied by a low droning bass sound).

38. Bochco's involvement is representative of another role that Levinson and Link played—that is, as mentors. It shows, too, how *Columbo* as a series served as the training ground for many up-and-coming writers and directors. In his interview with the Television Academy that touches on *Columbo*, Bochco discusses how Levinson and Link taught him about structure, how to drive a story, and how to write for a particular character. And when they rewrote his work, "they would always do it with great respect." For a range of conversations that include discussions of *Columbo*, see https://interviews.televisionacademy.com/shows/columbo#who-talked.

39. Bochco describes them as a "collective brain, but Dick had the mouth" ("Steven Bochco Interview," Television Academy, https://interviews.televisionacademy.com/interviews/steven-bochco).

40. Second script version of "The Most Dangerous Game," held at the WGF, p. 43.

41. Flicker wrote and directed the 1967 paranoid comedy-thriller *The President's Analyst* and later would develop the television series *Barney Miller*. "Dead as a Duck" is far more akin to his 1967 film than it is to *Columbo*.

42. Theodore J. Flicker, "Dead Swan / Dead as a Duck" script (Aug. 12, 1973), held at the WGF, p. 7.

43. Barthes, *The Pleasure of the Text*, 35–36.

44. Barthes, *The Pleasure of the Text*, 36.

45. Kristeva, "Word, Dialogue and Novel," 58.

46. Eco, *Limits of Interpretation*, 100.

47. Eco, *Limits of Interpretation*, 100.

3. *"I'm Fascinated by Money"*

1. The Los Angeles Police Department describes the titles on its website: https://www.joinlapd.com/career-ladders.

2. For a terrific study of modern cop series, see Nichols-Pethick, *TV Cops*.

3. After one season as part of the mystery wheel, *Quincy, M.E.* became a mid-season replacement series in early 1977 and then ran for six additional seasons.

4. Heissenbüttel, "Rules of the Game of the Crime Novel," 80.

5. Caillois, "The Detective Novel as Game," 10.

6. Caillois, "The Detective Novel as Game," 4.

7. In Caillois's words, "The detective no longer disguises himself, but thinks" ("The Detective Novel as Game," 2).

8. Heissenbüttel, "Rules of the Game of the Crime Novel," 81.

9. Heissenbüttel, "Rules of the Game of the Crime Novel," 89.

10. Heissenbüttel, "Rules of the Game of the Crime Novel," 89.

11. "Dean Hargrove Interview Part 2 of 3," Television Academy, https://interviews.televisionacademy.com/interviews/dean-hargrove?clip=2.

12. Falk, *Just One More Thing*, 172.

13. Falk, *Just One More Thing*, 172.

14. The scout is played by an uncredited African American actor. Notably, the series cast a number of Black actors in bit parts—as other cops, surely, but also in various venues like this one. As I have discussed, the cocreators made a conscious decision to not cast Black actors as murderers.

15. "By Dawn's Early Light" also features some attention to shoes; in this case it's a young student at the military academy who is chastised by the killer, Col. Rumford (Patrick McGoohan), for not wearing clean shoes.

16. In fact, the episode neatly opens with a phone call, recalling the Hitchcock film.

17. Not long after this episode aired, Joan Didion published an essay called "Quiet Days in Malibu," later included in her collection *The White Album*, in which she describes her love of greenhouses, particularly one that grew orchids in Southern California where the caretaker, Amado Vazquez, would allow her to sit and eat her lunch. When she learns that some of the orchids were valued at as much as "three quarter of a million dollars," she proclaims, "I suppose the day I realized this was the day I stopped using the Arthur Freed greenhouses as a place to eat my lunch." As the owner, Marvin Saltzman, later also admitted, "Frankly it's an expensive business to get into." But she would continue to visit Vazquez: "We were standing in a sea of orchids, an extravagance of orchids, and he had given me an armful of blossoms from his own cattleyas to take to my child, more blossoms maybe than in all of Madrid." Didion, *The White Album*, 217–21.

18. Cited in Weber, "Peter Falk, Rumpled and Crafty Actor."

19. Set within the context of civil rights and the recession during the era, this class conflict is a means of representing the political tenor of the period. As I discuss in my chapter on Levinson and Link, it is through class that the series often understands gender, as well, though, as mentioned, the cocreators also made a conscious decision not to include any African American murderers during the series' initial run, as they didn't want the series to further popular associations between violence and Black Americans.

20. *Fresh Air*, National Public Radio, March 15, 1995.

21. *I'm Okay—You're Okay* was a bestseller by Thomas Anthony Harris, which was also a guide to Transactional Analysis.

22. Trained psychoanalytically and influenced by Freud, Berne developed Transactional Analysis, which became a mainstay of therapeutic work for decades. Transactions, for Berne, signal an ongoing pattern of communication between a "sender" and "receiver"; those who communicate also alternate roles between the ego-states "Child," "Parent," and "Adult," which were practical expansions of the Freudian concepts of the Ego, Super-Ego, and Id. For Berne, these ego-states are active in every person, thus enabling a less abstract and more applicable concept in therapeutic practice than Freud's more abstract divisions.

23. See White, *Tele-advising*.

24. Shortly after the pickup speech, Columbo appears on the scene to implicitly threaten George concerning his role in covering up the embezzlement that preceded the murder he's investigating.

25. Berne, *What Do You Say after You Say Hello?*, 23.

26. Berne, *What Do You Say after You Say Hello?*, 23.

27. Berne, *What Do You Say after You Say Hello?*, 33.

28. Moreover, if Dr. Hiedeman is a benevolent doctor, Columbo is the benevolent law. Certainly his "benevolence" is signified by the evident guilt of the criminals, but it is also demonstrated by that which is absent—those elements of the law that, during the civil rights era, were in fact malevolent.

29. And don't get me started on other textual coincidences: the woman who plays the mother of the Manchurian Candidate is none other than Angela Lansbury, who will go on to play amateur sleuth Jessica Fletcher in *Murder, She Wrote*, cocreated by Levinson, Link, and Peter S. Fischer. Geer himself also took a menacing turn in another John Frankenheimer picture, *Seconds* (1966).

4. Special Guest Stars

1. Desjardins, *Recycled Stars*, 58.
2. Conversation with Mr. Link, July 9, 2013.
3. Desjardins, *Recycled Stars*, 57.
4. Also see Hastie, "The Trouble with Lupino."
5. Desjardins, *Recycled Stars*, 80.
6. Of course, in the case of *All about Eve*, Davis also plays a mere forty-year-old.
7. Brooks, "Performing Aging/Performance Crisis," 233.
8. In her groundbreaking essay "The Concept of Live Television: Ontology as Ideology," Jane Feuer considers how television's "liveness" is equated with its realness. In her critique of this ideological mode, she describes a series of assumptions and parallels, such as that stated above: "Live television is *not* recorded; live television is *alive*; television is living, real, not dead" (14).
9. With many thanks to Mary Desjardins for this insight.
10. Granted, there are competing stories as to the origin of the name.
11. Given that Vaughn only appeared on two episodes overall, I won't focus on his work in this chapter, though I would note that, strangely enough, both episodes take place around the water (and both are directed by actors).
12. Falk, *Just One More Thing*, 155.
13. Dawidziak, *The Columbo Phile*, 257–58.
14. Later he drops by to literally cheer Rosemary on in her work with a little spontaneous song: "Just keep thinking you're Rosemary, Rosemary, Rosemary. R.O.S.E. Ro—Ro—Ro—You're a grand ol' . . ." and he trails off into another, more recognizable show tune.
15. The fact that both of these episodes take place in the literary world also showcases "plotting"—of the murder, of course, but also of the mystery series itself, as I have discussed elsewhere.
16. Conversation with Mr. Link, July 9, 2013.

17. Interestingly, in the prior episode in which Cassidy guest stars, the final clue to his guilt centers around a key.

5. *Between Columbo and Cassavetes*

1. *A Constant Forge* (Charles Kiselyak, 2000).

2. As Gazzara claims, "John wasn't afraid to change the script" (*In the Moment*, 142). Both Falk and Cassavetes discuss writing the work in tandem with one another.

3. Carney, *Cassavetes on Cassavetes*, 213.

4. Carney, *Cassavetes on Cassavetes*, 232.

5. Carney, *Cassavetes on Cassavetes*, 253.

6. Gazzara, *In the Moment*, 153.

7. Green, "Dick Cavett's Worst Show." Amazingly, Cavett appears to have complained about this event for over four decades.

8. The three actors also appeared together for a Los Angeles–based broadcast of an Easter Seals telethon.

9. For an insightful analysis of the variety show, see Sutherland, *The Flip Wilson Show*.

10. Before Cassavetes comes onstage, Falk says to Carson, "I don't understand John. I don't understand him when he talks. . . . He talks a lot." And he claims—however "jokingly"—that he doesn't have any "endearing qualities."

11. Carney, *Cassavetes on Cassavetes*, 310.

12. Carney, *Cassavetes on Cassavetes*.

13. As noted in *Broadcasting* at the time: "Peter Falk, who plays the title role of the detective in *Columbo* earns $100,000 for each of the 90-minute shows he does, for a maximum of eight shows a year" (Oct. 1, 1973, p. 17). In an issue of the same publication on September 17, 1973, it was reported that Falk "signed new agreement with network that his agent claims is 'largest contract ever negotiated by an actor in a continuing series'" (p. 36). Several months later, on July 1, 1974, *Broadcasting* reported that Falk walked off the show, claiming that Universal owed his own production company $132,777 (p. 38). Contractual problems with Falk continued to be reported in 1976 by *Broadcasting* (March 1, 1976, p. 7). In an interview, Dean Hargrove also comments on Falk's salary. He notes that in the first year Falk made $26,500 per episode, $500,000 in the final season, and then $1 million for each episode of the reboot. He also emphasizes that Falk "never misbehaved." See "Dean Hargrove Interview Part 2 of 3," Television Academy, https://interviews.televisionacademy.com/shows/columbo?clip =107899#who-talked.

14. The direction of this episode has been almost routinely mistaken to be by Cassavetes himself. For instance, the website Internet Movie Database (imdb .com) inaccurately lists him as director, as did Falk's obituary in the *Guardian*.

15. Is it a coincidence that Janice is the name of Ben Gazzara's wife at the time?

16. Interestingly, in both "Étude in Black" with Cassavetes and "Playback" with Rowlands, the final clue hinges on the wife's refusal to lie for her husband. In "Étude in Black," at least Benedict tells his wife to tell the truth (not unsurprising, given Cassavetes's emphasis on "truth" as a director), and he whispers to her that he loves her just before he turns himself over to the detective. The killer Van Wick, on the other hand, implores his wife to lie for him, while she sits in the doorway, crying and speechless, except for the utterance "No." After her husband is taken away, she looks silently at the detective, tears still streaming down her face; the final shot shows Columbo turning off the monitor, so that the image is frozen with him next to a blank screen.

17. Gazzara, *In the Moment*, 137.

18. Gazzara, *In the Moment*, 137.

19. American Film Institute (AFI) transcript of a master class with Cassavetes and Falk, p. 98.

20. AFI transcript, p. 2.

21. Gazzara, *In the Moment*, 260.

22. Falk, *Just One More Thing*, 201.

23. Falk, *Just One More Thing*, 202.

24. Falk, *Just One More Thing*, 200.

25. Falk, *Just One More Thing*, 200. He also notes that he had been physically lucky (this claim by a man who as a child had cancer that took his right eye).

6. An "Obsessive Preoccupation with Gadgetry"

1. Of course, *Columbo* is not the only moving-image text to reveal these connections. For central cinematic examples, both preceding and contemporaneous with the series, in which time-based media are linked to murder, menace, and investigation, see *Laura* (Otto Preminger, 1944), in which a radio show is used for an alibi; *Klute* (Alan J. Pakula, 1971), in which a recorded conversation is paired with the telephone by a murderer in order to taunt his next would-be victim; and *The Conversation* (Francis Ford Coppola, 1974), which painstakingly details the ways in which sound is recorded, reordered, and ultimately reconsidered. The latter two are also, arguably, in conversation with Michelangelo Antonioni's *Blow-Up* (1966). On television in the 1960s and 1970s, many detectives and crimefighters traded on their own expert knowledge and

use of gadgets to catch criminals, ranging from *Mannix* (originally created by Levinson and Link) to *Mission Impossible* to *Batman*.

2. For other means of thinking through television and knowledge, see, for instance, Joyrich, "Epistemology of the Console."

3. As I've noted, McEachin is also the lead of Levinson and Link's *Tenafly*, which appeared between his two turns on *Columbo*.

4. Drawing on the work of Stephen Heath and Gillian Skirrow, Feuer argues that "by postulating an equivalence between time of event, time of television creation and transmission-viewing time, television as an institution identifies all messages emanating from the apparatus as 'live'" ("The Concept of Live Television," 14).

5. Such is the case in "Double Shock" and "Étude in Black," for instance.

6. Friedberg, *The Virtual Window*, 192–93.

7. Gitelman, *Always Already New*, 5.

8. Ephron, *Crazy Salad and Scribble Scribble*.

9. Toffler, *Future Shock*, 21.

10. Toffler, *Future Shock*, 230.

11. McLuhan, *Understanding Media*, 43.

12. Moreover, the very anxiety about the fragmentation of space is, as Jane Feuer notes, resolved by television's illusion of liveness.

13. The idea of the kid programming a robot to manage all those tasks we find annoying—but that is misused to enable a man to commit murder—is perhaps only palatable because we know this "boy genius" really goes into another, perhaps safer technological field than global warfare: the film industry. Importantly, too, Spielberg himself becomes famous for films about the evils of war rather than the thrill of military enactment and strategy, as we see in "Mind over Mayhem."

14. See Wasser, *Veni, Vidi, Video*, 2.

15. Bochco script held at the Writers Guild Foundation, p. 72.

7. Columbo's Reign

1. I am indebted to my research assistant Kiera Alventosa for helping me make sense of a nascent idea.

2. The four nucleotides making up the DNA strand are adenine, thymine, guanine, and cytosine. They do not allow for an exact duplicate of the parts that make up the basic structure of *Columbo*'s "DNA," but please bear with me in my analogy.

3. In 1971, Falk appeared in Neil Simon's Broadway comedy *The Prisoner of Second Avenue*.

4. This is itself a confusing claim, as he's been "playing" the detective in private scenes with Tess.

5. The series is a mere footnote in the writers' *Stay Tuned*, in which they note that they made one firm recommendation: that Maureen Stapleton be offered the lead (Kate Mulgrew was miscast instead). As they note, "*Mrs. Columbo* went on the air and fared poorly, but to the surprise of the industry Silverman renewed it. There was the obligatory salvaging operation—a divorce was decreed for the poor woman and the series was christened with a new title, *Kate Loves a Mystery*—but the ratings continued to dwindle and Kate was finally given the *coup de grace* in the ritual bloodletting of mid-season" (91).

6. Fantle and Johnson, *Reel to Real*, 216. The authors go on to note that when fans are not calling him by the lieutenant's name, they shout "Serpentine" instead (217).

7. Baxter, "Obituary."

8. *Fresh Air*, National Public Radio, March 15, 1995.

9. I must thank my friend Matt Roberson for this description of my method.

10. *TIME*, "A Cop (and a Raincoat) for All Seasons."

11. Importantly, Falk was one of the few major male actors of his generation (if not, in fact, the only one!) to work with three different women directors: Elaine May for *Mikey and Nicky*, Susan Seidelman for *Cookie*, and Sandra Seacat for *In the Spirit* (1990), in which he plays Elaine May's husband and in which Jeannie Berlin, May's daughter, also appears.

12. See Baxter, "Obituary."

13. Canby, "'Big Trouble,' with Arkin and Falk."

14. Rogowski, *Wings of Desire*, 48.

15. I am grateful to Nancy Meyer, who worked as a director of development with Falk in the latter years of the reboot, for details regarding development, timing, and budget. As with his work with three women film directors, it's significant that he maintained this producing relationship with a woman during these years. As Meyer also pointed out, many women during this time had production companies making movies for television. Conversation, July 18, 2016.

16. As Nancy Meyer mentioned, John Cassavetes was the model for Falk's control over his work (conversation, July 18, 2016). In fact, as the television director Robert Butler noted, Falk also maintained a great deal of control over the original series. When Butler directed two episodes of the original series, the experience was one of "accommodation and collaboration" with the star. To recognize Falk's "control" is not to suggest that he was "difficult," as Hollywood parlance goes, Indeed, Robert Butler and UCLA television archivist Mark Quigley emphasized that any criticism of Falk in trades of the day was a

result of the Universal machine, as part of the studio's hard-line tactics. More-over, according to Butler, Falk was a generous actor who would support other actors appearing with him in the series. Conversation with Robert Butler and Mark Quigley, July 2016.

17. Scientists can supply the DNA template of their choosing, thereby writing in any gene they want or correcting a mutation.

18. Steven Bochco, script for "MURDER BY STARLIGHT" (original title, "Requiem for a Falling Star"), held at the Writers Guild Foundation (WGF).

19. I am indebted here to Maeve McNamara for her insights and research assistance.

20. "Steven Bochco Interview Part 3 of 12," Television Academy, https://interviews.televisionacademy.com/interviews/steven-bochco.

21. Steven Bocho, script for "Murder by the Book," held at the WGF.

22. Here, too, I am grateful to Maeve McNamara for her analysis of these primary materials.

23. Barthes, *The Pleasure of the Text*, 9.

24. Kristeva, "Word, Dialogue and Novel," 50.

25. Kristeva, "Word, Dialogue and Novel," 50.

26. The two earlier novels were penned by Alfred Lawrence, and the later ones were attributed to William Harrington. These distinctions—with some plots parallel to those in the series and others that resituate the characters historically—are similar to other sanctioned and unsanctioned television tie-ins; see Hastie, "The Epistemological Stakes of *Buffy the Vampire Slayer*."

27. Lawrence, *The Dean's Death*, 26.

28. Lawrence, *The Dean's Death*, 27.

29. Granted, the later novels also extended the material of the original series; like the reboot, they drew more explicitly on sex and violence. In Harrington's *Columbo: The Game Show Killer*, a woman describes her mur-dered husband as "a lecher nonpareil": "My husband would have mounted a sheep or a goat if he hadn't had a woman during the past twenty-four hours" (105). Descriptions of women in Harrington's *Columbo: The Helter Skelter Murders* are particularly reductive; two characters, for instance, are even called "Puss" and "Boobs." And Mrs. Columbo hardly fares better herself. The lieutenant's thoughts turn to her as he watches a lingerie modeling session: "He wasn't going to say, even to himself, that he *wasn't* interested, though he couldn't imagine Mrs. Columbo wearing what the model was now showing or what Miss March was wearing in the calendar. No. Mrs. Columbo was a huskier woman than these models, more athletic. She was a first-class bowler. She was just as sexy as the model, in her way. But . . . in her way" (75). With thanks to my research assistant Sabrina Lin for her close reading of *Columbo: The Helter Skelter Murders*.

30. Collins, "Falk's Career Strategy."

31. Three years prior to the interview, he played himself playing a detective in *The Player*, Robert Altman's serious parody of Hollywood.

32. Regarding Wim Wenders's own apologies concerning the inconsistencies of Falk's character in the film, Rogowski notes, "Angels of course don't have a personal past, and thus can't have grandmothers" (*Wings of Desire*, 47). Of course, the fictionalization of Falk within the film is multifold. After all, Falk's ancestors were Eastern European Jews, so while this detail might point to the actor's investment in the film-within-the-film, it's also somewhat fictionalized. Rogowski also reads the inclusion of the American star and his appearance in an American film being shot in Germany as a means for Wenders to critique the ways that both the US and German film industries have engaged in "willful historical mystification." As he explains, this film-within-a-film "evokes a controversy" initiated by the American 1978 miniseries *Holocaust*, which reduced "a vast, complicated, and multifaceted historical catastrophe into the manageable pop-cultural form of a melodrama revolving around a single family" (56).

33. *TIME*, "A Cop (and a Raincoat) for All Seasons."

Epilogue

1. Hammerton, *Cooking with Columbo*. In fact, I made "Johnny Cash's Chili" myself, adjusting the ingredients slightly—replacing squirrel meat with "meatless" ground beef. See Whittemore, "Goodbye, Columbo."

Bibliography

Archives

American Film Institute, Los Angeles, CA
The Paley Center for Media, Los Angeles, CA
The Paley Center for Media, New York, NY
Television Academy, Los Angeles, CA
UCLA Film and Television Archive, Los Angeles, CA
Writers Guild Foundation, Los Angeles, CA

Books and Articles

Aira, César. *Dinner*. Translated by Katherine Silver. New York: New Directions, 2015.

Arnold, Sarah. "Netflix and the Myth of Choice/Participation/Autonomy." In *The Netflix Effect: Technology and Entertainment in the 21st Century*, edited by Kevin McDonald and Daniel Smith-Rowsey, 49–62. London: Bloomsbury, 2018.

Banks, Miranda. *The Writers: A History of American Screenwriters and Their Guild*. New Brunswick, NJ: Rutgers University Press, 2015.

Barthes, Roland. *The Pleasure of the Text*. Translated by Richard Miller. New York: Hill and Wang, 1975.

Baxter, Brian. "Obituary: Peter Falk: American Actor Known All Over the World for His Role as the Rumpled Detective Columbo." *Guardian*, June 27, 2011.

Bazin, André. *What Is Cinema? Volume 1*. Translated by Hugh Gray. Berkeley: University of California Press, 2004.

Becker, Christine. *It's the Pictures That Got Small: Hollywood Film Stars in 1950s Television*. Middletown, CT: Wesleyan University Press, 2009.

Berne, Eric. *What Do You Say after You Say Hello? The Psychology of Human Destiny*. New York: Grove Press, 1972.

Berzsenyi, Christyne. *Columbo: A Rhetoric of Inquiry with Resistant Responders*. Bristol, UK: Intellect Books, 2021.

Boddy, William. "Is It TV Yet? The Dislocated Screens of Television in a Mobile Digital Culture." In *Television as Digital Media*, edited by James Bennett and Niki Strange, 76–101. Durham, NC: Duke University Press, 2011.

Borges, Jorge Luis. "Blindness." In *Everything and Nothing*, translated by Eliot Weinberger, 113–29. New York: New Directions, 2010.

Borges, Jorge Luis. "The Garden of Forking Paths." In *Everything and Nothing*, translated by Donald A. Yates, 49–63. New York: New Directions, 2010.

Brooks, Jodi. "Performing Aging/Performance Crisis (for Norma Desmond, Baby Jane, Margo Channing, Sister George—and Myrtle)." In *Figuring Age: Women, Bodies, Generations*, edited by Kathleen Woodward, 232–47. Bloomington: Indiana University Press, 1999.

Browne, Nick. "The Political Economy of the Television Super(Text)." *Quarterly Review of Film Studies* 9, no. 3 (Summer 1984): 174–82.

Brunsdon, Charlotte. *Law and Order*. London: British Film Institute, 2010.

Caillois, Roger. "The Detective Novel as Game." In *Poetics of Murder: Detective Fiction and Literary Theory*, edited by Glenn W. Most and William W. Stowe, 1–12. New York: Harcourt Brace Jovanovich, 1983.

Caldwell, John Thornton. *Production Culture: Industrial Reflexivity and Critical Practice in Film and Television*. Durham, NC: Duke University Press, 2008.

Canby, Vincent. "'Big Trouble,' with Arkin and Falk." *New York Times*, May 30, 1986, 60.

Canby, Vincent. "Suspense Melodrama Stars Widmark and Fonda." *New York Times*, June 11, 1977, 12.

Carney, Ray. *Cassavetes on Cassavetes*. New York: Farrar, Straus and Giroux, 2001.

Caughie, John. *Edge of Darkness*. London: British Film Institute, 2007.

Collins, Glenn. "Falk's Career Strategy: Who Needs a Strategy?" *New York Times*, November 28, 1990.

Curran, Shaun. "Why the World Still Loves 1970s Detective Show *Columbo*." BBC, September 9, 2021. https://www.bbc.com/culture/article/20210909 -why-the-world-still-loves-1970s-detective-show-columbo.

Dallas Voice. "Award-Winning Actor Known as Activist for Peace, Social Justice." June 14, 2007. https://dallasvoice.com/martin-sheen-is-btd-speaker/.

Dawidziak, Mark. *The Columbo Phile: A Casebook*. New York: Mysterious Press, 1989.

Desjardins, Mary. *Father Knows Best*. Detroit, MI: Wayne State University Press, 2015.

Desjardins, Mary. *Recycled Stars: Female Film Stardom in the Age of Television and Video*. Durham, NC: Duke University Press, 2015.

Didion, Joan. *The White Album*. New York: Farrar, Straus and Giroux, 1990.

Dostoyevsky, Fyodor. *Crime and Punishment*. Translated by David McDuff. New York: Penguin Classics, 2002.

Eco, Umberto. "Can Television Teach?" *Screen Education* 31 (1979): 15–24.

Eco, Umberto. *Limits of Interpretation*. Bloomington: Indiana University Press, 1991.

Ellis, John. *Visible Fictions: Cinema, Television, Video*. London: Routledge, 1982.

Ephron, Nora. *Crazy Salad and Scribble Scribble: Some Things about Women and Notes on Media*. New York: Vintage, 2012.

Falk, Peter. *Just One More Thing*. New York: Carroll and Graf, 2006.

Fantle, David, and Tom Johnson. *Reel to Real*. Oregon, WI: Badger Books, 2004.

Feuer, Jane. "The Concept of Live Television: Ontology as Ideology." In *Regarding Television: Critical Approaches—an Anthology*, edited by E. Ann Kaplan, 12–24. Baltimore, MD: University Publications of America, 1983.

Fiske, John, and John Hartley. *Reading Television*. 2nd ed. London: Routledge, 2003.

Flitterman-Lewis, Sandy. "The Real Soap Operas: TV Commercials." In *Regarding Television: Critical Approaches—an Anthology*, edited by E. Ann Kaplan, 84–95. Baltimore, MD: University Publications of America, 1983.

Freud, Sigmund. *Beyond the Pleasure Principle and Other Writings*. Translated by John Reddick. London: Penguin Books, 2003.

Friedberg, Anne. *The Virtual Window: From Alberti to Microsoft*. Cambridge, MA: MIT Press, 2009.

Galiero, Emmanuel. "Columbo, les dernières images dans l'intimité de Peter Falk." *Le Figaro TV Magazine*, July 10–16, 2011.

Gazzara, Ben. *In the Moment: My Life as an Actor*. New York: Da Capo Press, 2005.

Ginzburg, Carlo. "Clues: Roots of an Evidential Paradigm." In *Clues, Myths, and the Historical Method*, translated by John and Anne C. Tedeschi, 87–113. Baltimore, MD: Johns Hopkins University Press, 1989.

Gitelman, Lisa. *Always Already New: Media, History, and the Data of Culture*. Cambridge, MA: MIT Press, 2008.

Gray, Herman. *Cultural Moves: African Americans and the Politics of Representation*. Berkeley: University of California Press, 2005.

Gray, Herman. "Television, Black Americans, and the American Dream." *Critical Studies in Mass Communication* 6 (1989): 376–86.

Green, Elon. "Dick Cavett's Worst Show." *New Yorker*, May 29, 2014.

Hammerton, Jenny. *Cooking with Columbo: Suppers with the Shambling Sleuth*. N.p.: Silver Screen Suppers, 2018.

Harrington, William. *Columbo: The Game Show Killer*. New York: Tom Doherty Associates, 1996.

Harrington, William. *Columbo: The Glitter Murder*. New York: Tom Doherty Associates, 1997.

Harrington, William. *Columbo: The Grassy Knoll*. New York: Tom Doherty Associates, 1993.

Harrington, William. *Columbo: The Helter Skelter Murders*. New York: Tom Doherty Associates, 1994.

Harris, Thomas Anthony. *I'm Okay—You're Okay*. New York: Harper and Row, 1967.

Hastie, Amelie. "Columbo, Cassavetes, and a Biography of Friendship." *Celebrity Studies* 8, no. 4 (Fall 2017): 493–509.

Hastie, Amelie. "The Epistemological Stakes of *Buffy the Vampire Slayer*: Television Criticism and Market Demands." In *Undead TV: Critical Writings on "Buffy the Vampire Slayer*," edited by Lisa Parks and Elana Levine, 74–95. Durham, NC: Duke University Press, 2007.

Hastie, Amelie. "The Trouble with Lupino." *Cinema Comparat/ive Cinema* 4, no. 8 (2016): 50–56.

Heissenbüttel, Helmut. "Rules of the Game of the Crime Novel." In *Poetics of Murder: Detective Fiction and Literary Theory*, edited by Glenn W. Most and William W. Stowe, 79–92. New York: Harcourt Brace Jovanovich, 1983.

Houston, Beverle. "Viewing Television: The Metapsychology of Endless Consumption." *Quarterly Review of Film Studies* 9, no. 3 (Summer 1984): 183–95.

Isaacson, Walter. *The Code Breaker: Jennifer Doudna, Gene Editing, and the Future of the Human Race*. New York: Simon and Schuster, 2021.

Joyrich, Lynne. "Epistemology of the Console." *Critical Inquiry* 27, no. 3 (Spring 2001): 439–67.

Kinder, Marsha. *Playing with Power in Movies, Television, and Video Games*. Berkeley: University of California Press, 1991.

Kompare, Derek. *Rerun Nation: How Repeats Invented American Television*. New York: Routledge, 2005.

Kouvaros, George. *Where Does It Happen? John Cassavetes and Cinema at the Breaking Point*. Minneapolis: University of Minnesota Press, 2004.

Kristeva, Julia. "Word, Dialogue and Novel." In *The Kristeva Reader*, edited by Toril Moi; translated by Alice Jardine, Thomas Gora, and Léon S. Roudiez, 34–61. New York: Columbia University Press, 1986.

Lawrence, Alfred. *The Dean's Death*. New York: Popular Library, 1975.

Leitch, Thomas. *Perry Mason*. Detroit, MI: Wayne State University Press, 2005.

Levinson, Richard, and William Link. *Stay Tuned: An Inside Look at the Making of Prime-Time Television*. New York: St. Martin's Press, 1981.

Link, William. *The Columbo Collection*. Norfolk, VA: Crippen and Landru, 2010.

Link, William, and Richard Levinson. *Prescription: Murder*. New York: Samuel French, 1963.

Lotz, Amanda. *Portals: A Treatise on Internet-Distributed Television*. Ann Arbor, MI: Maize Books, 2017.

Martin-Jones, David. *Columbo: Paying Attention 24/7*. Edinburgh: Edinburgh University Press, 2021.

McCarthy, Anna. *Ambient Television: Visual Culture and Public Space*. Durham, NC: Duke University Press, 2001.

McLuhan, Marshall. *Understanding Media: The Extensions of Man*. Cambridge, MA: MIT Press, 2004.

Mellencamp, Patricia, ed. *Logics of Television: Essays in Cultural Criticism*. Bloomington: Indiana University Press, 1990.

Mittell, Jason. *Genre and Television*. New York: Routledge, 2004.

Modleski, Tania. *Loving with a Vengeance: Mass-Produced Fantasies for Women*. New York: Routledge, 1984.

Munsterberg, Hugo. *The Photoplay: A Psychological Study and Other Writings*. Edited by Allan Langdale. New York: Routledge, 2001.

Murphy, Sheila. *How Television Invented New Media*. New Brunswick, NJ: Rutgers University Press, 2011.

Naficy, Hamid. "Television Intertextuality and the Discourse of the Nuclear Family." *Journal of Film and Video* 41, no. 4 (Winter 1989): 42–59.

Newman, Michael, and Elana Levine. *Legitimating Television: Media Convergence and Cultural Status*. New York: Routledge, 2012.

Nichols-Pethick, Jonathan. *TV Cops: The Contemporary American Television Police Drama*. New York: Routledge, 2012.

Olsson, Jan. *Hitchcock à la Carte*. Durham, NC: Duke University Press, 2015.

Polan, Dana. *Julia Child's "The French Chef."* Durham, NC: Duke University Press, 2011.

Powers, James. "The Chevy Mystery Show." *Hollywood Reporter* 160, no. 21 (May 31, 1960): 9.

Ragaine, Franck. "Adieu, Columbo." *TéléPouch*, July 9–15, 2011.

Rogowski, Christian. *Wings of Desire*. Rochester, NY: Camden House, 2019.

Simenon, Georges. *Maigret*. Translated by Ros Schwartz. New York: Penguin Books, 2015.

Sobchack, Vivian. "The Scene of the Screen: Envisioning Cinematic and Electronic 'Presence.'" In *Film and Theory: An Anthology*, edited by Robert Stam and Toby Miller, 67–84. Malden, MA: Blackwell, 2000.

Spigel, Lynn. *Make Room for TV: Television and the Family Ideal in Postwar America*. Chicago: University of Chicago Press, 1992.

Sutherland, Meghan. *The Flip Wilson Show*. Detroit, MI: Wayne State University Press, 2008.

TIME. "A Cop (and a Raincoat) for All Seasons." November 26, 1973.

Toffler, Alvin. *Future Shock*. New York: Bantam Books, 1984.

Torres, Sasha. "King TV." In *Living Color: Race and Television in the United States*, edited by Sasha Torres, 140–59. Durham, NC: Duke University Press, 1998.

Tryon, Chuck. "'Make Any Room Your TV Room': Digital Delivery and Media Mobility." *Screen* 53, no. 3 (Autumn 2012): 287–300.

TV Guide. "*Rollercoaster* Reviews." Digital reprint, https://www.tvguide.com/movies/rollercoaster/review/2000118561/.

Wald, Gayle. *It's Been Beautiful: Soul! and Black Power Television*. Durham, NC: Duke University Press, 2015.

Wasser, Frederick. *Veni, Vidi, Video: The Hollywood Empire and the VCR*. Austin: University of Texas Press, 2001.

Weber, Bruce. "Peter Falk, Rumpled and Crafty Actor in Television's 'Columbo,' Dies at 83." *New York Times*, June 25, 2011.

White, Mimi. "Crossing Wavelengths: The Diegetic and Referential Imaginary of American Commercial Television." *Cinema Journal* 25, no. 2 (Winter 1986): 51–64.

White, Mimi. *Tele-advising: Therapeutic Discourse in American Television*. Chapel Hill: University of North Carolina Press, 1992.

White, Mimi. "Television Genres: Intertextuality." *Journal of Film and Video* 37, no. 3 (Summer 1985): 41–47.

Whittemore, Katharine. "Goodbye, Columbo." *Amherst Magazine*, July 23, 2019. https://www.amherst.edu/news/news_releases/2019/7-2019/goodbye-columbo.

Williams, Linda. *On "The Wire."* Durham, NC: Duke University Press, 2014.

Williams, Mark. "Television Postwar Los Angeles: 'Remote' Possibilities in a 'City of Light.'" *Velvet Light Trap*, no. 33 (Spring 1994): 24–36.

Williams, Raymond. *Television: Technology and Cultural Form*. 2nd ed. London: Routledge, 2003.

Wright, John. "BTD Speaker Sheen Blasts Dems, GOP, Bush." *Dallas Voice*, October 25, 2007. https://web.archive.org/web/20071105004219/http://www.dallasvoice.com/artman/exec/view.cgi/97/7095.

Index

Academy Awards (Oscars), 26–28, 106, 123, 195
accoutrements, Columbo's: cigar, 81, 109, 137, 153, 190, 198; raincoat, 81, 117, 119; shoes, 16, 75–78, 81, 84, 209n15
All about Eve, 101, 102, 104, 108, 211n6
Arnold, Sarah, 202
authorship, 61–71, 96, 192

Banks, Miranda, 61
Barthes, Roland, 64, 69, 70, 192
Baxter, Anne, 94, 97, 104–8
Becker, Christine, 102
Berne, Eric, 84–87, 210n22
Berzsenyi, Christyne, 204n38
Bochco, Steven, xvii, 14, 62, 65, 133, 145, 164, 185, 190–91, 192, 194, 208nn38–39
Borges, Jorge Luis, 1, 11, 13
Bradshaw, Booker, 57, 208n31
Brooks, Jodi, 102
Browne, Nick, 5, 6
Butler, Robert, 215n16

Callois, Roger, 74, 209n7
Cannell, Stephen J., xvii, 158
Carney, Ray. *See* Cassavetes, John

Cash, Johnny, 32, 78, 80–81
Cassavetes, John, xvi, 21, 26, 37, 79, 97, 119–43, 172, 175, 180, 181, 184, 192, 195, 213n14, 213n16, 215n16
Cassidy, Jack, 14, 15, 109, 113–17, 186, 212n17
Charlie's Angels, 102. *See also* Lupino, Ida
Cheap Detective, The, 37, 98, 174
Citizen Kane, 47, 98, 99
class: and *Columbo*, xv, 15, 16, 21, 32, 34–37, 72, 74, 75, 78, 84, 93, 110; and Peter Falk, 25–26, 130; and race, 55–56, 58–59, 61, 203n13, 210n19; and technology, 146–47, 163
classical Hollywood, 21, 46, 97–108, 133. *See also* Davis, Bette; Desjardins, Mary; Head, Edith; Leigh, Janet; Lupino, Ida
Culp, Robert, 75, 109–10, 112–13, 114, 158, 159–60, 163

Danese, Shera, 97, 202n9
Davis, Bette, 101, 108, 211n6
Dawidziak, Mark, *The Columbo Phile: A Casebook*, 110

Demme, Jonathan, xviii, 174

Desjardins, Mary, 96, 102, 211n9

detectives: definitions, 72–75; influences on *Columbo*, 10, 13, 74; literary models, 31, 40, 73–75, 110, 174,
192; television models, xvii–xviii,
33, 61–62, 73, 75, 98, 129, 205n6

Dick Cavett Show, The, 124–26

Didion, Joan, 210n17

dog, Columbo's, 66, 119–20, 121, 138,
178, 189, 197

Dostoyevsky, Fyodor, 10, 13, 192

Eco, Umberto, 4, 70

Ellery Queen, 40–41, 43, 73, 75,
205n6

Emmy Awards, xvii, 26–27, 30, 55,
109, 110, 130, 166, 195, 201n4,
207n29

"Enough Rope," xv–xvi, 31, 39, 84,
187, 197, 201n1, 202n10

Ephron, Nora, 162

episodes, original series (in chronological order): "Ransom for a
Dead Man" (pilot), xvii, 31, 32, 33,
100–101, 112, 146–47, 163, 205n4;
season 1: "Murder by the Book,"
xvii, 14, 31, 45, 62–64, 114–15, 116,
146, 156, 173, 190, 192, 216n21;
"Death Lends a Hand," xvii, 24,
33, 80, 92, 110–13, 201n4; "Dead
Weight," 78, 165; "Suitable for
Framing," 19; "Lady in Waiting,"
97, 112; "Blueprint for Murder," 34;
season 2: "Étude in Black," 34, 57,
79, 132–39, 144, 165, 170–71, 187,
192, 195, 207n27, 213n16, 214n5;
"The Greenhouse Jungle," 73, 80,
97; "The Most Crucial Game," 33,
75–77, 97, 113, 163; "Dagger of the
Mind," 55; "Requiem for a Falling
Star," 33, 34–36, 104–7, 165, 188,
198, 216n18; "A Stitch in Crime,"
xx, 7, 87–91, 93–94, 95, 112, 187,
208n40; "The Most Dangerous
Match," 65, 67, 87–94, 95, 112,
187, 208n40; "Double Shock," 165,
188, 214n5; *season 3:* "Lovely but
Lethal," 81, 186; "Any Old Port
in a Storm," 78, 165, 188, 198–99;
"Candidate for Crime," 14, 34–35,
77, 82–84, 187; "Double Exposure,"
113, 158, 161, 164, 187; "Publish or
Perish," 32, 101, 112, 113–16, 187;
"Mind over Mayhem," 32, 81, 119,
164, 214n13; "Swan Song," 32, 78,
80–81, 97; "A Friend in Deed," 81,
133, 139, 140, 162; *season 4:* "An
Exercise in Fatality," 77–78, 163;
"Negative Reaction," 22–23, 146,
147–48, 204n37; "By Dawn's Early
Light," 109, 209n15; "Troubled
Waters," 14, 33, 139–40; "Playback," 77, 119–20, 133, 137, 138,
147, 155–59, 160, 161, 192, 208n31,
213n16; "A Deadly State of Mind,"
84–85; *season 5:* "Forgotten
Lady," 103–4, 152, 154; "A Case of
Immunity," 34; "Identity Crisis,"
68–69, 97, 109–10; "A Matter of
Honor," 16, 81, 112; "Now You See
Him . . . ," 115–18; "Last Salute to
the Commodore," xviii, 68, 109,
110; *season 6:* "Fade in to Murder,"
97, 119–20, 133, 137, 138, 147, 155–
59, 160, 161, 192, 208n31, 213n16;
"Old Fashioned Murder," 80; "The
Bye-Bye Sky High I.Q. Murder
Case," 17–18, 85, 185, 204n37;
season 7: "Try and Catch Me," 17,

204n36; "Murder under Glass," 14, 19, 97, 173–74; "Make Me a Perfect Murder," xv, 1–4, 33, 53, 57, 60, 77, 81, 112, 144–45, 148–52, 165, 168–70, 171, 197; "How to Dial a Murder," 98–100, 104, 187; "The Conspirators," xviii, 197
Execution of Private Slovik, The (Levinson and Link), 46–49

Feuer, Jane, 12, 102, 156, 211n8
Fischer, Peter S., xvii, 40, 114, 185, 186,
Flower Shop Mysteries, The, xviii
Francis, Anne, 7, 89
Freud, Sigmund, 22, 85–86, 210n22
Friedberg, Anne, 161
Future Shock (Toeffler), 162–63

Gazzara, Ben, 21, 121, 123, 124–29, 131–32, 134, 138–40, 213n15; memoir, 124, 141–43
Geer, Will, 7, 88–89, 91
Gillis, Jackson, xviii, 65, 68–69, 185, 188–89
Ginzburg, Carlo, 22
Gitelman, Lisa, 161
Golden Globes, xvii, 55
Gray, Herman, 8, 56, 203n13
Gun, The (Levinson and Link), 44–45, 46, 47, 70, 206n13

Hallmark Movies & Mysteries Channel, xix, xx
Hargrove, Dean, xvii, xviii, 61, 62, 65, 75, 164, 201n6, 209n11, 212n13
Head, Edith, 106–7, 189
Honey West, 7, 39, 89
Houston, Beverle, 5–7

Husbands, xvi, 123–24, 127–28, 130–31, 141–42

In-Laws, The, 132, 178, 179, 180–81
intertextuality: as analytic method, xxi, 2, 4–8, 12, 19–21, 70, 173, 199, 203n10; definitions of, 6–7, 10–11, 62, 203n16; and infinity, 11–13
It's a Mad, Mad, Mad, Mad World, 27–28, 33

Johnny Cash's Chili, 198, 217n1
Johnny Staccato, 129–30, 132, 135. *See also* Cassavetes, John
Joyrich, Lynne, 214n2

Kibbee, Roland, xvii–xviii
Kinder, Marsha, 7, 10, 203n10
Klute, 213n1
Kristeva, Julia, 10–11, 62, 70, 192, 196

Lansbury, Angela, xvii–xviii, 206n6, 211n29. See also *Murder, She Wrote*
Leigh, Janet, 97, 103, 105, 152–54, 186
liveness, 12, 113, 137, 157–58, 160–61, 211n8, 214n12
Los Angeles, xvi, xviii, 15, 16, 31–33, 36, 38, 54, 55, 58–59, 79, 80, 90, 106, 110, 129, 143, 139, 184, 209n14, 212n8
Lupino, Ida, 81, 97, 103, 105, 186

Manchurian Candidate, The, 93, 95, 211n29
Mannix, 39, 44, 112, 214n1
Martin-Jones, David, 202n2

May, Elaine, 37, 122, 131, 215n11
McEachin, James, 53, 56, 57, 133, 136, 150, 207n27
McGoohan, Patrick, xviii, 68–69, 109–10, 113, 114, 185
McKim, Kristi, 176
McLuhan, Marshall, 163–65, 171
media technologies: answering machines, 163; audio recorders, 113, 147–49, 160, 162–63, 169, 171; film projection, 53, 137, 148, 150–52, 154–55, 169; VCRs, 16, 148, 165–68; video surveillance, 113, 137, 148, 156–58, 160–61, 171
Mikey and Nicky, 37, 121–22, 128, 131, 139, 180, 195, 206n15, 215n11
Murder by Death, 37, 98, 173, 174, 175
Murder, She Wrote, xvii, xix, 40, 97, 114, 186, 211n29
Murphy, Sheila, 9, 209n17
My Sweet Charlie (Levinson and Link), 46, 56

Naficy, Hamid, 7–8, 10
NBC Mystery Movie, The, xvii, xx, 39, 57, 73, 96
Newman, Michael, and Elana Levine, 204n30
New York City, xv–xvi, 31, 38, 79
Nichols-Pethick, Jonathan, 209n2
Nimoy, Leonard, 7, 88, 91, 93, 95

parody, 9, 62, 174, 192–94, 195, 203n16
Prescription: Murder: movie, xvi, 84, 96, 123, 146, 187, 197, 201n3; play, xvi, xviii

Price of Tomatoes, The, 25–27, 28, 33, 130
Princess Bride, The, 177–78, 183

race, 8, 25, 55–60, 89, 150, 162, 202n13, 207nn27–28, 208n32, 209n14, 210n19, 211n28
reboot, *Columbo* (ABC), xviii, 9, 13, 14, 62, 69, 97, 109–10, 132, 174, 175, 184–92, 194–95, 197, 201n2, 203n16, 205n3, 208n35, 212n13, 215n15, 216n29
Rockford Files, The, xvii, 73
Rogowski, Christian, 182, 217n32
Rollercoaster, 42–43, 56, 206n10
Rowlands, Gena, xviii, 37, 97, 119–21, 123, 131, 132, 137–39, 140, 155, 175, 180, 192
Run for Your Life, 129, 132, 134. *See also* Gazzara, Ben

Seidelman, Susan, 180, 215n11
Shatner, William, 9, 166–67, 175, 189
Sheen, Martin, 47–48, 50, 97, 207n23
Sobchack, Vivian, 12
Spelberg, Steve, 119, 164–65
Spielberg, Steven, xvii, 14, 64, 165; *Jaws*, 43
Storyteller, The (Levinson and Link), 46, 48
streaming platforms, xix, xx, 5, 9, 12, 19, 70, 202n3, 204n30; algorithms of, 5, 19, 202
Sutherland, Meghan, 212n9

Television Academy interviews, 190, 121n8, 205, 208nn38–39, 209n11, 212n13, 216n20
television studies, 5–8, 11–12, 20

Tenafly, xiii, 36, 39, 43, 57–61, 70, 75, 205n6, 207n30, 208n31, 214n3

That Certain Summer (Levinson and Link), 46–47, 49–55, 56, 60, 61, 70

tie-ins, xviii, 2, 193, 197–98, 216n26, 216n29, 217n1

Tonight Show, The, 30, 127, 128, 131

Trials of O'Brien, xvi, 28–29, 70, 96, 123, 129

Twilight Zone, The, 25, 102, 123

Universal Studios, xvii, 27, 44, 61, 96, 103, 109, 125, 133, 165, 201n6, 206n13, 212n13, 215–16n16. See also *NBC Mystery Movie, The*

Wald, Gayle, 56, 59

wheel series, xvi, 4, 39, 57, 73, 184. See also *NBC Mystery Movie, The*

White, Mimi, 6–8, 10, 203n10

Wings of Desire, 131, 177, 181, 183, 194–95, 217n32

Woman under the Influence, A, 37, 120, 121–22, 123, 128, 131–32, 139. *See also* Cassavetes, John; Rowlands, Gena